Praise for

BREAKING FREE

"You don't read Marcie Bianco to cheer on the standard feminist line; you read her if you want to be intellectually challenged and philosophically engaged. *Breaking Free* calls into question a basic premise of feminist thought: that women should be equal. Instead, Bianco calls for something more radical and more necessary: freedom, in all its forms. A provocative read, *Breaking Free* asks us what it is, exactly, we all want and deserve." —Jill Filipovic, CNN columnist, author of *The H-Spot*

"There are many voices in the contemporary public square riffing on topics that are expansive and grand, like equality and freedom. Then there are the penetrative voices emanating from sagacious and adroit thinkers. Bianco's is one. She is a writer who is less interested in adding noise to the discourse and instead is focused on materializing equity and radical love. *Breaking Free* is an incisive read. And we are ever so ready."

—Darnell L. Moore, author of *No Ashes in the Fire*

"Anyone who believes equality with men is the benchmark for women's rights, well-being, safety, or power should read this book. Bianco's thought-provoking, myth-busting rejection of this idea, in defense of freedom as our goal, is an essential read."

—Soraya Chemaly, author of *Rage Becomes Her*

"What I have always loved about Bianco is her extraordinary ability to make difficult concepts accessible, applicable, and even attractive to the most cynical mind. She is an immensely empathetic human being who knows how to make a common-sense argument for liberation. I cannot tell you how excited I am for the world to read this."

—Charlotte Clymer, writer, leading LGBTQ influencer,
military veteran, and author of the popular
Substack newsletter *Charlotte's Web Thoughts*

"From Beyonce to Britney, Harry Styles to Hilary Clinton, Bianco wields an agile and incisive feminist pen. In *Breaking Free*, Bianco insists we see the perniciousness of patriarchy and expertly maps the ways feminism can liberate us."

—Mona Eltahawy, author of
The Seven Necessary Sins for Women and Girls

BREAKING
FREE

BREAKING
FREE

THE LIE OF EQUALITY AND THE FEMINIST FIGHT FOR FREEDOM

MARCIE BIANCO

PUBLICAFFAIRS

NEW YORK

PublicAffairs
Hachette Book Group
1290 Avenue of the Americas, New York, NY 10104
www.publicaffairsbooks.com
@Public_Affairs

Printed in the United States of America

First Edition: September 2023

Published by PublicAffairs, an imprint of Perseus Books, LLC, a subsidiary of Hachette Book Group, Inc. The PublicAffairs name and logo is a trademark of the Hachette Book Group.

The Hachette Speakers Bureau provides a wide range of authors for speaking events. To find out more, go to hachettespeakersbureau.com or email HachetteSpeakers@hbgusa.com.

PublicAffairs books may be purchased in bulk for business, educational, or promotional use. For more information, please contact your local bookseller or the Hachette Book Group Special Markets Department at special.markets@hbgusa.com.

The publisher is not responsible for websites (or their content) that are not owned by the publisher.

Library of Congress Cataloging-in-Publication Data
Names: Bianco, Marcie, author.
Title: Breaking free : the lie of equality and the feminist fight for freedom / Marcie Bianco.
Description: First edition. | New York : PublicAffairs, [2023] | Includes bibliographical references and index.
Identifiers: LCCN 2022060904 | ISBN 9781541702424 (hardcover) | ISBN 9781541702448 (ebook)
Subjects: LCSH: Feminism. | Equality. | Women's rights.
Classification: LCC HQ1155 .B526 2023 | DDC 305.42—dc23/eng/20230119
LC record available at https://lccn.loc.gov/2022060904
ISBNs: 9781541702424 (hardcover), 9781541702448 (ebook)
LSC-C
Printing 1, 2023

In dedication to the memory of
Angela Bianco and Barbara Johnson

CONTENTS

INTRODUCTION

Equality Will Not Free Us

Equality is a lie. It is a myth perpetuated to coax women into complicity with their oppression.

Women are not equal to men. No two people are equal. We are not born equal or with equal advantages. We do not experience life equally. And while we all eventually die, we do not encounter death on equal terms. We each come from different backgrounds, possess different qualities and talents, cultivate different knowledges and expertise, accrue unique experiences, have distinct desires and needs, and have been systematically advantaged or disadvantaged based on the social identities we have either willingly chosen or had imposed upon us by others.

It is not simply that we are not equal because we are different. Rather, we are not equal because our differences have been manipulated by a society intent on justifying and preserving its traditions and norms. Our differences have been systematized and moralized over generations such that we have been conditioned to believe, for example, that men are superior to women and that white people are superior to all Black and brown and Indigenous people. In the United States, what we designate as *inequalities*—political, economic, or social—are nothing but the measured effects of the discrimination of difference in relation to the white supremacist cis-heteropatriarchy.*

US social movements fighting against racial, gender, and LGBTQ+ discrimination have found more success in redressing measurable inequalities in laws and policies than in eradicating the pervasive oppressions at the root of this nation and its values—oppressions that have inflicted incalculable pain and trauma on generations of people. The feminist movement is one such movement that has measured women's progress in terms of equality. To be clear, the movement is not a monolith. Parallel and often intersecting versions of feminism have coexisted for decades, distinguished by their particular ideologies and players—from single-issue to multi-issue feminism, liberal to radical feminism, Black to white feminism.

Despite the plurality of feminisms, the unfortunate fact is that equality feminism has had a stranglehold on the movement's values, political strategies, and agenda for more than a century. While not without some resistance, equality feminism has been embraced across sectors—government, industry, and the media—and commercialized to the point of cultural saturation. Equality signs, everywhere. On billboards and T-shirts and mugs and dog collars. The sign, in fact, says it all: Equality's broad acceptance is due in part to its perceived logical simplicity, rendered as equal rights under the law, equal representation in government and industry, and equal participation in society. And American feminism has long held this idea as the solution to systemic misogyny.

---

* Invoking the words of bell hooks, I refer to the total ideological system as the "white supremacist cis-heteropatriarchy." Admittedly, it should be the "white supremacist capitalist cis-heteropatriarchy." Yet the magnitude of this word salad is at times too much even for my big mouth. So, occasionally, I may simply refer to the "patriarchy" or the "white supremacist patriarchy."

But equality will not free us.

Women's liberation cannot be achieved through assimilation into patriarchal institutions—plenty of radical, Black, and lesbian feminists have told us this for years. And the current political moment—the unyielding assault on civil rights and the criminalization and imprisonment of people seeking health care—proves the lie of equality. This moment reinforces to us that equality is contingent upon the whims of the people in power. It's a cruel joke, because despite various rights, laws, and legal mechanisms—from voting rights to equal protection and due process—promised as correctives to societal oppression and systemic discrimination, equality remains elusive.

Even worse is how the language of equality is weaponized to protect the status quo, either to assert that equality really exists because it is written into the law or to stymie justice efforts intended to help society's most marginalized and disadvantaged communities. Examples abound, from the "separate but equal" clause of *Plessy v. Ferguson* to the "equal right" to vote of the Fifteenth and Nineteenth Amendments, to the most recent efforts by conservatives arguing that "equality begins in the womb" as part of their oxymoronic argument about "fetal personhood"—which is like my referring to living persons as "undead corpses." Equality as sameness is easily fabricated by collapsing difference, here the differences in stages of life constituted by time.

The lie of equality is everywhere, and it was brought into stark relief by the coronavirus pandemic, the compounded negative health and economic effects of which disproportionately affected racially marginalized and low-income communities. The wealthy and powerful had more resources and far greater access to care throughout the pandemic—from having the option to abscond to their private estate on Hawai'i (or a second or third home) to being able to afford childcare when schools closed during lockdowns and quality health care when people fell ill, to getting government bailouts and PPP loans with few to no strings attached. Meanwhile, the brunt of unpaid, underpaid, and invisible care work falls on those who need care—including government support—the most.

Rapid advancements in digital technology have transformed our society into an inescapable surveillance state and exposed the harmful and deeply racist realities of the police force empowered by the state. Viral circulation of videos, photos, and live streams of the murder of Black and racially marginalized people have magnified the lie of equality while also retraumatizing communities that have experienced state-inflicted racial violence for generations. We are not treated equally by the police. And we are not treated equally in courts of law. On top of it all, disasters ranging from global warming–induced extreme weather to viral pandemics are exacerbating the suffering of Black, Indigenous, and other racially marginalized communities. These harms—these injustices—have accrued generation upon generation.

Equality feminism, proposing that inclusion can lead to a reformation of our misogynistic and racist institutions, is nothing less than white feminism—which amounts to little more than the white supremacist cis-heteropatriarchy in a dress—because these institutions cannot bend. The capitalism undergirding them has proven inescapable because it is an economic system that incentivizes exploitation for profit.

Plenty of feminists have debated equality as our endgame. Black and radical feminists in particular have called out equality as a principle of sameness that relies on the erasure of our differences and a centering of whiteness and patriarchal values. And yet equality has persisted. Feminist scholars have reached a kind of ideological détente with a vague and uninspiring definition of equality as a "negotiation of differences," which ultimately calls for a third entity to determine how to account for people's differences while ensuring their equal value, equal rights, and equal opportunity to participate in society.

This commitment to equality demands too much complicity and affords too much grace to white supremacist cis-heteropatriarchal institutions to do the right thing. I mean, we only need to turn to the US Supreme Court to see who has historically set the conditions for the negotiation of our civil rights and, by extension, our humanity. Equality is both the wrong ideal and the wrong endgame if we truly desire to end systemic racism and misogyny.

Feminists cannot smash the patriarchy by fortifying its walls. Revolution and inclusion are at odds here. Seeking equality within our existing institutions means desiring to join the very institutions that have depended on women's subjugation.

Feminists need a tool, a new guiding idea, that allows us to build a society on something other than patriarchal values and to cultivate lives not circumscribed by them. One that finds dignity in difference, and from that recognition helps us create a society that cherishes independence and interdependence; autonomy and belonging; accountability, care, and justice.

And that idea, I believe, is freedom.

— ⁓

I am a capital-A, capital-F Angry Feminist. Feel free to stereotype me further: I am an angry lesbian feminist, although please attribute some of my anger to my warring Italian and German sides as well as to my fiery astrological Sun and Moon signs (a double Leo—to the surprise of no one).

I wasn't always a feminist. As a teen and young adult, I couldn't fathom associating myself with the word. What I despised about feminism was my perception that all feminists seemed to do was whine and revel in playing the victim. I had been a competitive athlete in my youth and had always prided myself on being strong, so the last thing I wanted to do was identify with weakness. But the projection of strength that I felt was essential to my core being was also a defensive barrier against seeing myself as a part of the world. You can't get hurt if you don't let other people in—this was my own island mentality.

I was a product of my culture, my misogynistic beliefs clearly informed by the cultural backlash against feminism in the 1980s and

1990s. My small South Jersey town—where mudder trucks bore Confederate flags on their way to the local rodeo at "Cow Town"—was Reagan Country. I grew up in a place so Anglo-homogeneous that white Catholics were treated as social outliers.

Regardless of countless childhood experiences in which I was told I couldn't or wasn't allowed to do something because of my gender, I never connected my anger to any broader sense of injustice. I wasn't yet capable of seeing beyond myself. I just had an intuition, this deep gut feeling apparent to me around the time I was nine years old, that it was ridiculous that I had to wear a shirt outside because, I was told, "You're a girl," while all the neighborhood boys, including my two younger brothers, got to run around unencumbered by cheap synthetic tops. Or that I did not receive my high school's inaugural student-athlete award, even though I had a higher GPA and more varsity letters than the boy who won it, because, as the school's PTA president (a good friend's dad) apologetically confided to me after the ceremony, "We had to give it to a boy first."

Nevertheless, my passionate opposition to feminism continued into my twenties. Even after I completed my graduate degree in Women's Studies, I thought feminism wasn't integral to my life because, during my studies, I became a lesbian and believed that in doing so I had fully freed myself from every single vestige of the patriarchy. (Women's Studies, my gateway to lesbianism.) I rejected the heterosexual game. I didn't care what men thought of me. I didn't dress for them or schedule my time around them. Men weren't the referent of my life. In fact, I cannot remember a time, even before I became a lesbian, when I ever regarded men as authorities of what was right or good—whether that man was my biological father or a religious Father. I became an atheist when I was eight years old because my endless existential questions were met with "because the Bible says so," which, even then, I knew was absurd. This vacuous answer is typically served up by people who have no justifiable reason for what they do, or what they demand *you* do, so they just uncritically parrot the words that were told to them.

Ultimately, my feminism emerged from my lesbianism. Women were—and, frankly, always have been—the cardinal focus of my desires, platonic and otherwise. It was a mindset very much aligned with what Audre Lorde referred to as having a "lesbian consciousness." Whereas equality feminism positions men as the authoritative referent of women's lives, the types of feminism I have studied and integrated into my life and work are not concerned with fitting into men's world, or acquiring men's acceptance, or earning a seat at men's table. Rather, these are feminisms that have endeavored to figure out ways that women can carve out their freedom by creating their own communities and their own values. The feminist visionaries I admire believed in the transformative power not of capitalism but of the imagination. Lorde, bell hooks, Simone de Beauvoir—these feminists examined how women could create lives not necessarily independent from men, because men are a part of the world we live in, but as free as possible from the oppressive strictures of the patriarchy.

From these feminisms, I have developed a feminism that, I see now, captures the spirit of the rebellious, "disrespectful" child I was and the person I am becoming. It is a feminism not seeking to be equal to men but one charting pathways to freedom, bodily autonomy, and creative self-determination *as a collective endeavor*. A freedom-centered feminism not based in the morality of right and wrong but in an ethics of how to live a joyous and meaningful life as a citizen of the world. A feminism that understands that power is not inherently evil but a force we can utilize to design our lives and strive toward justice. A feminism that believes freedom is not the province of the individual but a responsibility of the collective.

I found my feminism in the work of Black, lesbian, and radical feminists, as well as in the work of some unlikely sources, from Friedrich Nietzsche to Henri Bergson to James Baldwin. A few incredible mentors have guided me along the way and influenced my thinking (you will see them quoted variously throughout this book). Their ideas, writings, and mentorship have made me the person I am today and am in the process of becoming. One of the greatest lessons I have learned is that our encounters and relationships—like those I have had with these women and their writing—are the most dynamic, powerful forces forging not just our individual becoming but our collective survival. They fuel the creativity we need to break free of the strictures that bind us.

For more than two decades, I have trained, written, taught, and lectured about feminism, gender and sexuality, language and literature, and ethics. In my work, I arrived at the conclusion that one problem with equality is that there is no clear, universal definition of what it is, or what it consists of, in social relationships. This is because, as feminists like Ute Gerhard and Linda Zerilli have explained, equality is a relational concept that—taking shape within patriarchal institutions—requires the complexity of humanity to be reduced to variables of likeness, a quantifiable equation applicable to all people. Sure, equality makes sense abstractly, in terms of a mathematical equation, or perhaps, more accurately, in an enclosed system. But humans—sorry-not-sorry to billionaire CEOs and corporations—aren't numbers, fixed objects, or profit-earning machines. The richness and intricacies of our lives cannot be compacted into an identity box on a census or job application. Relationships, too, aren't mathematical problems that can be easily solved when disagreements arise. Equality gives lie to the notion that life is simple, that gender exists in a neat binary, and that society's greatest problems can be solved if we had the right formula or code.

The correlation between the ubiquity of equality and its ambiguity is prevalent throughout our culture. In 2019, for example, I reported that a celebrated 2018 study based on forty years of social survey data concluding that people wanted more equality in both the home and workplace relied on one profound oversight: Not once in that forty-year period were respondents given a definition of equality prior to answering questions about gender equality. Both the scholar who authored the study and the research organization (NORC at the University of Chicago's General

Social Survey) that provided the data set to the scholar shockingly admitted to me that no definition of equality was included in their survey. Yet, without a set definition, how can any assessment be made about societal views on gender equality? If anything, the study's results indicated that people's perceptions of gender equality are *subjective* and *gendered*—the findings of such surveys always show that a higher percentage of men than women believe gender equality already exists. This isn't surprising. First, increased visibility of women's political power, professional advancement, and cultural representation conjure the perception of equality—suggestive of the psychological phenomenon of overestimating the size and/or power of an underrepresented population—even if it statistically does not exist. Second, if men believe they are innately smarter, faster, and stronger than women, then their understanding of gender equality is based on gender *inequality*. In short, how you understand gender determines how you understand gender equality.

In my days as an adjunct professor, my students and I would often talk about gender equality. Early in a semester, I would pose the question: "How do you define feminism?" Invariably, no matter the college (like the typical adjunct, I taught at multiple colleges each semester), no matter the latest trend, everyone used the word *equality* in their answer. Feminism meant "equality for women," or "equality for people of all genders," or "equality in the workplace."

The repetition of *equality* in the responses, to me, connoted the uncertainty of ambiguity. That is why, in an attempt to make the concept concrete, my students applied it to groups of people ("women," "all genders"), settings ("the workplace," "the law"), or things ("rights," "pay"). But when I asked a follow-up question about what equality *meant* and what it actually *looked* and *felt* like outside all the rhetoric, they always fell silent.

This silence may simply have been unknowingness. Or it may have suggested a budding insight: That beyond its symbolism, equality is empty of real meaning outside of its application, and that its application is imposed externally—enacted and enforced by institutions—rather than being a genuine feeling or experience.

To distill my students' dawning realization: Equality means whatever those in power want it to mean. In the United States, the people in power have been, for centuries, white men—originally, land-owning white men, several of whom enslaved Black people. Indeed, the so-called Founding Fathers' fear of the tyranny of the majority was born out of a desire to protect the power of wealthy white men such as themselves—who were, and continue to be, the statistical *minority* in America. Accordingly, what equality looks like in our nation is determined by how it is processed through white supremacist cis-heteropatriarchal systems and institutions.

A second classroom example proves my point. Continuing our discussion of what gender equality looks like, I would ask my students to raise their hand if they would walk around topless in New York City—not for any lascivious reason but because the city has had, since 1992, what I jokingly refer to as "topless equality." That is, in the Big Apple, everyone, no matter their gender, can legally walk around topless in public.

And, *shocker*, not one woman raised her hand. And, *double shocker*, no one was ever surprised by this result.

Despite this equal right, my female students said they would not go topless because they didn't want to risk harassment, assault, or any form of harm, including judgmental or lecherous stares, from men or women. They knew—as women and queer people and disabled people and racially marginalized people *have known*—that our bodies are constantly policed in ways that legal equality fails to account for and cannot prevent or remedy. Further, any protection promised by the law can only be sought *after* violence has occurred. The language of protection, moreover, is often supremacist code for reinforcing boundaries. Take the police motto of "serve and protect." Whom, exactly, are they serving and protecting? Believe me, I didn't feel protected by the cop who stalked me during my senior year of high school. Or, years later, by the cops who hissed "dyke" at me. Protection implies prevention. It implies care. Yet even their policy—that they cannot get involved until a physical altercation takes place—runs afoul of their motto.

The profound disparity between what the law says and how it is implemented and experienced confirms the lie of equality. "Since men are not equals in the white supremacist, capitalist, patriarchal class structure, which men do women want to be equal to?" hooks asked. "Do women share a common vision of what equality means?" We clearly don't. A gap exists between equal rights and actual rights experienced by people and recognized by our legal institutions. Just take the "equal right" to vote. The racism that fuels voter suppression efforts—from making it difficult to register and stay on the rolls to blocking the counting of votes, gerrymandering districts, and allowing armed vigilantes to patrol polling sites across the nation—is the very racism constructing the mirage of the equal right to vote. And, as if these suppression efforts weren't bad enough, the US Supreme Court has shown its willingness to reconsider this right. In its 2022 fall term alone, it heard two voting rights cases: *Merrill v. Milligan* (a case about the legality of racial gerrymandering in Alabama) and *Moore v. Harper* (out of North Carolina and also about gerrymandering and state legislatures' power to pass voter restriction laws without judicial interference). The so-called equal right to vote has, for years, been under assault at every level of government.

If voting is a symbol of democracy, when we peel back the lie of equality, we may even begin to wonder *how* exactly the United States is a democracy, given that it was founded on the genocide of the land's original inhabitants and enslaved and denied the humanity and citizenship of millions of Black people who built its wealth.

Equal rights have not guaranteed "liberty and justice for all." Constitutional amendments and federal and state laws have not safeguarded Black people from being murdered for simply walking down the street with some Skittles and iced tea in hand, or sleeping in their bed, or riding public transit, or going for a run. As we have witnessed time and again, these rights and laws have been ineffective in a society with deeply ingrained prejudices, in a nation that interprets justice, sug-gestively, through the framework of a *criminal* justice system—which I prefer to call, borrowing from legal scholar Dean Spade, "the crimi-nal punishment system." Violence is legitimized—not prevented or redressed—when "justice" is exacted through criminalization and punishment.

Equality cannot be our strategy or our endgame because it doesn't allow us to imagine a life beyond the patriarchy and its institutions. The pur-suit of equality leads to a kind of entrapment that will always confine us to the restraints of the patriarchal institutions in which we live and constrain us into making reactionary choices along a spectrum from complicity to resistance. Arguably worst of all, equality locks us all into a debilitating, bad-faith gender binary. The politics of this pursuit also circumscribes our language and logic about issues pertaining to bodily autonomy, from the right to have an abortion to the right to receive gender-affirming health care (which is life-affirming health care, or just health care, or just *care*). Within these patriarchal systems, women are relegated to defining themselves in relation to and in the reflection of men. Feminist efforts should not aspire to sameness or acquiescence through compromise within systems that depend on our oppression.

Tethered to equality, feminists remain stuck endlessly recycling the same talking points about the same issues battled by our mothers and our mothers' mothers. Talk about cruel optimism, or what cultural critic Lauren Berlant described as "when something you desire is actually an obstacle to your flourishing."

Equality does not offer ways to articulate women's desires, dreams, or self-determination as political imperatives outside of the patriarchal framework and standpoint of oppression. Consequently, the feminist politics of equality has struggled to conceive of women's power and pleasure outside of men and distinct from patriarchal understandings of these terms.

Equality cannot change the institutions in which we live and work. Its mechanisms in no way function to emancipate us from the gender binary that legitimizes gender oppression, discrimination, and violence *to keep white men in power.* What equality does do is allow more people to join the team if they play by the rules of the game. And who has written and enforced the rules?

Expanding the system does not fundamentally change the system. The price for admission is assimilation. Inclusion requires complicity. *Don't you want to keep your job? Rent won't pay for itself. Neither will that root canal, even if you have dental insurance.*

Simply put, equality is not good enough. As feminist journalist and lawyer Jill Filipovic said, "Women deserve more than just equality." But I also want women to realize, to quote an old feminist saying, "If you think equality is the goal, your standards are too low."

In this book, I unpack the lie of equality to show how this long-cherished ideal no longer serves the feminist movement. I take up Zerilli's call to action—"What if instead of thinking about and practicing feminism under the banner of equality or difference (or both), we thought about and practiced feminism under the banner of freedom?"—to propose that freedom is the tool we need to revitalize feminism and cultivate more dignified, caring, and joyful lives. It can usher us beyond visibility, representation, false equivalences, and the harmful expansion and replication of systems of oppression.

I define freedom as an ongoing process of self-creation and world-building rooted in accountability and care. Freedom practices are those that foster our authenticity and honor the dignity of all people. They demand the recognition of our mutual coexistence. Freedom means, for example, reorienting our thinking about our health not as personal health but as public health, of health care not as a personal matter but as a public responsibility—and reconceptualizing our politics to recognize health care not as a personal benefit afforded by our employer but as a public good provided by our government.

In this sense, freedom is both a personal ethics and a collective politics. The practices of freedom are grounded in the development of a critical consciousness of how our mutual coexistence necessitates working toward our mutual freedom. The internal work and external practice continuously inform each other and evolve through our encounters and relationships over time. The political power of this freedom work is that it can build movements that intermingle, deconstruct, and redeem spaces that have been historically exclusionary and toxic, and that generate intersectional frameworks and policies that intend to make all of us safer and more cared for, and imbue us with a sense of belonging.

One freedom practice threaded throughout this book is the creation of our gender, both in our choice of an identity and in the stylistic expression of who we are and are becoming. Equality feminism, I argue, relies on the gender binary, which binds *woman* to *man*. But what if we freed ourselves of the mindset that has conditioned us to understand *woman* through men's gaze and values? And what if we understood that this liberation did not erase women but removed the traditional strictures of womanhood? And that *woman* is not half of a whole, but rather can be a constellation, abundant in its variety? How might this mutual recognition and respect for all women transform our politics? How might it liberate us from a standpoint of oppression and a scarcity mindset that has us fighting each other about who gets to be a woman and instead allow us to imagine new ways to strengthen and enlarge our freedom to care for ourselves and each other?

Inherent in a freedom practice is holding oneself accountable for one's choices and actions, no matter how limited the range of choices are. Accountability, I believe, is essential to feminists' ability to generate a political standpoint rooted in strength and integrity rather

14

than in shame and oppression. Accountability is liberating in this regard because, for example, when I declare that my sexuality is *my* choice—from the identity I choose to how I pursue my desires—no one can make me feel shame for who I am or how I live.

Because freedom is not a possession but a continuous practice, we can think of freedom-centered feminism not as an event but as a narrative, a movement. It extends over time, which means there is always an opportunity for change. "Freedom is a constant struggle," as Angela Davis told us. Unlike the applied artifice of equality, freedom is not given—Beauvoir and Baldwin, among others, maintained—but is claimed and activated. You decide *how* you will live your freedom. The catch is that the capacity of this *how* depends on the collective.

Freedom is not new to feminism, or to US social movements. For more than a century, Black, Indigenous, lesbian, and queer feminists have championed freedom, only to be excluded by mainstream white feminists religiously dedicated to equality. These freedom feminists learned from and were inspired by those fighting for Black liberation—the freedom fighters of slavery abolition in the nineteenth century and those of civil rights in the twentieth. Distinct from their predecessors and rooted in more radical traditions, the freedom fighters of today do not want a seat at the proverbial table. They know their freedom is not won through inclusion in white supremacist institutions but through creativity and imagination. The feminist freedom presented in this book is indebted to these freedom fighters, today's activists and forward-thinking minds—from the Nap Ministry's Tricia Hersey to Decolonize Design's Aida Mariam Davis—who know the table is just another trapping of the capitalism that is so deeply essential to the white supremacist cis-heteropatriarchy.

It is time that feminists heed the longstanding call for freedom, what Beauvoir believed gave meaning to life. Beauvoir dedicated herself and her work to the pursuit of freedom. In various writings, she explained that freedom is only possible when we understand it as a collective endeavor, not an individual enterprise. It is not experienced in isolation but only through dynamic engagement with the world. Beauvoir also recognized that we are fundamentally unequal—meaning we are not born with the same amount of freedom or equal resources to cultivate it. Rather, she contended, our lives are "situated" by our personal histories and socioeconomic conditions, and it is from this unique "situatedness" that our freedom work begins. That our situation marks the starting place of our freedom, however, is the opposite of fatalism. Beauvoir asserted that through our encounters and relationships we can surpass the limits of our freedom.

"Simone de Beauvoir's words," Lorde wrote in *A Burst of Light*, "echo in my head: 'It is in the recognition of the genuine conditions of our lives that we gain the strength to act and our motivation for change.'" From this recognition, Lorde understood that "I am not free while any woman is unfree, even when her shackles are very different from my own."

If equality anchors our dignity, our bodily autonomy, and our rights to the patriarchy, then freedom liberates them from it. Equality feminism has us seeing the ceiling as the limit. But if we stepped outside the house, we'd see the entire sky.

— ~

In this book, I call upon feminists to realize equality's utter inadequacy and instead center freedom as the primary value to shape our narratives and guide our activism and politics.

My intention is to encourage us to pivot our ideas, logic, narratives, and politics from an equality mindset to a freedom mindset. The question, ultimately, for feminists is not "What are we fighting *against*?" but "What are we fighting *for*?"

As a book of ideas, the following pages raise several questions. What would happen, for instance, if we substituted mutuality for equality? What if we recognized that each person has dignity, or what the Combahee River Collective described as a person's "inherent value"? What if instead of whitewashing differences and disparities, we systemically and culturally incentivized behaviors, policies, laws, and institutions that worked to affirm and *collectively account for* each person's dignity, distinct from identity politics? What if we defined this work as care work that attends to each person's and community's needs in accordance with their own situation, rather than offering them rights based on what wealthy white men wanted in the eighteenth century? What if we recognized that perhaps we don't all want the same thing or need the same thing to live meaningful lives? What if, to respect the freedom and dignity of all people, we invested in communal forms of care and support, rather than in policing and criminalization, because we understood that incarceration destroys human dignity and forecloses accountability?

Some of you might be thinking that nothing, including freedom, escapes white supremacy and capitalism. And that when you hear the word *freedom*—bandied about in rhetoric about free speech to defend hate speech and in rabid assertions about the right to bear arms in public or to not wear a mask during a global pandemic—you understand it to be a tool of white supremacy.

Frankly, you're not wrong. But this bastardized notion of freedom—what historian Tyler Stovall and writer Ta-Nehisi Coates have called "white freedom"—is a misuse of the word. It describes a kind of narcissism that demands the oppression of others. Through a nationalist lens, it is egoism touted as American individualism, a birthright enshrined by white supremacy. And a freedom defined by winners and losers—people who have freedom and those at whose expense that freedom comes—is not freedom at all.

My definition of freedom directly challenges this predominant understanding of American freedom based in a history of white supremacy and rugged male individualism. By recuperating and centering the long tradition of feminists who have fought for freedom, my objective is to reclaim freedom from the ideological right. And this challenge is essential: If we are to change our culture, we need to change the narrative. Foundational to my definition of freedom is that individual freedom is both realized and expanded by the freedom of others. This is a critical distinction between white freedom and feminist freedom.

— ⁓

My sincere hope is that you will critically engage with the ideas in this book to further our collective feminist politics. Ideas are catalysts for change. They are not perfect or unassailable, nor do they have to be to make new ones possible. I offer mine here as a starting point by way of asking questions to shift our mindset, values, and objectives. By asking, What else? What else other than equality? The provocative Nietzschean in me wants to crack open settled ways of how we think, live, and interact with each other. At stake is the power of words to shape not only action but also how we think and, in turn, reshape the political narratives that have dominated the feminist movement.

So, what happens if we free ourselves of equality?

Let's find out.

CHAPTER 1

THE EQUALITY MINDSET

Why have women settled on—or, more importantly, settled *for*—equality?

The desire for equality, the unrelenting commitment to it, is like a willful entrapment. A bad romance we just can't quit. We cling to the fantasy despite its endless disappointment. It's kind of funny, to be honest: The patriarchy presented women this ideal, conditioned us to believe in it, and simultaneously made it impossible to achieve.

The COVID-19 pandemic only magnified this disappointment, born from the reasonable presumption that, certainly, in the twenty-first century, men would pick up the slack at home, share the load of house chores, and help the kids with their homework. In heterosexual partnerships, women statistically handle a majority of the domestic and childcare workload, a statistic that increased in 2020, the first year of the pandemic. Consequently, in that year alone, women left the workforce at twice the rate of men, largely because of the gendered expectation that they are the primary if not the sole caregivers of the family. The 2022 *Women in the Workplace* report—the largest annual study of women's standing in corporate

America—found that for every woman in leadership who got a promotion, two women quit. And work-from-home job flexibility—promised as an antidote to having to choose between family and career—has only increased the amount of work women do at home. The consequence, cultural critic Anne Helen Petersen reported at *Bloomberg*, is that they have turned into "one-woman safety-nets," available 24/7 to everyone.

The cruel optimism of equality has wrought this gap between women's expectations and our reality.

The tension generated by this antagonism was depicted by Rachel Cusk in *Aftermath*, a memoir about her divorce. In processing the breakdown of her marriage, Cusk realizes that swapping gender roles with her husband—she was the breadwinner, while he was the stay-at-home parent—not only failed to effect the desired equal distribution of domestic and childcare responsibilities but also disillusioned her of her belief in gender equality. "I earned the money in our household, did my share of the cooking and cleaning, paid someone to look after the children while I worked, picked them up from school once they were older," she wrote. "And my husband helped. It was his phrase and still is: he helped me. I was the compartmentalized modern woman, the woman having it all, and he helped me to be it, to have it. But I didn't want help: I wanted equality."

"He helped me" is a symptom of the sexist belief that women are solely responsible for taking care of the home, such that a husband like Cusk's articulates his participation in this labor in terms of a supporting role rather than a primary one. Faith in equality has misled women like Cusk to believe in the promise of *having it all*. At most, this class-based fantasy has produced an unquantifiable shit ton of burnout. Because *having it all* really means *doing it all*.

What goes unspoken in mainstream conversations about having it all is the fact that the inclusion of women in the capitalist workforce has no direct impact on the domestic labor they have been historically expected to perform at home. Cusk's story exemplifies findings from a 2022 study on gendered housework in US families revealing that hetero-married mothers who earn more than their husbands also do more housework. "The gender housework gap actually gets bigger for mothers who earned more than their spouses," the study's author, University of Bath economist Joanna Syrda, wrote. "The more they earned over their partner, the more housework they did."

Study after study shows a gender disparity in perceptions of gender equality: A higher percentage of men believe women and men are more equal than ever before and that, in fact, gender equality has already been won and, therefore, the need for equality efforts is done. This discrepancy is not surprising given how the *idea* of equality takes shape in a patriarchal society where it is both "natural" and "expected" that women will do more, if not all, of the childcare and household labor—unpaid care work has historically been coded female and, by a nearly two-to-one ratio, has been women's work for decades. As a result, Petersen observed, job flexibility intended as a perk can instead "default into a far more regressive division of labor," since men, preferring to work in the office, accept less flexibility than women. The consequence, she explained, is that "no matter how theoretically equitable the marriage is, you can see who would naturally pick up more of the domestic and caregiving responsibilities: the partner who is often in the home, with greater proximity to the kids, and whose career is already consciously or subconsciously deprioritized because, well, it pays less."

Cusk's story also demonstrates the fallacy of social equality. Relationships are dynamic, not static. And equality, in the sense of a permanent equilibrium or balance, is impossible to achieve or sustain in relationships, personal or professional, sexual or platonic. How do you create, let alone prove, an equal relationship? Between a manager and their employee? A parent and their child? Or children? A husband and wife? Or any two spouses, for that matter?

It's strange, too, that equality is a barometer of a good relationship. When it comes to a sexual relationship, what does equality even mean or look like? What if you top from the bottom? What if having an orgasm is not your endgame? Or fucking isn't a teleological narrative ending in

21

someone coming? Pleasure is qualitative, not quantitative. A feeling, not a number.

No one is immune to or too privileged to experience the frustration produced by the lie of equality. In her book *Becoming*, for example, former US First Lady Michelle Obama described the different experiences and responsibilities she and her husband, former US president Barack Obama, had while attempting to get pregnant via IVF: "He was gone and I was here, carrying the responsibility. I sensed already that the sacrifices would be more mine than his," she said. "None of this was his fault, but it wasn't equal, either, and for any woman who lives by the mantra that equality is important, this can be a little confusing. It was me who'd alter everything, putting my passions and career dreams on hold, to fulfill this piece of our dream."

WHAT (WO)MEN WANT

Women have settled on and settled for equality because we've been conditioned to want it.

Social conditioning molds mindsets, or structured ways of thinking that over time become automatic and unconscious—"natural." Our mindset shapes our ideas and beliefs and is the lens through which we perceive the world. I define the *equality mindset* as that which has engendered the unyielding, even uncritical, fidelity to equality as the cure-all to the mechanisms of gender oppression and discrimination we interpret in terms of gender inequality. This mindset, as I wrote for NBC, has hemmed the expanse of our imaginations to the patriarchy. It has shaped women's self and social perceptions, and it has established an identitarian, rights-based agenda as the predominant feminist agenda. Its history, however, reveals more sinister consequences: The equality mindset supports and strengthens the very white supremacist cis-heteropatriarchy that feminists claim we want to dismantle.

I use mindsets as the framework to analyze feminism because this method allows for a cross-historical, sociological, and political assessment of the dominant ideology that has monopolized US feminism. Only by understanding equality feminism as an intergenerational product of the equality mindset can we break free of this mindset and change the vision and politics of the movement. I refrain from using the traditional wave framework because it is reductive and inaccurate to think of feminism in waves, as if the diverse and divergent seas of activism were completely calm and nonexistent in between some great white wave of middle- and upper-class white women fighting for their next desired equal right. Feminists like Benita Roth, in *Separate Roads to Feminism*, and Koa Beck, in *White Feminism*, have disabused us of this overly simplistic narrative.

The equality mindset devises a politics that is both reformist and reactionary because men are the frame of reference for inclusion within patriarchal institutions, and it is a politics that strives to attain the same rights, privileges, and power as white men. The aspiration of parity has resulted in a lot of unfortunate mimicry. "In order to succeed in a patriarchal world," writer and cultural critic Jessa Crispin asserted in *Why I Am Not a Feminist*, "we took on the role of patriarchs ourselves. In order to win in this world, we had to exhibit the characteristics the patriarchal world values and discard what it does not."

The payoff in both the compromise and the complicity is (white) women winning the rights that have granted them greater access to society and its institutions. And with this access comes power and wealth. The agenda is thus justified by these successes—voting rights, educational opportunity, the ability to own property—that are in no small part a product of the power, predictability, and inflexibility of our capitalist systems and institutions.

The social conditioning instantiating this mindset is one that, Beauvoir asserted, concretizes women's "second sex" status. She examined, in *The Second Sex*, how this conditioning is ubiquitous, prevailing in all institutions, all discourses—from history to religion, literature, the law, science, news media, and psychoanalysis. A palimpsest of patriarchal reinforcement, she observed, has trained women into "a deep complicity with the world of men," such that they "can only submit to the laws, the gods, the customs, and the truths created by males." And they are threatened with moral indictments—the male god or authority figure always watching—and violence if they fail to submit.

Complicity is appealing, even desirable, because in exchange for submission, women are gifted male protection, proximity to patriarchal power, and social acceptance as feminine—as "real" women who "act like ladies." Such tokens of complicity are why, Beauvoir said, as if alluding to white feminism without giving it a name, "white women are in solidarity with white men and not with Black women." Women's alliance with and allegiance to men, furthermore, points to how heterosexuality functions as a patriarchal and political institution, as a handbook on social cues about "correct" and "natural" gender relations.

The nineteenth-century women's movement for suffrage established the culture of gender equality, and once white women were given a taste of power by white men, the validation of this political strategy inculcated it more deeply into women's minds. Yet, the equality mindset has fixed us into a permanent state of wish fulfillment, a dream deferred that demands a suspension of disbelief (or masochism—take your pick). We are locked into this mindset because the illusion of equality is sustained by our being fed breadcrumbs—look, one Black, South Asian female vice president of the United States! One Black woman and one Latina on the Supreme Court *at the same time*? Success! So we keep *persisting*, as our T-shirts tell us to do, harboring the belief that gender equality is "possible within our lifetime." And these breadcrumbs, these "small wins," as some say, give us false comfort that equality is achievable. But the assumption that "nearness to this thing will help [us] or the world to become different in just the right way," as Berlant said, is the relation of cruel optimism we have been stuck in for more than a century.

A significant reason why equality is so challenging to achieve inheres in the process of turning an idea into reality. Filtering the idea of equality through the sieve of the white supremacist cis-heteropatriarchy means that how it is interpreted and applied has historically rested in the hands of the white men who designed and continue to control our institutions, laws, and policies. Think of it like Play-Doh. Pushing an amorphous concept like equality through a man-made mold means it will come out the other side looking like the shape of that mold.

No wonder equality has not been the great panacea to women's liberation. What might have started as an inspired endeavor quickly morphed into a movement that replicated and reinforced the "glass" barriers (ceilings, floors, cliffs) of the very systems we were convinced we were shattering.

A critical limitation of this mindset is rooted in its architecture. The equality mindset is built upon the gender binary. What I mean by this is that feminists have adopted the hierarchical opposition of man above woman as the ideological structure of the movement. The gender binary is the foundation upon which women have leveraged their "second sex" status as a political imperative. It is the ultimate logic of equality feminism. And it is the reason why some self-identified feminists remain so passionately wedded to the gender binary. They believe that without it, not only would feminism have no political standing but also that the category of woman would cease to exist—a paranoid belief that has been legitimized by both traditional and social media in recent years. Frankly, this idea is simply ridiculous—I mean, if you've been erased, then who the hell is tweeting from your account?

This kind of binary thinking, of course, isn't really *thinking* at all. The equality mindset operates as a zero-sum game. And feminism has been in lockstep with this oppositional, reductive thinking. Both the mindset and the gender binary subscribe to what literary theorist Barbara Johnson described as the patriarchal, heteronormative logic of $1 + 1 = 1$. The sum of "1" is the perfect union of man and woman, which, because woman is conceived as man's complement, is really about making man whole. A perfect union, traditionally, is symbolized by a woman taking her husband's surname upon marriage. It is still, in the twenty-first century, considered radical, and maybe even a bit queer, for each person to keep their respective surname, arguably even queerer for a man to take his wife's surname.

Yet, as Beyoncé told us in "1+1," "One plus one equals two."

If we break free of the gender binary, however, we can break free of the equality mindset.

And the moment we realize the fallacy of equality, we'll begin to ask how it happened and why we even wanted it in the first place.

HOW EQUALITY HAPPENED

How did the equality mindset take hold of us? And how did equality feminism emerge as the dominant model of US feminism?

The history of US feminism cannot be summarized in a neat, linear narrative, a progressive arc of the rise and slow decline of white feminism. Among the many types of feminism, there has been a defining tension between a single-issue feminism focused exclusively on gender and multi-issue feminisms that acknowledge that all forms of oppression—misogyny, racism, xenophobia, classism, ableism, homophobia, and transphobia—are linked and cannot be separated and resolved individually. These latter feminisms encompass the work of Black women writers and lecturers of the nineteenth century like Anna Julia Cooper and Mary Church Terrell, who argued that Black women experience a unique set of racist and sexist oppressions, and that of more anarchist and Marxist-leaning feminists like Emma Goldman and, later, Silvia Federici, who advocated for workers' rights and expressly pointed out that domestic labor is largely unpaid because it is gendered as women's work.

Equality has played a role in both single-issue and multi-issue feminisms. And many feminists have pointed out the challenge—what historian Joan Scott called the "paradox"—of equality for feminist politics: It has forced us either to argue for sameness between men and women to win equal rights or to claim that biological differences exist between men and women to justify the need for extra supports and protections (often in the name of equity) to pave the road for equality. The paradox has produced a kind of agnostic compromise, whereby faith in equality has been secured by loosely conceiving of it as a space in which differences between women can be negotiated so that common ground can be located from which to advocate for equal rights and opportunity.

This definition, however, does not address the fundamental problem of equality's architecture: the gender binary. Additionally, to conceptualize equality as a negotiation of differences requires a system of measurement established on the gold standard of white men and rendered largely in terms of capitalism and identity. This system has materialized in the feminist politics of "equal pay" and "equal rights"—equal, of course, in relation to white men. The zero-sum thinking driving the equality mindset means, at its worst, the negotiation of our differences manifests as a kind of bad-faith Oppression Olympics to see who has suffered the most. From a political strategy standpoint, the equality mindset configures women's power from a place of oppression, where, for example, our empowerment is determined by how much money we earn in relation to a white man's dollar.

That equality is easy to grasp, at least in theory, is part of equality feminism's ascendance. Simplicity is great for branding. But equality feminism also works in service of the patriarchy. It justifies patriarchal institutions because it exists in them. Equality feminism was never about dismantling patriarchal systems and institutions but about including women in them, fortifying them in the process.

We can trace the origins of the equality mindset to the dawn of the US feminist movement, in the mid-nineteenth century. Distinct from other Christian sects, the Quaker faith believed in egalitarianism—that all people are equal in God's eyes. This belief spurred Quakers' presence at the frontlines of the abolition movement to end slavery. The Quaker-led abolitionist argument rooted in egalitarianism was so effective in persuading (white) public opinion that women appropriated it for their own case. Quaker women—including Susan B. Anthony, Alice Paul, and Lucretia Mott—became some of the leading proponents of women's rights.

Mott was one of several women who attended—but were prevented from participating in—the World Anti-Slavery Convention in London in 1840. There, Mott met Elizabeth Cady Stanton, who was raised in the Scottish Presbyterian Church, which was doctrinally Calvinist (with strong beliefs in predestination and men's moral superiority over women). In 1848, the two had a meeting with Mott's sister and two other Quaker women to plan a convention concerning the status of women, *for women*. From this meeting, Stanton drafted the Declaration of Sentiments, considered a foundational political document of US feminism.

Sentiments was modeled on the Declaration of Independence, with one notable addition: "We hold these truths to be self-evident: that all men *and women* are created equal; that they are endowed by their Creator with certain inalienable rights; that among these are life, liberty, and the pursuit of happiness" (emphasis mine).

The Declaration of Sentiments was presented and signed at the 1848 Seneca Falls Convention, regarded by many as the origin-event of US feminism. Stanton, tellingly, declared the convention to be "the most momentous reform that has yet launched in the world"—emphasis on *reform*, indicating a desire to amend yet ultimately maintain an established system. Stanton and other suffragists argued that including women in society, and especially in the voting booth, would improve and strengthen the moral righteousness of the nation.

Both declarations invoked the Quaker belief in God- or creator-given egalitarianism. Stanton even asserted that "the equal station to which [women] are entitled" is that which "God entitle[s] them," and, later, "that woman is man's equal—was intended so by the Creator."

This same belief of God-given equality threads through the *Letters on the Equality of the Sexes* by Sarah Grimké, published in 1837. (For readers unfamiliar with her: Grimké is considered a canonical feminist foremother. I think she's mostly known today through the late Supreme Court Justice Ruth Bader Ginsburg's quote "I ask no favor for my sex. All I ask of our brethren is that they take their feet off our necks," which was paraphrased from Grimké's original: "I ask no favors of my sex. I surrender not our claim to equality. All I ask of our brethren is, that they will take their feet from off our necks, and permit us to stand upright on that ground which God designed us to occupy.")

Grimké and her sister Angelina were from an enslaver family in South Carolina. In 1821, Sarah converted to Quakerism, which stoked an internal moral conflict between her new religion and her personal history with slavery that subsequently incited her to action. Later that decade, she began speaking on the antislavery lecture circuit, and, not long after, she began applying her egalitarian ideas to women and incorporated women's plight as an oppressed caste into her speeches and writings.

Grimké's fifteen letters meticulously sourced the Christian Bible as evidence that women's equality is ordained by God. "I shall touch upon a few points in the Scriptures," she wrote, "which demonstrate that no supremacy was granted to man." From Letter I, "The Original Equality of Woman," to Letter 15, "Man Equally Guilty with Woman in the Fall," Grimké's objective was to prove that women's equality is God's word and therefore the undeniable truth. "They both fell from innocence, and consequently from happiness," she said of Adam and Eve, "*but not from equality.*"

Equality feminism's foundation in Christianity made it a compatriot to white Christian nationalism. Crucially, the "equality" of American feminism did not inhere in the egalitarianism of the people who first inhabited the land—the matrilineal society of the Cherokee—but the patriarchal Christian colonizers whose goal was to establish their supremacy.

WHITE FEMINISM BY DESIGN

Many if not all women traditionally heralded as the foremothers of US feminism in school textbooks and during Women's History Month promoted the interests of middle- and upper-class white Christian women. These women homed their efforts on gender to the exclusion of issues concerning women whose experiences of gender discrimination were compounded by racism and labor exploitation. While the phrase "white feminism" feels like a contemporary invention, its ideology lies at the origins of the mainstream

US feminist movement. Historian Kyla Schuller even regards Stanton as the inventor of white feminism because, as she wrote in *The Trouble with White Women*, Stanton "framed white civilization as imperiled until it made room for white women's leadership, which she figured as more moral, just, and ultimately profitable than men's leadership."

The inception of the US feminist movement coincided with the rise of a white nationalist mandate that codified gender and race as categorical, biological truths and then pointed to those so-called truths as justifiable cause for medicalizing and criminalizing groups of people. The ship of colonization was steered by racism and capitalism and delivered both to these shores—where they served as constitutive instruments of the nation. The United States was founded upon the genocide of Indigenous and tribal peoples, who were the original stewards of the land, and then amassed its wealth from the labor of enslaved African people, who built its agricultural and industrial economies. White feminists vowed that their equal rights, therefore, would serve white men's interests. They wanted to join white men, not tear them down—to *reform* the system, as Stanton commented, not revolutionize it.

Racism and power are entwined at the core of white feminists' strategy. Racism has been white women's ticket to power—specifically, in the early decades of the movement, to the power of the vote. And those white feminists clearly understood the supremacist assignment, because they reversed their position on Black enfranchisement as soon as the Fifteenth Amendment was on the table. Stanton, in fact, led women's charge against it. In countless speeches, she vociferously argued that giving the vote to "Sambo" and "the ignorant African"—her words—would imperil the nation, whereas the moral purity of white women, miraculously transfused into their votes, would sanctify the nation. In setting women's suffrage in opposition to Black suffrage—completely, to note, discounting Black women—we see how the binary works as a supremacist logic to reinforce white supremacy.

To accrue power—whether in terms of suffrage or access to traditionally male spaces like schools—white women formed alliances with white men, particularly Democrats, whose favor they courted to gain national support for their cause. These alliances began as early as 1866, when Anthony and Stanton founded the American Equal Rights Association (AERA) and launched state-level suffrage campaigns across the nation. In Kansas, for example, they accepted the financing and endorsement of the wealthy—and racist—railroad financier George Francis Train. Historian Laura E. Free noted in *Suffrage Reconstructed* that they even shared the same platform with him as he unabashedly rehearsed "racist arguments to support white women's enfranchisement." Among these arguments was one in which he asserted that Republicans wanted to "vote for *negro suffrage* and against *woman suffrage*," telling audiences that this would "place your family political still lower in scale of citizenship and humanity" than Black men. Train did not mince words in the epigram he delivered in a speech in Johnson County, Kansas: "White women work to free the blacks from slavery / Black men to enslave the whites with political knavery, / Woman votes the black to save, / The black he votes, to make the woman slave." Therefore, he argued, only by voting Democrat—and, implicitly, supporting women's suffrage—would society remain intact.

White suffragists were not reluctant to adopt this argument. As Carrie Chapman Catt, who twice served as president of the National American Woman Suffrage Association, once reportedly reassured her audience: "White supremacy will be strengthened, not weakened, by woman suffrage." White women's logic was simple: Only people in power can give you power. And the people in power were white men. They were the gatekeepers, the politicians, the judges, the bankers, the property owners and landowners. They were the protectors—as well as the predators. To interpret power as a thing that can be possessed, is of limited quantity, and is a force wielded for domination is to conceive of it from a supremacist mindset. The political strategy of white suffragists was undeniably born from this thinking.

Rather than form coalitions with women of color and working-class women, these suffrage leaders chose to align themselves with the most powerful, just like the white women who followed in their footsteps chose for decades to exclude racially marginalized, working-class, and queer women from their feminist efforts. They institutionalized this strategy in their suffrage organizations, beginning with Stanton and Anthony's AERA. As Schuller wrote, "for nearly two centuries, white feminists have set lifting white women into the nation's structures of power as the ultimate goal, and they've framed that rise up the hierarchy as the very meaning of equality—even when it requires, by definition, lifting up some through pushing down many others."

This history has served as the template for white feminism as we know it today, as an ideology that reinforces white supremacy and the gender binary that consigns women to their "second sex" status. Within a patriarchal society, therefore, to be *equal* to men is to always be *second* to them. The equality mindset that has taken hold of mainstream feminism and its politics explains its shortcomings and compromises, as well as its racism, lesbophobia, and transphobia. The white feminist politics that Beck so rightly identified as "replicating patterns of white supremacy, capitalistic greed, corporate ascension, inhumane labor practices, and exploitation, and deeming it empowering for women to practice these tenets as men always have" operate from the equality mindset.

We can see this mindset evident at every turn, at every flashpoint of feminist history, from white women telling Black and Indigenous women to march at the back of the 1913 Woman Suffrage Procession in Washington, DC, so as to not offend white southerners, to the *Lean In* feminism of the 2010s. The equality mindset even rears its head in nonsense statements like the notion that Wall Street would be much more ethical if the "Lehman Sisters" were in charge rather than Lehman Brothers—the global investment bank whose 2008 bankruptcy was the largest ever in US history. This mindset takes no issue with the trappings of capitalism. In fact, those who live by it believe that capitalism is the most promising pathway to and realization of equality.

THE LOGIC AND LANGUAGE OF EQUALITY

The critical difference between Stanton's time and ours, and even Beauvoir's time and ours, is that which time has wrought: The ideas, writings, and activism of antiracist and radical feminists have provided us the tools and templates to break free from the equality mindset—that is, if we choose to use them. We have the resources to break free of this complicity. The price for women, Beauvoir wrote in *The Second Sex*, is "renouncing all the advantages an alliance with the superior caste confers on them."

What this means more specifically is that both white women and white feminists—two overlapping but distinct groups—who have possessed the crux of societal and institutional power and resources under the banner of feminism must make a choice about their values and about feminism's purpose. Will they cling to "white supremacy under the guise of 'equality,'" as journalist Ruby Hamad asked in *White Tears/ Brown Scars*, "or will they stand with women of color as we edge ever closer to liberation?"

If we seek to break free of this mindset, becoming aware of its apparatus is the first step. But the work does not end there. We must go further, exposing its roots and examining its logic and language so we can dissect its mechanics to comprehend how the mindset works within ourselves and in our politics and culture. This work helps us to develop a critical consciousness from which we can begin to imagine new strategies in the fight for our dignity and bodily autonomy.

I have already referenced some synonyms for equality, including *parity, sameness, egalitarianism,* and even *equity,* despite the latter's methodical difference—additional structural supports based on need—in how to achieve systemic equality. Here I want to focus on the cultural buzzwords used to invoke equality as a smokescreen to disguise systemic discrimination. This language and the logic that informs it weave a mosaic of equality in support of the patriarchal status quo.

The Logic of the Gender Binary

The gender binary is the organizational principle of gender equality. Equality, as I noted earlier, is a relational concept. It only has meaning within a closed system and specifically within the context of the other fixed values within that system. For example, take the number 3. We only know what 3 means because it exists in relation to other numbers. It is, for instance, *less than* 7 but *more than* 1. In our patriarchal society, the value of all people, and the rights accorded to them, are determined by and set in relation to white men. All gender equality efforts, therefore, position white men as the ultimate referent—the baseline and gold standard.

The gender binary is a modern invention. White colonizers brought it to the North American continent to dehumanize and discriminate against Indigenous and tribal peoples by imposing Christian morality and stripping them of their bodily autonomy. More than one hundred tribes on the continent held cultural beliefs espousing the multiplicity, rather than the duality, of gender.

White settler colonialism not only wrested stewardship of the land from Indigenous people but alienated them from their own cultures and traditions, especially through the enforcement of colonizers' heterosexist notions of gender and sexuality. Indigenous feminist Jihan Gearon, who is Diné (Navajo) and Nahiłii (Black), has written about how the colonizers' gender binary enacted a kind of cultural genocide. Within her own community, for example, "Diné people traditionally have four genders based on the role a person plays in the larger community. The roles of *naadheeh* (feminine man) and *dilbaa'* (masculine woman) have a unique ability and responsibility to act as translators between *asdzáá* (feminine woman) and *hastiin* (masculine male), and they have a unique ability to bring about balance between the masculine and feminine." The gender binary, she observed, was part of the colonizers' ideological agenda to establish their dominance and superiority through Christianity. Compulsory assimilation or elimination expunged defining matriarchal elements from Indigenous communities.

As a relational concept, the gender binary has defined the meaning and value of *woman* in relation to *man*. The relation is cast in the negative—what feminist philosopher Luce Irigaray articulated as "A / not-A" or, more clearly, "man / not-man." The gender binary has meant that women end up representing everything that men are not or do not want to be. Emotional vulnerability, for instance, is considered a weakness in men: a sign that they are effete, effeminate, and maybe even—*gasp*—homosexual. Women must be depicted as weak, needy, dumb, and dependent so men feel strong, competent, smart, and independent.

The gender binary plays out in an array of oppositions—including good versus evil and active versus passive—to affirm and reinforce men's superiority over women. This is the social conditioning that has led us to believe that men are innately superior to women and are, by birth, entitled to this superiority. (Not all men, of course, are entitled in the same way—racism, homophobia, xenophobia, ableism, and classism all affect a person's social privilege and their own sense of entitlement.) This entitlement manifests in the dynamics of traditional gender roles and stereotypes, such as taker and giver, breadwinner and homemaker, and virile and virgin. In other words, men are always and in all ways on top, and women are on the bottom. (And this thinking underlies the question all lesbians are eventually asked—"Who's the man?"—to which we universally respond with an eyeroll.)

White supremacist society needs binaries. They comprise America's architectural bones. These binaries—white/Black, heterosexual/homosexual, cisgender/transgender, able-bodied/disabled, et cetera—function to segregate and exclude people in accordance with society's hierarchical structure of identity categories. Within a white supremacist cis-heteropatriarchy, white is superior. White is man. White is masculine. America's white supremacist society remains intact through not only physical violence but also linguistic violence that employs these binaries. This language work is seen in the racist emasculation of Black men through the patronizing language of "boy," as well as in the deliberate aging of Black children by referring to them as adults, which construes them as dangerous societal threats to warrant their criminalization—a justification for putting terrified, sobbing Black schoolchildren in handcuffs.

You can see how difference plays out in our society in accordance with the power structure of the patriarchy. Our differences have been reductively rendered into artificial identities that are then slotted into a hierarchal system designed to preserve the status quo and especially to safeguard white Christian nationalism. The white supremacist cis-heteropatriarchy is the original pyramid scheme.

If we stopped relying on binaries, how might we upend this power structure and society as we know it?

Fairness

The language of fairness is weaponized to police, ostracize, and expel people from participating in society under the guise that their inclusion discriminates against the people for whom society's very institutions were built. The targets are usually racially marginalized, disabled, gender-nonconforming, and trans people. It is as if their very existence threatens the fabric of the white supremacist cis-heteropatriarchy. Cries of "Fairness!"—or, more specifically, "Unfair!"—are nothing less than dog whistles for the discrimination that is systematically levied against our most marginalized communities.

Demanding fairness is a response to a measured or perceived discrimination that, from an equality mindset, is construed as an inequality. And these days, fairness seems to appear everywhere. In the media, for instance, we have seen fairness evoked in the name of *objectivity*, which has recently given way to *bothsidesism*. The modern fairness argument emerged in opposition to affirmative action law and policy, specifically pertaining to college admissions—since education is a critical lever of societal change and key indicator of social and economic mobility, our white supremacist society has felt it imperative to erect as many barriers to education as possible.

Modern affirmative action policies linked to advancing racial equity were enacted and took effect in the late 1960s, and claims of "reverse discrimination" and "reverse racism" followed almost immediately, with the first suit, challenging the University of Washington Law School's affirmative action policy, filed in 1971. The Supreme Court's 1978 ruling in *Regents of the University of California v. Bakke* forced higher education institutions to change their affirmative action policies, declaring quotas to be unconstitutional according to the Equal Protection Clause of the Fourteenth Amendment. In its fall 2022 term, the US Supreme Court heard two cases challenging the legality of race-conscious admissions at Harvard University and the University of North Carolina brought forth by the nonprofit Students for Fair Admissions. The nonprofit, according to its website, "believe[s] that racial classifications and preferences in college admissions are unfair, unnecessary, and unconstitutional." It was founded by conservative legal strategist Edward Blum—the man who has brought forth dozens of anti–affirmative action cases and led the legal challenge that resulted in the Supreme Court gutting the Voting Rights Act in 2013.

In their Supreme Court brief, lawyers representing Students for Fair Admissions cited the Fourteenth Amendment's Equal Protection Clause and Title VI of the Civil Rights Act of 1964 to contend that "because *Brown* is our law, *Grutter* cannot be." (Harvard, as a private institution, is only subject to the charge of violating Title VI, which states that "no person in the United States shall, on the ground of race, color, or national origin, be excluded from participation in, be denied the benefits of, or be subjected to discrimination under any program or activity receiving federal financial assistance.") The nonprofit deployed the *Brown* ruling—which overturned *Plessy v. Ferguson*'s "separate but equal" clause by claiming the Equal Protection Clause prohibits racial segregation in schools—against the *Grutter v. Bollinger* verdict in 2003 permitting race to be a factor considered in school admissions. This is a clear-cut example of how equality is weaponized against system-wide antidiscrimination and racial justice efforts.

In this context, fairness is usually coupled with another red-flag word: meritocracy.

The myth of American individualism has perpetuated the belief that a person's individual merit is the sole reason they are admitted to a prestigious college or land a six-figure job. Meritocracy is grounded in the fallacy of equality that disguises individual privilege and systemic discrimination.

For people who believe in meritocracy, affirmative action is nothing less than special privilege, or even, egregiously, "reverse racism." Having attended K-12 public schools, completed four degrees (without much debt, thanks to scholarships and part-time teaching jobs in graduate school), taught at high schools and colleges, and tutored wealthy children (because being an adjunct professor doesn't pay the rent), I have plenty of insight into the accumulated and compounding effects of classism and racism within the education system. Children from wealthy families are sent to astoundingly expensive private and independent schools, where they receive individual care, instruction, and attention; where classroom sizes are limited in number; and where the quality of education and resources are unquestionably superior to those available to increasingly underfunded public-school students.

Students from wealthy families can afford to hire multiple private tutors, who may or may not have a heavy hand in completing their school assignments and writing their college application essays. (The stories tutors could tell. Once I even had a high schooler order me to do his history assignment while he took a bath.) They not only have high school tutors but also SAT tutors and college admissions consultants—entire entourages that, behind the scenes, guarantee their success. These advantages are supplemented by parents' donations to colleges prior to their children applying for admission, to grease the path through the gates, so to speak. And if prospective students have parents who are alumni (or "legacies," as my undergraduate alma mater Harvard calls them), their applications are marked as such to denote their special status. And this is only to speak of the preadmissions and admissions

38

processes. The advantages continue into college, whether through pre-existing networks of friends, connections with professors, or access to invite-only clubs reserved for the privileged classes. (At Harvard, these are called "finals clubs.")

According to a 2019 National Bureau of Economic Research study, 43 percent of white admits to Harvard were either recruited athletes (myself included), legacies (another word for nepotism—the opposite of so-called meritocracy), children of faculty and staff, or children whose relatives had recently donated to Harvard. The same study revealed that 75 percent of these white admits would have been rejected (myself included) had they not fallen into any of these categories.

As depressing as it sounds, one of the greatest lessons I have learned, not only from my undergraduate experience but from the diverse experiences I've had across various types of institutions, both public and private, is that there is no such thing as meritocracy. Moneytocracy, perhaps, but certainly not meritocracy. Working hard does not guarantee your success. Nor is it the determining factor of your success. Networks have a greater impact. Knowing people, having connections to people in high places who can open doors, does wonders for a person's career. And, studies show, these social networks are by and large homogenous, race based, and class based.

In the same context, fairness has been used in arguments against student loan debt cancellation. The logic is that debt cancellation would be unfair to people who have paid off their loans. We don't have to dig deep to point out the basic fact that the price of college tuition has skyrocketed in recent decades—between 2006 and 2016, college tuition and fees increased by a whopping 63 percent, according to the US Bureau of Labor Statistics—and student loan debt has soared in kind, thanks to predatory loan companies that capitalize upon people's dreams. It's such a strange, vengeful, and inhumane argument to say, *I suffered, so you should suffer too!* Perhaps this is what America's version of equality really means.

More recently, the language of fairness has been weaponized against trans people's participation in sports. Both national and international fairness policies are being deliberated by legislative bodies to decide which women have the right to compete as women. In the name of fairness, for example, in 2020 the Swiss Federal Tribunal upheld World Athletics' decision to bar South African runner Caster Semenya from defending her Olympic gold. This is despite her undergoing years of inhuman body examinations and tests to prove her gender, including her agreement, in 2011, to take medication to reduce her testosterone levels to become eligible to compete. This medication, she told HBO in a 2022 interview, had several harmful effects, including illness, weight gain, and panic attacks. She has since refused to undergo such medicalized violence to artificially lower her testosterone levels.

The measure of fairness is so arbitrary, in fact, that Semenya is allowed to compete in some women's events (the 100m, 200m, and distances greater than 1,600m) but not others (anything between 400m and 1,600m), based on the acceptable testosterone range for those events. "According to World Athletics and its members," she tweeted in March 2022, "I'm a male when it comes to the 400m, 800m, 1,500m and 1,600m! Then [I'm] a female in 100m, 200m, and long-distance events." Equality is not only at work here in the language of fairness—in the rhetoric of creating an equal or level playing field—but also in how the gender binary is enforced to both exclude and violate people whose bodies are perceived as subversive or threatening to the supposed veracity of it.

"These binaries that we have in sport don't match up to the world," historian Amira Rose Davis said in an interview with NPR. "Sports must maintain this really, really violent binary at all costs, no matter who it hurts," she added. "And right now, that burden, that pain, that harm is most keenly felt by women of the Global South," she said, noting that these standards are based on white patriarchal notions of womanhood, and as such have disproportionately impacted people of color.

The same notion of fairness is found throughout arguments in favor of legislation to ban trans and nonbinary youth from participating in school sports. Advocates claim these laws are necessary to protect girls' and women's sports by mandating a fair and equal competitive playing field—this is all, obviously, code for reifying the gender binary, the architectural bastion of the white supremacist cis-heteropatriarchy.

As of September 2022, eighteen states have passed legislation banning trans youth from participating in sports, with dozens more similar pieces of legislation under consideration in state legislatures across the nation. These anti-trans sports bans represent just one portion of the more than three hundred anti-LGBTQ+ bills presented in state legislatures nationwide in 2022. (Nearly four hundred have been put forth in the first quarter of 2023, with a majority directed at dehumanizing trans people by restricting their health care and inclusion in society, which includes participating in school sports.) And the language of fairness echoes throughout most if not all of these bills and in the arguments for them. "I want to make sure that all the opportunities are provided for our young females* and we protect the fair competition for them so they have all those possibilities," Republican Indiana state representative Michelle Davis, who authored her state's anti-trans bill, said in an Indiana House Education Committee meeting on the proposed legislation in early 2022. Davis repeated the language of fairness ("fair competition") multiple times in her testimony. States like Florida and Kansas even call their respective laws the Fairness in Women's Sports Act.

Title IX, which prohibits sex discrimination in any educational institution that receives federal funding, is invoked by both sides. It protects transgender and gender-nonconforming students from discrimination, but it is also being used by gender essentialists who contend that the inclusion of trans girls puts cisgender girls at a competitive disadvantage to win trophies and break records. This was precisely the argument of the plaintiffs in the 2022 federal appellate court case *Soule et al v. Connecticut Association of Schools et al*, who asserted that Title IX protections—providing "equal athletic opportunity for members of both sexes"—for cisgender girls are weakened by allowing trans girls to compete against them. Those fighting to exclude trans and

---

* "Female" when used in the noun form is a red flag for gender essentialism, as it implies that gender is biology.

gender-nonconforming athletes, in short, are basing their interpretation of Title IX on the gender binary.

Fairness is code for discrimination. At the collegiate level, the cry of fairness was the lynchpin of the effort to ban UPenn swimmer Lia Thomas from collegiate competition in the 2021–2022 season. Thomas followed NCAA protocol to be eligible for competition after her transition. Yet she encountered relentless attacks intended to both intimidate and prevent her from competing.

In June 2022, World Aquatics—swimming's world governing body, which at the time was known as FINA, the Fédération Internationale de Natation—voted that only trans women who "have not experienced any part of male puberty" are eligible for women's competitions, effectively banning trans women like Thomas who did not transition before going through male puberty. World Aquatics' president Husain Al-Musallam justified the ruling using the language of equality and fairness: "Equality is also a key principle for us," he said of the eligibility change. "It is a policy that we need to introduce to protect the competitive fairness of our event."

Such arguments about fairness in women's sports are based on the medical classification of the gender binary, which has strangely rendered puberty as the absolute determinant of gender and, therefore, in this context, of fairness. An athlete's eligibility is determined by an arbitrary hormone level range and classification system set by the medical establishment, whereby women and girls undergo body examinations, hormone testing, and menstrual-cycle reporting. Yes, that's right. In most states, high school athletes are asked questions about their menstrual history on medical evaluation forms they must compete prior to participating in school sports. Anti-trans fanatics are terribly small-minded if they think gender policing ends with trans kids.

The thing is, no two women are the same. It is the fallacy of equality that any two women have the same bodies, or same-sized muscles or body parts, or the same exact hormone levels. Individual hormone levels, in fact, fluctuate daily, weekly, and monthly—there is no set level of estrogen that biologically confirms *woman*. Without the gender binary codified by patriarchal laws and medical institutions, there is no standard definition of *woman* to substantiate such hateful pieces of legislation.

In May 2022, the *New York Times* ran one of its many anti-trans sports articles. This particular article had a section on "science," with writer Michael Powell quoting Mayo Clinic physician Michael J. Joyner, who said "testosterone is the 800-pound gorilla" to emphasize that testosterone, and testosterone alone, is the ultimate factor in athletic success. Powell asserted that the "biological advantage" of testosterone must be true, because men's swimming record times are about 10 to 12 percent faster than women's. But there are a lot of logical leaps operating in this assertion, including the assumptions that muscle mass equals athleticism, athleticism is the same across sports, and all sports require the same athletic skills.

"Sports encompass an enormous array of activities requiring vastly differing combinations of skills and physical capacities," sociomedical scientist Rebecca M. Jordan-Young and cultural anthropologist Katrina Karkazis observed in *Testosterone: An Unauthorized Biography*. "When is power more important? When is finesse? How crucial is endurance? What about flexibility, hand-eye coordination, communication with teammates, strategy?" Testosterone is an anabolic steroid hormone that builds complex muscle mass, but it certainly doesn't equate to the ability to land a quadruple axel in figure skating. You need the technique, you need the endurance, and you need the mental acumen to do that. Muscle power is just one factor in athletic ability. Jordan-Young and Karkazis are right: "The idea that there is one core ingredient in the magic sauce for every conceivable sport is frankly absurd." Yet this is precisely the magical thinking underlying the argument against trans kids participating in sports, whereby debates about fairness are categorically reduced to testosterone as a signifier of manhood.

I am curious, too, why this—the historically racist and eugenicist testing of blood to enforce a supremacist pseudoscientific classification system—is the only vector of fairness of public concern. What about the economic advantage of families who can afford to pay for their kids to train with private coaches, join elite teams, and participate in costly competitions and tournaments? In tennis, for example, your ranking is determined by the points you accrue from the number of matches you win in tournaments. Growing up, I could afford maybe one or two tournaments a year, but the girls I beat on the court were always ranked higher than me because they could afford to play in tournaments year-round—and rankings matter in college recruitment. Should I have cried, "Unfair!"? Or what about racism? What about the racist bullying experienced by Black and brown kids that ostracizes them and pushes them out of sports? Funny how these types of unfairness are swept under the rug.

Again, the issue isn't fairness. It's about excluding trans people from living fulfilling and joyous lives and from participating and finding ways to belong in society. Black excellence, too, is unacceptable in a society that demands Black suffering. That gender is a racial construct means the racism experienced by Black female athletes is often tethered to misogyny. Endless misogynistic, racist, and dehumanizing assaults—too disgusting to warrant repeating here—have been hurled at tennis champions Serena and Venus Williams throughout their careers. These assaults all employ the binaries of the white supremacist cis-heteropatriarchy when they accuse the Williams sisters of not being real women because they are too strong, too aggressive, or win too much.

Also recall the 2021 controversy surrounding Simone Biles, the most decorated gymnast in history, whose score was docked by judges at the US Classic for successfully completing the Yurchenko double pike—the first woman to do so, and a move only a handful of men have pulled off. The reason? According to Juliet Macur at the *New York Times*, the federation assigned the move a "low start value" to "discourage others from risking it." This sanctioning was intended to limit an excellent and iconic Black female gymnast. *It's punishment for her excellence.* The long-term effects of this gender barrier perpetuate the social conditioning that women are inferior—physically weaker—than men. We see this, for example, in claims that men are better than women at sports because they can do X move, which they, and not women, have been allowed to practice and perfect for decades. How about we prohibit male gymnasts from performing the Yurchenko double pike for a century and then reassess their presumed innate athletic superiority?

Conservative media reserves its attacks for excellent racially marginalized, queer, and trans athletes because they are the athletes who, according to bigoted logic, take a (white, cisgender) woman's spot on the podium—precisely the argument of the *Soule* plaintiffs. As case in point: There was a media firestorm about Thomas's participation in the 2022 NCAA championship meet, but she was not the only trans swimmer there. Yale undergrad Iszac Henig, a transgender man, tied for fifth place in the women's 100-yard freestyle race. He was eligible to compete in the women's category by following NCAA regulations to refrain from taking testosterone-based hormone therapy. The marked difference in public outcry about and media coverage of these two trans swimmers suggests how powerful the cultural belief is that testosterone equals manhood—just turn on the TV (for those of us who still have one) and witness all those commercials for "man-boosting" testosterone supplements for men, if you need more proof.

"There is so much more to a great athlete than hormones or height," Henig pointed out in a January 2023 *New York Times* opinion piece about his decision to compete with the men's team during the 2022–2023 NCAA season. "I swim faster than some cis men ever will." And, he added, while competition is important, community and belonging are also meaningful aspects of sports participation. "The more time I spent with the guys," he said of his time so far on the men's team, "the more I realized how much better I felt in men's spaces."

What is interesting about anti-trans arguments is how fairness undermines the spirit of competition. In fact, it's completely antithetical to competition. But participation trophies, as ridiculous as they are, aren't to blame for this—transphobia and misogyny are. The very unfairness arguments levied against trans athletes have been lobbed at lesbians accused of being too manly to compete against women. Tennis legend Martina Navratilova was even called "a walking mixed-doubles team" by a sports columnist who lamented her rival Chris Evert's retirement as a loss of femininity for the sport. (This is gobsmacking considering Navratilova has become a poster girl for banning trans people from sports.)

I, too, personally experienced barely veiled accusations about my gender and also recall them being hurled at female athletes, and specifically Black female athletes, in high school competition. Anytime a girl is just "too good," her gender will be questioned, as if it is unnatural for her to be strong, or fast, or skilled. For example, in August 2022, the *Washington Post* reported that the Utah High School Activities Association investigated the gender identity of a female student who won first place at a state-level competition in 2021 after complaints by the parents of the second- and third-place finishers. (Utah, one of the eighteen states with a trans sports ban, had its ban temporarily blocked by a Salt Lake City judge in August 2022.) A representative of the association told the *Post* that the number of complaints and requests for gender investigations have increased in recent years—no doubt a consequence of the media-fueled gender-binary hysteria.

And just to point out the hypocrisy: No one seemed bothered by the fact that twenty-three-time Olympic gold medalist Michael Phelps had numerous advantages—including an unusually wide wingspan (wider than he is tall), twice the lung capacity of the average person, and the ability to produce significantly less lactic acid, which causes muscle fatigue—over other swimmers. Funny how no one sought to ban his trans-human self from competitive swimming and from becoming the most decorated Olympian of all time.

Gender essentialists do not see how reinforcing the gender binary through the argument of fairness ultimately limits the athletic potential of girls and women. These people are so uncomfortable with the thought of leaving their Platonic cave that they cannot see how radically promising the future of sports could be *for women* if we broke free of the gender binary.

The Logic of Whiteness

As a logic of whiteness, equality functions to neutralize racial differences in order to erase centuries of discrimination. Apparent in the language of equality, in words like *fairness* and *sameness*, this logic is employed to create a façade of objectivity. This whitewashing effectively gaslights people's experience of racism. In this capacity, the role of equality is to establish and maintain a traditional, homogenous, white supremacist society by suppressing and/or assimilating difference. This erasure is critical to those in power being able to claim that they are *not* powerful or privileged because of their whiteness—rather, they are just like everyone else. The point is to conceal the very real material, economic, physical, and psychological effects of racism.

In recent years, we have witnessed equality deliberately invoked to thwart equity and justice efforts, from economic stimulus packages to prison abolition. The backlash to "any policy protecting or advancing non-white Americans," Boston University professor Ibram X. Kendi said in *How to Be an Antiracist*, manifests in the loaded language of "reverse racism."

The logic and language of equality has been the modus operandi of the nonprofit America First Legal (AFL), founded by former Donald Trump aide Stephen Miller in February 2021. AFL has financially backed several successful lawsuits—among them, one out of Texas to stop the federal government's COVID-19 relief response from prioritizing Restaurant Revitalization Fund applications from businesses owned by women, veterans, and people of color. Upon the US district court's ruling in May 2021, Miller released a statement: "This ruling is the first, but crucial, step towards ending government-sponsored racial discrimination."

Miller's organization espouses its message against "anti-white racism" variously, even running radio ads during the 2022 midterm election campaign season that stated: "Progressive corporations, airlines, universities all openly discriminate against white Americans. Racism is always wrong. The left's anti-white bigotry must stop. We are all entitled to equal treatment under the law." The objective of the logic of whiteness, once again, is apparent: to neutralize centuries of racism using the rhetoric of equality in order to argue that any structural support given to racially marginalized people is tantamount to anti-white racism.

AFL also backed another successful lawsuit—one of several—to halt the Emergency Relief for Farmers of Color Act of 2021, which would have provided $5 billion in funds to Black, Indigenous, and Hispanic farmers, and other socially disadvantaged farmers, who have faced decades of documented discriminatory practices by the US Department of Agriculture. In their court filing, the litigants, which included Texas Agriculture Commissioner Sid Miller and a handful of white farmers, claimed that the legislation discriminated against white farmers and ranchers and, therefore, was unconstitutional based on the equal protection principles of the US Constitution: "These racial exclusions are patently unconstitutional, and the Court should permanently enjoin their enforcement. Doing so will promote equal rights under the law for all American citizens and promote efforts to stop racial discrimination."

And this is precisely how the white supremacist mindset interprets justice efforts: as racial discrimination against white people, but especially white men. It is the same logic used by opponents of affirmative action. Any effort that directly challenges the US hierarchical power structure and racial caste system is accused of being discriminatory.

In *Democracy May Not Exist, but We'll Miss It When It's Gone,* filmmaker and writer Astra Taylor traced the history of this argument to the mid-twentieth century, during which time conservatives made a concerted effort to eradicate decades of racial reform policies and laws by "redefin[ing] equality in a way that justified radically disparate outcomes." This effort sowed the seeds for legal challenges against affirmative action and voting rights, in addition to other racial justice reforms. She elaborated, "Color-blind policies or a flat tax that treats everyone the same, regardless of their background, qualify as equity—maintaining, in other words, equality before the law while ignoring equality of opportunity or outcome. This is how equality has been twisted to mean leaving vast imbalances of power firmly in place."

This logic also resides at the origin of white feminism, both in the overarching strategy of acquiring the same rights and privileges as white men and in its tactics of ostracizing and dismissing women of color. In *The Trouble with White Women*, Schuller identified three mandates that demonstrate how the logic of whiteness has operated within the mainstream feminist movement. A "civilizing agenda" in the nineteenth century "promised that anyone could be made useful to white society." Civilizing not only included tactics of erasure but also of severance, assimilation, and dispossession, especially of Indigenous and tribal peoples. This mandate, she argued, became a strategy to cleanse society—most notoriously through the twentieth-century eugenics movement that sought "sexual autonomy for the so-called fit [and] reproductive violence for the so-called unfit." In the twenty-first century, the mandate has been self-optimization, whereby "improving the self, and lifting up some of the other women from those lofty heights, has become white feminism's ultimate goal." The calculated decisions of white feminists not only shored up their womanhood and whiteness but also gifted them with power, privilege, and, in some cases, equal rights to white men.

To protect whiteness, equality is strategically invoked to eradicate difference. This erasure is evident in the pervasive cultural tendency of people who refuse to comprehend the historical, systematic entrenchment of racism and misogyny. When confronted with information that jeopardizes their myopic worldview, they project their discomfort in sentiments like "I don't see race!" These are the same people who always end up invoking mythical "purple people" in their defensive complaints that they "treat everyone equally" and are "*definitely not racist!*" And don't forget the egalitarian proclamation that "we're all created equal in God's eyes"—that is, until Black people try to move into the neighborhood or have the *audacity* to run for president. (Separating the doer from the deed, as I will discuss later, is the quintessential strategy to avoid accountability.) The logic of whiteness, of denying the historical conditions of gender and racial oppression, hinges on the language of equality—popularized in the language of colorblindness.

Colorblindness

The oft-employed ruse of being "blind" to color—which more tellingly reveals a person's refusal to acknowledge racism, because they can't be made uncomfortable by what they can't (or don't want to) see—is so pervasive that it even found its way into the eleventh season of *The Real Housewives of Beverly Hills*, which aired in 2021. On two separate occasions, white women said "I don't see color" to assert that they are not racist because they see all people equally. Sutton Stracke shouted it through her white tears at Crystal Kung Minkoff, the series's first Asian American housewife; and Kathy Hilton said it to Garcelle Beauvais, the show's only Black cast member. "She's saying," Kathy's sister Kyle spoke up in her defense, "that everybody to her is equal." Beauvais quickly called out the lie: "We're not. We're not equal." As a Black woman in America who is raising her three Black sons, Beauvais has had personal and intergenerational experiences have given her the acute knowledge that no one is born equal or treated equally in society.

As a rhetoric of equality, colorblindness cloaks white fragility, blanketing white people from uncomfortable truths. This desire for comfort is, in the United States, sustained by an education of ignorance. White people are taught from a very early age to not acknowledge or talk about skin color in order to ensure that we as a nation never address racism. "The color-blind message is so esteemed in American society that even our children pick up the idea that noticing skin color is rude," Stanford University psychology professor Jennifer L. Eberhardt explained in *Biased: Uncovering the Hidden Prejudice That Shapes What We See, Think, and Do*. "By the age of ten, children tend to refrain from discussing race, even in situations where mentioning race would be useful, like trying to describe the only Black person in the group." Here, the logic of whiteness relies on the tactic of silence.

Manifested as shutting down, preventing, criminalizing, and controlling the flow of information, this tactic is critical to maintaining not just white supremacy but all forms of domination—systemic or interpersonal.

Colorblindness is also a form of gaslighting, often, I believe, apparent in superficial "DEI" (diversity, equity, and inclusion) initiatives that refer to individual people as "diverse" in a way that simultaneously tokenizes them, neutralizes their individuality, and, consequently, renders them interchangeable. The thinking is that *all diverse people are the same.* "It is a cruel way of making BIPOC believe that they are just imagining the way they're treated is because of their skin color," author and educator Layla F. Saad observed in an essay unpacking racial gaslighting, "thus keeping them in a position of destabilization and inferiority." It also enables, she added, a lack of critical self-reflection by white people, by "protect[ing] them from having to reflect on what it means to be white in a white supremacist society."

Sweeping centuries of discrimination under the rug is the goal. Out of sight, out of mind, the adage goes. Because facing facts, facing history, demands accountability. Demands repair and reconciliation. Doing so, in effect, would undermine the narratives that have built our white supremacist society. Fear of this has led the effort to ban critical race theory (CRT)—a misnomer broadly applied to the teaching of American history but actually a term coined by law professor Kimberlé Crenshaw to describe an interdisciplinary method to analyze intersecting forms of legal structural racism—from schools. Fear of learning history led to Florida banning its AP African American studies course in January 2023, as part of Governor Ron DeSantis's campaign against what he calls "state-sanctioned racism." It is also why there are "Don't Say Gay" and anti-trans bills cropping up in dozens of US states. Legislating ignorance through constraining speech protects the white supremacist cis-heteropatriarchy because, again, silence preserves the status quo.

"Our Constitution is color-blind"—Supreme Court Justice Clarence Thomas's words in his dissent in *Grutter v. Bollinger,* which upheld schools' right to consider race as a factor in admissions (and which, as mentioned earlier, was challenged in two Supreme Court cases in fall 2022), are the exact words invoked repeatedly to prevent the redress of systemic racism. His words echo those of Supreme Court Justice John Marshall Harlan, who asserted that "our Constitution is color-blind" in his dissent in *Plessy v. Ferguson.*

Equality manifest in the language of colorblindness is intended to neutralize centuries of racism to present the façade of sameness. The argument against affirmative action employs this very language and logic to allege that any consideration of race (in school admissions, in job applications) violates the Equal Protection Clause of the Fourteenth Amendment. The entire argument depends on how forcefully the racist rhetoric of equality lands with the courts, legislators, and the public—because the fact is that race has *always* been a factor in the service of white people. The logic of whiteness that pervades our society and its institutions works to mask this historical reality tracing back to the foundation of the United States: Race has always been a factor because whiteness has always been a privilege. The mirage of equality, therefore, must endeavor to disguise this historical fact through its absurd rhetoric, from *colorblind* to *race neutral.*

Exposing the logic and language of equality demonstrates the extent to which equality functions to maintain the white supremacist cis-heteropatriarchy. For feminists to rely on this very language and logic, therefore, is to foreclose our liberation. We are hemmed in, and, it appears, willfully so, as we repeat the words of equality back to the men who handed them to us. Equality locks us into the patriarchy's power structure, and we have been conditioned to be satisfied with what we are allowed to have and who we are allowed to become. Our freedom to create authentic lives is affixed to the man in the mirror.

THE MAN IN THE MIRROR

Because the equality mindset is structured by the gender binary, "man defines woman, not in herself, but in relation to himself," Beauvoir wrote in *The Second Sex.* "She is not considered an autonomous being." The gender binary, in short, means that *woman* only exists if *man* exists. The trappings of this binary lock women into a state of perpetual dependence, in which we have been conditioned to perceive our own personhood not as independent from men but wholly realized through them. That is, the ideal image of who we should aspire to become is not simply that of man but of how man has imagined woman.

The irony is that white men serve as both the lowest common denominator and the gold standard of a woman's worth and self-perception. They determine what women should become, what women should value, and what their dreams and aspirations should be—that is, according to how men envision women's dreams and aspirations. Women can only want just enough to keep the patriarchy intact. Their "empowerment" cannot jeopardize men's power—which is why, I think, this infuriating word has become so popular. *Empowerment* is code for keeping women powerless but selling them a kind of commercialized enlightenment as real power. Women can only want what is acceptable in a world composed of systems and institutions made intentionally to disadvantage them. Because within our patriarchal society, we all know what happens to women who want too much—*ambitious!*—or unapologetically express their desires—*whores!*—or complain about sexist limitations—*bitches!* And, if they exceed heteronormative gender expectations, their womanhood itself is questioned.

These double standards are, frankly, just the standards. Remember, not that long ago, when people proclaimed they were not sexist because, they said, while they would never vote for "that woman" (Hillary Clinton), they would absolutely vote for Elizabeth Warren or Kamala Harris if either ran for president? Four years later, during the 2020 Democratic primaries, we saw exactly how this panned out. Every female candidate dropped out of the race earlier than the sea of male candidates, many of whom had demonstrably less political, policy, and leadership experience than US senators Warren, Harris, and Amy Klobuchar. According to the Brookings Institution, women—who comprise a greater percentage of

Democratic primary voters than men—secured the Democratic presidential nomination for Joe Biden. The sexism of such a (double) standard in American politics reflects the gap between men and women—the gold standard and the substandard.

The "mediocre-white-male-industrial complex," coined by writer Ijeoma Oluo in *Mediocre: The Dangerous Legacy of White Male America*, describes how "the rewarding of white male mediocrity not only limits the drive and imagination of white men; it also requires forced limitations on the success of women and people of color in order to deliver on the promised white male supremacy." The insidiousness of this mediocrity is akin to what Hannah Arendt called the "banality of evil," the incalculable harm resulting from thoughtless actions produced by herd-mentality thinking. For Oluo, this translates to complicity and complacency with oppressive systems through "a dedication to ignorance and hatred . . . that white men have been conditioned to believe . . . are their birthrights." She elaborated,

> When I talk about mediocrity, I talk about how we somehow agreed that wealthy white men are the best group to bring the rest of us prosperity, when their wealth was stolen from our labor. When I talk about mediocrity, I am talking about how aggression equals leadership and arrogance equals strength. . . . When I talk about mediocrity, I talk about success that is measured only by how much better white men are faring than people who aren't white men.

If our society's institutions are structured by the values, laws, and principles of the white supremacist cis-heteropatriarchy, then why are we seeking equality within them? To settle for equality is to settle for mediocrity.

This mediocrity is not just systematic. It exists interpersonally and on a personal level. The equality mindset has conditioned women to define ourselves in relation to and in the reflection of men. It consequently limits the expanse of our lives, restricting our self-determination and bodily autonomy—not just in the law but more fundamentally within our own minds. Some might describe this conformity in terms of settling—agreeing to terms and conditions that you might not want but would rather settle for than "be a problem."

This social conditioning emblematic of the equality mindset is why power and desire have been historically fraught points of discussion not just for feminists but for women in general.

DIRTY THINGS

The equality mindset harbors patriarchal definitions of both power and desire, meaning that we recognize them, actualize them, and measure them on men's terms. And these terms, especially where power and desire intersect, are more than anything defined by capitalism. The not infrequent consequence of this is our disappointment with the idea of gender parity—often articulated as a complaint about representation or that "just having a woman in charge won't change the system." Equality does not liberate women's power and desire. It constrains women to what men want (for them).

Within our white supremacist cis-heteropatriarchal society, power is conceived of as finite, hierarchical, and synonymous with domination. Historically, women have been trained to fear and despise power as something inherently corrupt. Power is especially taboo when expressed as a desire. We have been socially conditioned to believe that power and desire—two sources of self-expression and sovereignty—are dirty things for women. Dirty, to evoke anthropologist Mary Douglas's *Purity and Danger*, meaning "out of place." As in, power and desire are "out of place" when in the hands of women.

The adoption of the patriarchal definition of power consequently reproduces all images, associations, behaviors, and representations of patriarchal power, which continue to be understood in terms of dominance. Power, especially through a capitalist worldview, is still conceived of as aggression, control, colonization, and exploitation. And women continue to conceive of our own lives and aspirations based on the man in the mirror.

Feminism's longstanding problem with power, I think, is a result of its commitment to equality. "Power has been seen as the enemy of feminism, something to be abhorred, challenged, dismantled, or at best, something to be shared more equally, a thing which can be divided in different ways," feminist philosopher Elizabeth Grosz asserted in "Histories of the Present and Future: Feminism, Power, Bodies." "Power is not an enemy of feminism but its ally." She explained,

> The goal of feminism is no longer the dismantling of power or its equal distribution, for power must be understood as that which administers, regulates, enables . . . as well as disqualifies and subordinates, limits, and contains. If feminists believe that their goal is to abandon power, then they have already lost in a game from which they cannot withdraw. Feminism must aim at the reordering of power and not its elimination, at the expedient use of power and its infinite capacities for transformation and rewriting, its fundamentally openended character.

Instead of assuming the patriarchal definition of power and then wanting to smash it or avoid it entirely, feminists need to decouple power from the patriarchy. Power is not inherently good or evil—its value and valence depend on how it is accessed, harnessed, and deployed. As writer Mona Eltahawy said in *The Seven Necessary Sins for Women and Girls*, "We must define power in a way that liberates us from patriarchy's hierarchies. We must imagine a world we want and redefine what power is, what a powerful woman looks like, and how power can be used to subvert rather than uphold patriarchy." But power, Eltahawy added,

> must be more than doing what men do or being what men can be. I don't want to be something simply because a man can be that thing. Men are not my yardstick. If men themselves are not free of the ravages

of racism, capitalism, and other forms of oppression, it is not enough to say I want to be equal to them. Equal to the ways they themselves are victimized by patriarchy? No thanks! I want to be free. As long as patriarchy remains unchallenged, men will continue to be the default and the standard against which everything is measured.

Liberating power from its patriarchal moorings means desire is, in turn, liberated from its sexist trappings. Women's desire ceases to be dirty or shameful, or considered less important or valuable than male desire. This detachment also allows us to comprehend how desire is subjective, such that not every woman desires the same thing in bed (or wherever you end up doing it), just like attraction is subjective. Not everyone is attracted to older wiser lesbians (OWLs) like I am—and I, dear reader, am sorry for your loss.

Power is relational, both affective and affecting, to evoke Grosz's definition. Supremacy is not the only form or expression that power takes. A feminism that centers freedom, as I will discuss later, allows us to redefine power and desire as positive and productive because desire forges connections that can constitute new types of relations. Among women, these connections, platonic or otherwise, can build feminist movements and nurture stronger, more feminist communities of belonging. This is feminist power.

EQUALITY IS NOT ENOUGH

"A world where men and women would be equal is easy to imagine," Beauvoir proffered in *The Second Sex*. It would be a world where

> woman raised and educated exactly like men would work under the same conditions and for the same salaries; erotic freedom would be accepted by custom . . . ; women would be *obliged* to provide another livelihood for themselves; marriage would be based on a free engagement that the spouses could break when they wanted to; motherhood

would be freely chosen—that is, birth control and abortion would be allowed—and in return all mothers and their children would be given the same rights; maternity leave would be paid for by the society that would have responsibility for children, which does not mean that they would be *taken* from their parents but that they would not be abandoned to them.

This is precisely the cruel optimism of equality. It is so easy to *imagine*—just like we can *imagine* a woman president! We have all the language and logic to articulate what parity would look like. Yet, Beauvoir unveiled the ruse: The reality of equality is only possible if all conditions—from conditions one is born into to social conditioning—are exactly the same. The requisite not only discounts history—histories of misogyny, racism, homophobia, ableism, and all forms of discrimination and oppression that have constructed the conditions of the world into which we have been born and in which we live—but neglects our distinct differences and in doing so denies our dignity and humanity.

An eternal dangling carrot, equality is the unrealizable feminist dream. The desire for equality is so deeply ensconced in our mindset that we cannot see beyond it—beyond the world that men have created and the values they have established. For more than 150 years, the feminist commitment to inclusion within patriarchal institutions and structures and the necessary adoption of patriarchal beliefs and values have only served to expand and fortify the white supremacist cis-heteropatriarchy. And expanding the system does not fundamentally change the system.

Gender equality only acquires meaning within systems and institutions created by men, for men. The politics of equality feminism necessitates the harmful—and, yes, misogynistic—usage of the gender binary in arguments for either women's rights or legal protections based on men's definitions of them. No wonder "women can't flourish in a system that needs us as support pillars for someone else's building," Jill Filipovic asserted in *The H-Spot: The Feminist Pursuit of Happiness*. "We're here to prop it up, not to live in it. This is not a place that was built for us to thrive."

Equality feminism rose to prominence because it put forward a simple vision for fairness that appealed to the people in power and made itself a handmaiden to America's white supremacy in the process. And as long as men retain their power and, crucially, patriarchal values remain the bedrock of our institutions, equality feminism will continue to eke out "small wins" on the path to advancing (white) women's full participation in society.

The catch, however, is that the system was not designed for this to happen.

CHAPTER 2

THE EQUALITY SYSTEM

"The system is broken." How many times have we heard this line? "The system is broken"—no matter whether we're referring to the health care system, the education system, the electoral system, or the criminal punishment system.

But what if the system is not broken? What if, as Ijeoma Oluo said, it's working "according to design"?

If a system is intentionally designed to support and protect white men—in the US Constitution, this originally meant landowning (and, not unfrequently, enslaving) white men who feared the "tyranny of the majority"—then that system will serve the interests of white men. John Adams made this quite clear in a letter responding to his wife Abigail Adams's request for him to "Remember the Ladies" as he and other wealthy white men in the Continental Congress penned the code of laws: "I cannot but laugh," he replied. "Indians slighted their Guardians and Negroes grew insolent to their Masters. But your Letter was the first Intimation that another Tribe," he wrote, alluding to women, "more numerous and powerfull [sic] than all the rest were grown discontented."

Dismissing her for being "so saucy," he quipped, "We know better than to repeal our Masculine systems."

Despite these "masculine" systems including women over time, the structure and the mechanisms that maintain them have remained the same. The mistake of equality feminism has been its belief that inclusion into any patriarchal system fundamentally changes its design, architecture, and processes. Rather, inclusion only serves to expand and strengthen the systems designed to discriminate against and incarcerate women and queer, trans, Indigenous, racially marginalized, and disabled people.

Feminists' lamentations about the *brokenness* of systems indicate the difference between what we want them to do and what they were designed to do. Equal rights in practice are incommensurate to how we envision them. And where our continued frustrations lie is in the chasm between equal rights and equal outcomes.

Like the civil rights and LGBTQ+ movements, equality feminism has measured its success based on the acquisition of equal rights under the law. Striking, however, is the fact that the Equal Rights Amendment (ERA) has remained elusive for more than a century. And its tumultuous history is due to more than just misogyny. I believe that collective, multiracial equality efforts have been undermined by the two conflicting strategies of equality feminism: one asserting that all people are equal, the other contending that women are biologically and categorically different from men.

Both strategies rely on and therefore reinforce the gender binary. Both petition the state and its institutions for rights as forms of equal status and participation in society. And both err in the presumption that having rights in name directly and seamlessly converts into their implementation in practice. These strategies yield authority over our rights—in terms of responsibility—to the state, the general sentiment being that rights have meaning in themselves. Yet this is incorrect. The meaningfulness of a right exists not in theory but in practice: not in its abstract possession but in its use, in how it is lived and experienced in the world. I agree with Linda Zerilli, who, evoking the radical Italian feminists of the Milan Collective, said the power of rights is not found in what they are but in what they *do*. And yet the public shock and disbelief at the Supreme Court's overturning of *Roe v. Wade* is case in point that we largely understand rights as things that, once possessed, are permanent and immutable. This is emblematic of rights-based politics in general, the efforts for which tend to end once a right is won, when, in fact, the political work to ensure its exercise is truly just beginning.

Like *mie sorelle*, I believe that equal rights do not guarantee women's freedom, nor, more broadly, can they fully liberate us from systems of oppression.

I'm certainly not arguing that rights and laws are meaningless. They are documents that should, ideally, represent the values of a people. Laws are critically important tools that structure a society and its institutions and should work to serve people's needs and well-being. But the equality mindset has resulted in our fetishization of equal rights, and by seeking rights and protections within the framework of equality, we have effectively made ourselves dependent upon the patriarchal principle of the gender binary. This has not only resulted in the creation of laws that primarily benefit cisgender white women but has foreclosed our ability to leverage political power from a vantage point outside of the place of subordination that the box of the gender binary has put us in.

Because laws operate within patriarchal systems, they afford women limited capacity in which to realize our freedom, particularly in terms of safeguarding our bodily autonomy and providing institutional and community supports essential to our dignity and care. Further, they hem us into an identity politics that conceives of our basic rights and protections in relation to men and, critically, places oppressed groups in competition with each other. The latter has manifested in the harassment and exclusion of trans people and, specifically, in transphobic women asserting that they alone can claim the identity of *woman*. Indeed, one premise in the argument against using the inclusive language of *pregnant people* is that doing so would undermine women's argument for the right to an abortion based in equality.

Antidiscrimination laws, furthermore, arguably have their greatest impact retroactively, largely coming into force after harm has been done. Yet lawsuits, I believe, do not inspire behavioral change or foster accountability. Neither are punishment or retribution effective measures to encourage positive behavior. And contrary to the mid-twentieth-century sentiment that the law, and specifically public interest law, has the power to change social attitudes, I think change begins with people. Because laws don't write themselves, just as institutions don't make or run themselves. People do.

PERFORMATIVE EQUALITY

Equality has been the strategy and endgame of the feminist movement, among other social movements, generally because of how easy it is to comprehend as a basic point of comparison. The only requirement is the ability to understand the principle of sameness and apply it as a logic to figure out if and how two (or more) things are the same or different. For example, when it came to gay marriage, the argument in favor of it was easy for mainstream media, corporations, and society to grasp because marriage is a right that heterosexual spouses live daily—to Zerilli's point, again, about the power of a right being what it does. Therefore, the inequality was clear, calculable, and—critically—*palpable* not just to gays but to mainstream, heterosexual society. Heterosexuals can legally marry; therefore, laws denying homosexuals the right to marry are discriminatory and should be overturned so everyone has the same legal right to join the marriage institution and access the much-lauded 1,138 rights afforded to married couples. (The value of these rights, I learned myself while gay-married, very much depends on one's wealth and parental status.) It is also worth pointing out that marriage, historically, was conceived as an institution to shore up men's power and wealth through the exchange of women, so we should not overlook the fact that white gay men's leading role in the campaign for marriage equality was also a factor in its being won so quickly.

The principle of sameness was similarly relied upon to fuel suffrage campaigns leading to the Fifteenth and Nineteenth Amendments: If all people are created equal, then everyone should have the equal right to vote. Here is where the Fourteenth Amendment has been so consequential, as many of these gains can be attributed to its Due Process Clause and, more so, its Equal Protection Clause, which states that groups of people cannot be treated unequally under the law, at least not in the public sector.

While equality makes for an easy and relatable campaign strategy to sell to voters, it is just as easily sabotaged in its interpretation and implementation.

Laws take effect and have power in their practice. Historically, the interpreters and implementers of US law have been white men (and their accomplices) whose objectives have been to maintain the systems that have given them social, political, and economic power. Our rights have rested in their hands since the founding of the nation. Operating concurrently with this systemic method is the conservative strategy of employing the rhetoric of equality both to distract from its inexistence in practice and to bring about gross discriminations without oversight or correction. The origins of this strategy extend as far back as US Reconstruction and manifested in the various racial apartheid laws of the late nineteenth century and the infamous "separate but equal" legal reasoning of *Plessy v. Ferguson*. And the public has been so persuaded by this strategy because it is predicated on the longstanding assumption that *a right is a real thing*. That a right in name is tantamount to a right in practice. It is a performative theory of equality.

As the Supreme Court's flagrant and fatuous decisions in June 2022 illustrate, even "constitutionally protected rights" can be overturned or withdrawn—which calls into question, arguably even undermines, the whole notion of a constitutionally protected right. And this can happen *despite* precedent, as we saw with *Dobbs v. Jackson Women's Health Organization*. Despite *Roe v. Wade*, despite *Planned Parenthood of Southeastern Pennsylvania v. Casey*, despite nearly fifty years of an established constitutional right to an abortion, the court's now settled conservative majority ruled that an abortion is not a constitutional right because the word *abortion* appears nowhere in the US Constitution. Here is Supreme Court Justice Samuel Alito, writing on behalf of the majority:

> We hold that *Roe* and *Casey* must be overruled. The Constitution makes no reference to abortion, and no such right is implicitly protected by any constitutional provision, including the one on which the defenders of *Roe* and *Casey* now chiefly rely—the Due Process Clause of the Fourteenth Amendment. That provision has been held to guarantee some rights that are not mentioned in the Constitution, but any such right must be "deeply rooted in this Nation's history and tradition" and "implicit in the concept of ordered liberty."

White men, a number of whom were enslavers, wrote the Constitution to serve and protect their own interests. So, for any justice or judge to proudly declare their fidelity to originalism is to admit their allegiance to the Constitution's baked-in misogyny and racism. The originalist method itself demands a lot of fantastical mind reading—it requires a justice's *interpretation* of what they *think* the Constitution's Framers *intended*. As legitimate as a nineteenth-century séance, originalism relies on literary apostrophe—meaning to throw one's voice onto an inanimate object to bring it to life and bestow it with authority—where the object in question is the collective voice of the long-dead, white male Framers.

Funny, too, how originalism seems more often than not to align with aiding and abetting a conservative agenda. Sure, the US Constitution doesn't mention abortion, but it doesn't mention AR-15s either. Yet, in *District of Columbia v. Heller* in 2008, the conservative justices chose to cast aside the first clause of the Second Amendment ("A well regulated Militia") and decided, in a majority opinion written by the late Justice Antonin Scalia, that the amendment actually "protects an individual right to possess a firearm unconnected with service in a militia." Originalism in this capacity is deployed to disguise political motivations behind the spirit of nationalism—justices are, in fact, *political* appointments, and there is no such thing as objectivity. And given the fact that Trump's SCOTUS appointees are young (relatively speaking), we can expect such originalist interpretations to dominate the court's decisions for the next couple of decades—and have impact far beyond that.

Abetting conservatives' performative equality is the "chipping away" strategy. *Chipping away* is a phrase that describes pervasive and relentless efforts to undermine rights and protections by claiming equality already exists and/or ignoring systemic discrimination. It is an incrementalist, long-game strategy employed by those who know the application of equality is subject to how it is interpreted, whom it is interpreted by, and in which time period and political and cultural contexts it is interpreted. The strategy materializes through loopholes, red herrings, or other justifications for chipping away at equal rights and protections. Conservatives' successful antiabortion strategy—exacted through the Reagan-era Family Protection Act of the early 1980s and deployed through an array of tactics, like having to get spousal or parental approval for an abortion, TRAP laws that target abortion providers, undue burden tests, and health regulations designed to shut down clinics—exemplifies how constitutional law can be eroded at both the state and federal levels. Perhaps the most harmful federal effort has been the Hyde Amendment, passed three years after *Roe*, in 1976, which prohibits the use of federal funds, including Medicaid, for abortion, except (in theory) in cases of rape or incest, or if a person is suffering a life-threatening pregnancy. This act alone has rendered abortion an unequal right by making it inaccessible to poor and low-income people, which has affected racially marginalized people the most.

The chipping away strategy also has been employed in various nationwide efforts to restrict voting rights enshrined in multiple constitutional amendments. The Supreme Court justified its gutting of the Voting Rights Act in *Shelby County v. Holder* in 2013 by alleging that the centuries of racism the law redressed no longer existed in the "post-racial" America of President Obama. Indeed, in the court's majority opinion, Chief Justice John Roberts cited the act's effectiveness as a reason why it was no longer necessary: "The Act has proved immensely successful at redressing racial discrimination and integrating the voting process," he wrote. Therefore, he concluded, "our country has changed, and while any racial discrimination in voting is too much, Congress must ensure that the legislation it passes to remedy that problem speaks to current conditions." Justice Scalia went further, asserting that protections safeguarding minority voting rights were tantamount to "racial entitlement." Scalia's logic—the logic of whiteness—rests on the rhetorical emptiness of performative equality: Because the law states that equality exists, then it must exist. (It is the same logic used by anti-ERA advocates who claim the ERA is redundant because several other equal rights and protections laws already exist.)

We see this strategy similarly employed against LGBTQ+ people. They now can legally marry, but a slew of "religious freedom" laws provides exemptions for people who do not want to sell them services to make their dream wedding possible. (Although, my gays, do you really want homophobes marrying you and baking your wedding cakes and designing your wedding websites? Shouldn't we be more conscientious about whom we give our money to? The choice to hire homophobes is simply bad taste—and I mean that both ethically and aesthetically.) The resurgent opposition behind these laws is sizable—if the 157 members of US Congress who in July 2022 voted against protecting existing same-sex marriages should the federal right, via *Obergefell v. Hodges*, be overturned is any indication. (The bill, called the Respect for Marriage Act, passed 267–157 in the House, with 47 Republicans joining Democrats, and, in November, passed 62–37 in the Senate, with 12 Republicans joining the Democrats. For NBC, I wrote about how this bipartisan support resulted from the late addition of religious liberty protections to the bill.

So while the act does not codify federal same-sex marriage, it does codify discrimination.)

State law has been adept at subverting federal equal rights laws and, indeed, supposed constitutional guarantees. Just take the right to vote, technically an equal right for all citizens (if you've not been incarcerated and are over the age of eighteen). Voter suppression practices—from purging voter rolls and rejecting voting by mail to targeting social media campaigns, restricting voting hours, and outlawing food and drink consumption while waiting hours in line to vote—are increasingly being adopted into state law. As a direct consequence of the *Shelby* decision, hundreds of polling sites—not coincidentally, many in predominantly Black and Latinx voting precincts—were shuttered before the 2020 elections. Fewer polling sites results in lower voter turnout. Elections are not federal holidays, and people cannot afford to travel a significant distance or wait in line for hours to vote.

It is far from infrequent to witness both political and judicial backlash following Supreme Court rulings that affirm equality under the law or even attempt to take a greater step forward in the name of justice. Take the Supreme Court's *Brown v. Board of Education* decision in 1954. Effectively reversing and nullifying *Plessy*'s "separate but equal" holding, *Brown* mandated school desegregation because, the court's majority ruled, education is the cornerstone of democracy and racially segregated education is not equal education. However, the court did not provide a road map for *how* to implement and achieve desegregation. Journalist and 1619 Project founder Nikole Hannah-Jones noted in an NBC News interview that this mandate was roundly ignored for the first decade after the Supreme Court's verdict, with more than one hundred members of the US Congress signing the Southern Manifesto of 1956 to declare their commitment to resist the *Brown* decision. It was only when the Civil Rights Act of 1964 granted the Department of Justice the right to sue to enforce desegregation that holdout schools began to comply with the law.

This legal recourse did enforce desegregation, even though it did not prevent Black children from being harassed and abused by their white schoolmates. It also did not prevent politicians from devising ways to withhold federal and state investments in public schools to stymie integration, including antibusing provisions—an issue US vice president Kamala Harris personally spoke about during the 2020 Democratic primaries. The effects of this legal recourse, however, were not permanent. Progress slowed and began to reverse when, in the 1980s, President Reagan's Department of Justice stopped enforcing court desegregation orders. This occurred in parallel to parental rights efforts advocating for school choice, which was supported by multiple presidential administrations, and policies that provided federal funding for voucher systems so that wealthy—and, overwhelmingly, white—children didn't have to go to school with Black children. (We've seen this notion of parental rights rear its exceedingly ugly head again in 2022, this time to restrict school curricula that seek to explore America's racist history and acknowledge the existence of queer people.) In addition, in separate rulings in 1990 and 1992, the Supreme Court declared that school districts can cease their desegregation efforts if they have demonstrated a "good-faith commitment" to integrate schools. Obviously, what constitutes a "good-faith commitment" is subjective—utterly subject to the whims of the people in power.

The designers of the Southern Manifesto promised that *Brown v. Board* would "destroy the system of public education." This was less a premonition than a declaration of their intention to chip away at public education as a public good. Arguably, they have kept good on their promise—the effects of which were acknowledged in a 2019 US House of Representatives hearing to discuss how *Brown v. Board* remains "a promise unfulfilled." As Virginia Foxx, the ranking Republican member on the Committee on Education and Labor, said in her testimony: "In the 65 years since *Brown v. Board*, we have not yet achieved true equality."

Structural forms of equality, whether law or policy, are incapable of producing equal outcomes or equal treatment. When executed in the spirit of achieving a multiracial democracy, laws have been effective in removing barriers to access and to offering equal protections. Yet there is a pervasive misconception about their permanence and effectiveness, born from a belief in the awesome power of institutions, cradling us into a state of complacency. Just because a right exists under the law does not mean it will be uniformly and universally applied in practice or produce equal outcomes. Power affects each of us differently. The white supremacist cis-heteropatriarchy works on each of us differently, depending on our individual identities and situations. It is incomprehensible, then, how institutional power in the form of equal rights could account for these differences. We are not one size fits all.

HOOP LOOPS

The chasm between equality in theory and equality in practice is apparent in what are considered some of our greatest feminist victories. Take Title IX, which became law in 1972 and states, "No person in the United States shall, on the basis of sex, be excluded from participation in, be denied the benefits of, or be subjected to discrimination under any education program or activity receiving Federal financial assistance."

Yet abundant, unequal treatment of women in college sports continues, from funding for equipment to recruitment to use of shared practice and competitive arenas. In 2021, a TikTok video by University of Oregon basketball player Sedona Prince documented the disparities between the men's and women's gym amenities at the NCAA Tournament. It was only because of the video's virality—with sports icons like the Golden State Warriors' Steph Curry and tennis legend Billie Jean King calling out the disparities on social media—that the NCAA issued a statement declaring it was "actively working" on improving the conditions for the women's basketball teams. If it happens, any future improvement, in this case, will not have been catalyzed by the law but by the people. And that's a pretty big if, because according to the Supreme Court's 1999 decision in *NCAA v. Smith*, the NCAA is not beholden to Title IX since it does not itself receive federal funding. It is perfectly legal for the NCAA to promote and treat men's and women's college basketball unequally.

Another loophole currently being challenged in the courts allows colleges to fabricate the number of female athletes they report to the Department of Education to prove their Title IX compliance. A 2022 report by *USA Today* documented that colleges padded numbers by double and triple counting athletes—adding up to 2,252 roster spots—who played more than one sport, and by counting male practice players as women. Of the 107 colleges surveyed, 52 counted men—who together added up to more than 600 of the 1,137 total participants reported—as members of women's basketball teams. In an analysis by Jeff Eisenberg at Yahoo Sports, in 2021 "Penn State counted 21 male practice players across five women's sports. UConn, Michigan, and TCU [Texas Christian University] are among the schools whose women's basketball teams last year counted more male practice players than actual female players." And "during the 2018–19 school year, Michigan State counted a combined 173 women on its cross-country, indoor and outdoor track teams," even though, a lawsuit alleges, "66 of those athletes never participated in a competition for one of their supposed teams."

Observing these loopholes in no way negates the profoundly positive impact Title IX has had on women. It has amplified women's sports and imbued them with social legitimacy, which has helped challenge gender stereotypes. It also has increased the number of resources for women's sports, and it has given women like me educational access and opportunity we could never have dreamed of. Throwing the javelin really far was my ticket into Harvard. White women like me, in fact, have been the primary beneficiaries of Title IX, because the law does not account for race or class—only gender.

These loopholes indicate how substantial the equality gap is for racially marginalized women. It is no surprise, then, that according to a 2022 Pew Research Center survey, 46 percent of women said Title IX has not done enough to support women in sports. And arguably worse, we have seen how this law—intended to provide structural supports for sports participation—has been weaponized against trans athletes.

"EQUAL" PAY FOR "EQUAL" WORK

The longstanding feminist fight for "equal pay for equal work," too, reflects the gap between the theory and practice of equality. We should drop the mantra altogether—doing so would allow us to disengage from and sidestep misogynist arguments and frameworks. It is tiresome to hear misogynists levy the same handful of comments over and over. First, based on their misunderstanding of the Equal Pay Act, they falsely claim that equal pay for women already exists under the law. When that argument fails—because it is wrong—they then try to rationalize the gender pay gap with gender essentialism, claiming men just *naturally* gravitate toward higher-paying professions and women just *naturally* choose to not work so they can take care of their children. Of course, this argument depends on a willed ignorance of the sexism that has produced this segregation, from care work and childcare not being compensated to sexual harassment that derails women's careers, to professions like IT and computer programming quickly becoming higher paying once men became the majority of workers in those fields. (Similarly, teaching, once a men's profession, is now dominated by women. Are we really surprised that teachers are paid abysmal, insulting wages?)

Let's look at the Equal Pay Act, which President John F. Kennedy signed into law in 1963. The act initially called for equal pay for *comparable* work, but the final draft was controversially revised to equal pay for *equal* work: "jobs the performance of which requires equal skill, effort, and responsibility and which are performed under similar working conditions." The consequences of this one-word revision were cascading and monumental by limiting the act's scope and potential impact. Historian Alice Kessler-Harris described the shift to *equal* pay as "the perfect compromise" because, she wrote in *In Pursuit of Equity*, it "incorporated women into notions of individual merit without disturbing the notion that gender differences still mattered when it came to the workplace." This transpired threefold: First, because occupations were segregated, "demanding equal pay only if men and women did exactly the same work offered greater symbolic consolation than practical benefit." Second, it in no way addressed the gender barriers that kept women from being hired in the same jobs as men, especially if doing so required employers to pay women equally. Third, the act only applied to sex discrimination and not pay disparities among women, which did not affect "the wages of the vast majority of women, who worked in predominantly female occupations."

The 1963 Equal Pay Act, furthermore, does not account for how gender discrimination both informs and is informed by additional, categorical factors like race. Nor does it address the compounding effects of systemic discrimination, such as women being pushed out of the workforce after World War II so that men returning from war could find employment and resume their traditional role as the breadwinners and economic powerholders.

It also doesn't account for forms of discrimination like sexual harassment and intimidation. The US Equal Employment Opportunity Commission (EEOC), which is the agency responsible for investigating workplace discrimination and harassment, has been largely incapable of addressing most harassment cases because funding has remained stagnant since the early 1980s. President Trump gutted the EEOC beginning with his appointment, in 2019, of corporate lawyer Janet Dhillon as its chair. Dhillon proceeded to slash the number of cases pursued in litigation until her appointment ended in January 2021, with the incoming Biden administration. Not to mention, the act offers no redress to forms of unpaid, emotional labor tied to workplace culture. Even when men and women have the same job, studies show that women take on more of the unpaid tasks traditionally gendered female—from organizing and facilitating staff events to managing workplace morale. It is the care work often associated with the domestic sphere—work that continues to be uncompensated and undervalued.

Women, and especially people from historically underrepresented and marginalized communities, often shoulder the additional labor of managing discriminatory behavior from colleagues. They may also be expected to educate these colleagues about bias—but very gently, with kid gloves, so as not to incur the wrath of retaliatory white fragility. It is risky work, and the people responsible for, say, leading their team's DEI efforts can find themselves in professional jeopardy. A 2016 study found that nonwhite and female executives who placed value on diversity in the workplace were penalized in their performance ratings. Shortly thereafter, the study's researchers arrived at the same findings: "It's risky for low-status group members to help others like them. And this can lead to women and minorities choosing *not* to advocate for other women and minorities once they reach positions of power, as they don't want to be perceived as incompetent, poor performers."

Inherent in this work is what sociologist Arlie Hochschild has called the "emotional labor" of covering up or suppressing feelings in order to portray an acceptable, white-professional countenance to one's colleagues. This labor results in what researchers at Catalyst, a nonprofit that helps companies create inclusive workplaces for women, defined as the "emotional tax" of feeling "othered," or like one doesn't fit in a workplace, which negatively affects one's health, well-being, and career success. The combined cost of this additional work keeps employees marginalized, powerless, and burned out. This labor and its tax, Audre Lorde wrote in "The Master's Tools Will Never Dismantle the Master's House," are not incidental but intentional:

> Women of today are still being called upon to stretch across the gap of male ignorance and to educate men as to our existence and our needs. This is an old and primary tool of all oppressors to keep the oppressed occupied with the master's concerns. Now we hear that it is the task of women of color to educate white women—in the face of tremendous resistance—as to our existence, our differences, our relative roles in our joint survival. This is a diversion of energies and a tragic repetition of racist patriarchal thought.

Take a moment: Have you ever been in a situation where you called out a workplace injustice, bias, or discriminatory behavior directed at you or a colleague? What about workplace sexual harassment and assault? If you have ever dared to call out the violation, what were the consequences—*for you?*

In my own experience, I learned pretty quickly that Human Resources (HR) serves and protects not the employee but the employer. (I call HR the Organizational Police.) And when it comes to filing a complaint, feminist scholar Sara Ahmed observed, "those who challenge how power works come to know how power works." How it works, I found out, is *according to its design*, as a support to maintain the existing system. Organizations do not like disturbances, so a person who calls attention to a problem is more often than not deemed the problem. Once, an HR representative told me there would be no consequences for the white male intern who harassed me because—and I will never forget this—he, then a newly hired staffer, was "just starting his career."

On another occasion, a female colleague asked me about my salary. Believing that pay transparency is a feminist duty, I told her. Her eyes widened in shock. She said that I earned more than her but did not feel comfortable confiding her salary to me in return. She was upset that we were paid differently, considering that our jobs were classified in the same category. However, the pay difference was understandable to me because I had a decade-plus more job experience and expertise than her, and I had worked at the organization longer (a part of that time in a different department). Not to mention that our precise duties were different, including overseeing and managing the different workflows of a differing number of contributors, and having different responsibilities within the team's work culture.

An intrinsic problem with equal pay is the lie of equal work. How can equal work be quantified, given that no two people have the same work ethic? What does it even look like? Which factors are accounted for in this equation, and which are omitted because they are invisible or not valued? Equal pay for comparable work, as the original language of the 1963 act read, and which nations like New Zealand are currently pursuing, aims for pay equity to close the gender pay gap. Yet New Zealand's pay equity efforts apply only to public sector leadership positions, and its national pay gap has seen only marginal changes in the past decade.

Furthermore, calls for both equality and equity arguably amount to nothing when domestic work and care work are not compensated but expected duties of women (especially those in heterosexual relationships). The COVID-19 pandemic made this abundantly clear: More than two million women left the workforce in 2020 to care for their children and/or their elderly parents. Data from a 2022 Stanford University survey found that 39 percent of women caregivers in the United States had quit work or reduced their work hours since March 2020, up from 33 percent in spring of 2021. (All low-income and single parents, especially those without local support networks, struggled to maintain their jobs while providing or finding daycare for their children, not just women.) Equal pay feels like nonsense talk when your salary is zero dollars for raising your three children (largely by yourself) while also shouldering what sociologist Marianne Cooper referred to as the "worry work" of being responsible for the family's finances and security.

The politics of equal pay also suffers from an equality mindset that seeks sameness and undermines our work and our worth. I mean, what does pay equity or equality even amount to when the federal minimum wage in the United States has remained stagnant at $7.25/hour since 2009? The minimum wage, in accordance with productivity and inflation rates in 2022, should be closer to $25/hour.

Just as the equality mindset hems women to patriarchal standards and values, it convinces us to shortchange our worth in the name of equal pay. And I think a part of this mentality is due to feminism's uneasy relationship with capitalism, which makes many feminists feel like hypocrites for participating in an exploitative labor system just to pay rent. While I am not advocating for capitalism, I am pointing out how patriarchal culture shames women for the compromises they make to become financially independent and able to take care of themselves without forced dependence on men. This shaming is particularly loud when it comes to criticizing women who spend money on travel or to pay for experiences as acts of self-care that bring them rest, joy, and pleasure. When we interrogate capitalism, we need more pragmatism, grace, and nuance. There is a profound difference, for example, between a union-busting, exploitative multibillionaire CEO and a grassroots organizer who at middle age can finally afford to buy a house for the first time in her life.

Another example of how the equality mindset sells women short, I'd argue, is the much-celebrated achievement of the US Women's Soccer 2022 pay agreement.* The forty-six players on the US men's and women's teams (twenty-three players on each team) must equally pool and divide all future competition prize earnings through 2028. This agreement is an example of joining the existing patriarchal payment structure to acquire equal pay. However, this equal pay is based in unequal work—at least, unequal success.

The US women's team won consecutive World Cups in 2015 and 2019, while the men's team made it to the round of sixteen in 2014, failed to qualify in 2018, and made it to the round of sixteen once again in 2022. In fact, the men's team was only in the semifinals once, in 1930, when they were one of only four teams in the entire tournament. Women have to do exponentially better, achieve extraordinary success in their field, just to have a seat at the contract-negotiating table. And there remains vast gender disparities not only in the FIFA prize money payment structure—$440 million for the men's 2022 World Cup and, comparatively, a mere $60 million for the women's tournament—but in sponsorships and viewership. The value system is completely financial—the payment structure is based more on profit generated than on number of victories.

The sexist rationale for the soccer pay discrepancy was that men were better (more tournament wins) and more popular (in terms of

---

* The US Women's Soccer lawsuit and subsequent agreement catalyzed the Equal Pay for Team USA Act of 2022, signed into law by President Biden in January 2023. The act guarantees equal pay and benefits for all athletes representing Team USA in global competitions—with the catch that "it shall be permissible to consider merit, performance, seniority, or quantity of play." And, as an acknowledgment that Team USA has no control over international sports organizations, the fine print of the act also states that "the corporation shall take all reasonable steps . . . to advocate to international sports federations and other event organizers to equalize prizes, compensation, funding, and other support provided to athletes by such federations and organizers." While this is a positive step, we see again how the language of equality is always qualified. The act's promises have yet to come into effect.

media coverage and audience ratings). Yet the opposite has been true in the past decade for the US teams—although not worldwide, which is how FIFA money distribution is determined. The US women's soccer team has won more international tournaments and is watched more than the men's team. The US women's 2019 World Cup victory over the Netherlands was the most watched English-language soccer game in US history—men's or women's. And according to the US Soccer Federation's financial statements obtained by the *Wall Street Journal* in 2019, US women's soccer games have generated more revenue than US men's games since 2016.

So why are the women subsidizing the men?

THE BONDS OF THE BINARY

The civil rights and LGBTQ+ movements both garnered equal rights in the form of federal law and shifting interpretations of constitutional amendments within decades of their inception. But achieving gender equality—namely the ERA—has been a struggle for more than a hundred years.

What makes gender different from these other identity categories?

We can begin to tease out the answer by looking more closely at the gender binary, the architecture of the equality mindset and the organizing principle of equality feminism. The traditional belief that gender is biological has shaped the rights-based movement and, in my estimation, resulted in diametrically opposed political strategies. The first strategy is based in a logic of sameness: that men and women are the same and therefore deserve the same rights and treatment under the law. The second envisions an indirect path to women's equal participation in society via legal protections that redress gender discrimination. This strategy points to the historical political and economic disparities between men and women to contend that women need extra protections and accommodations in order to assume equal citizenship and equally participate in society.

It's not simply that the scope of equality feminism is inadequate because it circumscribes our legal rights, our dignity, and our personhood to scripts written by men. It's that the gender binary has structured the entire rights-based movement. The logic underlies both strategies, just from opposite sides. It has contributed to the ERA's failure (and perpetual limbo status), and it resides at the hinge of the current political schism between women who cling to the gender binary to prove their categorical oppression as "biological women" and those who are trying to cultivate a feminism outside the patriarchal gender binary. Only the latter, I believe, offers a pathway to liberation from gender scripts, stereotypes, and norms.

The two strategies even collided in the early decades of the organized feminist movement. In 1908, the Supreme Court decided in *Muller v. Oregon* that women were a class distinct from men ("The two sexes differ in structure of the body, in the functions performed by each, in the amount of physical strength . . .") and therefore required special labor protections. Protective legislation was justified, the court said, because of a woman's "physical structure, and a proper discharge of her maternal function—having in view not merely her own health, but the well-being of the race." Writing about the case in 2019, NYU law professor Melissa Murray noted that for working-class women, "such legislation was a practical—and necessary—response to the very real dangers of economic (and other forms of) exploitation that women faced when they left their homes to participate in the workplace."

Conversely, she added, "those who identified as first-wave feminists and suffragists were less sanguine about protective labor legislation and the gendered rationales that undergirded them. For these economically privileged women, protective legislation, and the Court's defense of such laws, was rooted in gender stereotypes that harmed women."

The dividing line between the two strategies crystalized after the *Muller* verdict, setting the stage for the political conflicts that have debilitated the feminist movement.

THE ERA 'TIS HERE! 'TIS HERE! 'TIS GONE!

The ERA is emblematic of a broader cultural confusion about the politics of gender equality: Are women the same as men, or are they different? We can't have it both ways when it comes to accessing civil rights within patriarchal institutions. One position effectively undermines the other, and the contradiction presented by the two is weaponized against women. Perhaps this is why gender equality continues to stall while other rights-based movements find success, because they focused on one argument: Gay people should have the same rights as straight people, Black people should have the same rights as white people, and to have a different set of rights very clearly indicates inequality. These movements have asserted a simple logic of sameness and—I want to be abundantly clear—are not attempting, like feminists, to topple the patriarchy. Simplicity is essential for public persuasion, especially in an age in which the depth of our cultural discourse often ends at a headline or a tweet. The feminist movement has not offered the same simplicity. Its messaging has been ineffective because it has been contradictory and confusing.

The gender binary has structured the adjudication and legislation of our rights in lockstep with—and locked into—the patriarchal equality system. It is no wonder then that, in tandem with systemic misogyny, the ERA has failed and women's basic rights have proven to be legal and legislative quagmires. Because we have constructed an equal rights movement on the gender binary, we keep fighting with each other about who gets to be a woman and not fighting together for the bodily autonomy and basic care of *all people*.

The ERA's storied history also embodies the illusiveness, and the elusiveness, of equality, so stubbornly etched into our mindsets as to consume the feminist movement's resources for generations. How could such a plain and simple amendment go through such a roller-coaster ride for a century? Why was the most significant fight against it led by a woman? And why, even if it were to be included in the Constitution, does there remain profound uncertainty about its potential impact? Indeed, while most Americans are in favor of the ERA, according to a 2020 Pew Research Center poll, a whopping 49 percent believe its passage "would not make much of a difference." To me, this statistic indicates the extent to which people understand that equal rights have very little direct effect on our daily lives without freedom from misogyny and sexual violence.

Let's briefly review the ERA's history. Suffragists Alice Paul and Crystal Eastman wrote and first proposed the amendment at the seventy-fifth anniversary of the Seneca Falls Convention, in 1923. In December of that year, two Republicans—Senator Charles Curtis and Representative Daniel R. Anthony (the nephew of Susan B. Anthony)—introduced the resolution into the US Congress.

The original language of the legislation stated: "Men and women shall have equal rights throughout the United States and every place subject to its jurisdiction." In its current incarnation, the language has been tweaked to be more inclusive: "Equality of rights under the law shall not be denied or abridged by the United States or by any state on account of sex."

From the start, the ERA was not universally supported by women—perhaps an obvious statement, given that women are not a monolith. A division formed along class and racial lines that reflected the nascent, conflicting political strategies of the movement as well as the tension between single-issue and multi-issue feminist politics. Middle- and upper-class women welcomed the ERA. However, working-class women were reluctant to support the amendment because they believed it "ignored the biological, social, and cultural differences that women faced—in the marketplace and elsewhere," as Murray explained. "Echoing the logic of decisions like *Muller v. Oregon*, working-class women argued that women employed outside of the home needed the law's special protection—especially with regard to workplace conditions and hours of employment."

Since 1923, the ERA has been introduced in every successive congressional session. The women's movement of the 1960s, largely inspired by the Black Civil Rights Movement of the previous two decades, fueled public support for the amendment. And female politicians like Democratic congresswomen Bella Abzug and Shirley Chisholm were among its vocal proponents. In fact, the ERA Coalition has attributed Chisholm's "barnburner" speech on August 10, 1970, with carrying the amendment through a victorious House of Representatives vote that day. (It failed to pass in the Senate that year.) Yet, it should be noted that Chisholm's speech was more pragmatic than it has been remembered. While she proclaimed the necessity of equal rights, she also admitted "this amendment will not solve the problem of sex discrimination" and "direct economic effects would be minor." Yes, the ERA would establish equal rights and treatment under the law, but she even acknowledged that the law would be tempered in its interpretation and application.

That equality cannot be legislated was understood by feminists who have been largely relegated to the margins of feminist history. "We are aware that the system will try to appease us with their [sic] paper offerings," declared a group of feminists who testified *against* the ERA during a US Senate subcommittee meeting in 1970. "We will not be appeased. Our demands can only be met by a total transformation of society which you cannot legislate, you cannot co-opt, you cannot *control.*"

These radical, multi-issue, and antiracist feminists criticized the equality mindset and the white feminist politics of reform. In her 1973 book *Lesbian Nation*, Jill Johnston called out the mainstream feminist movement for being "directed toward bigger and better participation in the male privilege through equality in his system and a further denial of her own identity in the wages of power in the same sexual caste system which she claims to be the source of her deprivation."

Despite this critique, equality prevailed as the centerpiece of feminist politics. And, buoyed by the winds of popular sentiment, in 1971, Democratic congresswoman Martha Griffiths, who used a discharge petition to bring the ERA to the House floor in 1970, reintroduced the ERA into the House, where it passed that October. The Senate followed a few months later, in March 1972. The amendment was then sent to the states for ratification.

The states were given a seven-year deadline to ratify the ERA—thirty-eight are needed for constitutional ratification. The situation looked optimistic for proponents: By the end of that year, twenty-two states had ratified it. The number rose to thirty-five at the end of five years. A year before the deadline, in 1978, President Jimmy Carter granted a deadline extension, until June 30, 1982.

But the cultural tide was rapidly turning red. Shortly after Congress passed the ERA, avowed antifeminist and conservative activist Phyllis Schlafly launched the STOP ERA movement. Her argument was that the ERA would harm women, stripping them of their protections and privileges associated with being legally dependent on men, like Social Security benefits and alimony. Furthermore, she falsely claimed the ERA would deprive women of the "right to be a housewife" and send them into military combat—and maybe, to the horror of many, even turn them into lesbians. You'll notice a correlation between Schlafly's argument and that of working-class women earlier in the century—both espoused the need for gender-specific special protections.

Ronald Reagan and conservatives swept the 1980 elections. The 1982 deadline came and passed, with the ERA stalled at thirty-five states.

The ERA was dead.

Or was it? Notwithstanding decades of feminist backlash, ERA proponents persisted. In 2017, Nevada ratified the ERA. Illinois followed suit in 2018. And Virginia—number thirty-eight—in 2020.

The legality of these three ratifications is questionable, however, given that the deadline passed more than forty years ago. And, as of May 2022, six states—Idaho, Kentucky, Nebraska, Tennessee, South Dakota, and West Virginia—have rescinded their ratifications. Even the late Supreme Court Justice Ruth Bader Ginsburg doubted the validity of the post-deadline ratifications. In a February 2020 interview, she said:

> I would like to see a new beginning. I'd like it to start over. There's too much controversy about a latecomer like Virginia ratifying long after the deadline passed. Plus, a number of states have withdrawn their ratification. If you count a latecomer on the plus side, how can you disregard states that said, "We've changed our minds"?

In addition, US archivist David S. Ferriero, who retired in April 2022, declined to certify the ERA as the Twenty-Eighth Amendment because, in 2020, then President Trump issued an executive memo to block it, citing the 1982 deadline as its legal expiration date. (As of May 2022, Debra Steidel Wall, the deputy archivist under Ferriero, is serving as acting archivist until a successor, nominated by the president, is confirmed by Congress.) Certification is the final step in an amendment's adoption. Without it, the ERA will not be added to and printed in the Constitution.

Perhaps you're wondering why milquetoast Joe Biden, the Delaware of presidents, has not issued an executive memo like his predecessor.* He issued a statement in January 2022 punting the responsibility to Congress, calling on it "to act immediately to pass a resolution recognizing ratification of the ERA." Of course, given that the 2022 midterm elections gave control of the House to the Republicans, Congress will do no such thing. It wasn't until February 2023 that the Senate held a hearing to discuss the repeal of the 1982 deadline. And, even if the repeal were to happen, the ERA still wouldn't pass based on the six states that rescinded their votes.

Without this certification, the ERA remains in a kind of Shakespearean limbo. It is like a ghost from beyond the grave that feminists simply cannot give up. Something between the Macbethian "sound and fury, signifying nothing" and the Hamletian "'Tis here! 'Tis here! 'Tis gone!"

The ERA, opined *New York Times* editorial board member Jesse Wegman in 2022, is the "Schrödinger's Cat of amendments." He postured that maybe its constitutionality is not what matters, quoting Columbia Law School professor David Pozen's comment that "when enough Americans act as though an amendment is part of the Constitution, it becomes part of the Constitution."

This may, at first glance, seem like a strange assertion. But the underlying sentiment is one I agree with: What matters most is not what the law says but what people *believe* and how they *act*. The power of a right,

---

* As someone born and raised in New Jersey, I feel it is my duty to insult Delaware at least once in this book.

as I noted earlier, is expressed and felt in how it is lived. This is especially true, I think, of the ERA—which legally applies only to the public sector. It has no jurisdiction over the private sector or private spaces, including nonfederal, nongovernmental workplaces and the home.

HOW EQUALITY UNDERMINES ABORTION

The Constitution was written by white men and expressly crafted with them as the model for rights and liberties. Seeking these same rights and liberties has stifled women's ability to legally pursue rights and protections outside of this patriarchal model. It is no surprise, to me, that guns arguably have more rights and fewer regulations than women—women are not even mentioned in the Constitution.

Neither is abortion. As Justice Alito repeatedly asserted in his majority opinion in *Dobbs*, abortion is not "deeply rooted in [our] history and tradition" and is not "essential to our Nation's 'scheme of ordered liberty.'" Through an originalist interpretation espoused by him and his fellow conservatives on the court, the scope of constitutional rights is conceptualized vis-à-vis cisgender white men—who arguably only think about abortion in terms of social reproduction and population control, not in terms of bodily autonomy, well-being (including financial well-being), or personal and public health.

The narrative Alito crafted and deemed "history" was intended to support his contention that abortion was always considered a criminal act in our society. Therefore, he conveniently ignored the parts of history that conflicted with his agenda, including the work of the nation's most esteemed polymath, Founding Father, and constitutional Framer Benjamin Franklin, who printed a recipe for abortion in his 1748 math book. Instead, he included only those sources—stretching as far back as the thirteenth century, centuries prior to the nation's founding—that demonized and criminalized abortion. He summarily concluded that "the inescapable conclusion is that a right to abortion is not deeply rooted in the Nation's history and traditions. On the contrary, an unbroken tradition of prohibiting abortion on pain of criminal punishment persisted from the earliest days of the common law until 1973."

This is factually incorrect. It wasn't until the nineteenth century that abortion began to be criminalized in the United States, thanks in large part to the efforts of the male doctors at the American Medical Association, who, as writer Gabrielle Bruney explained in an article for *Jezebel*, wanted to discredit midwives by claiming they were "dirty, backwards, and morally compromised." Even the Catholic Church did not oppose abortion until 1869.

Notably, the morality referred to is Christian. Judaism allows for abortion and requires it when a pregnant person's life is at stake. Yet the prominence of Christianity in our jurisprudence has denied people of other faiths their religious freedom to determine their own reproductive futures. Several lawsuits in states like Florida and Kentucky have cited religious freedom to contest abortion restrictions, claiming they violate the teachings of Judaism. Islam, too, does not prohibit abortion. In April 2022, prior to the *Dobbs* decision, the American Muslim Bar Association published "The Islamic Principle of Rahma: A Call for Reproductive Justice," which called "for mercy and compassion when it comes to all matters related to the womb."

Despite the Establishment Clause—the "separation of church and state" at the cornerstone of the nation—Christian morality has dictated abortion law in the United States. For people who are not Christian, and especially for those who are atheists like me, the historical disregard for this supposed, nation-defining separation is an affront to our dignity, as well as to our citizenship and, more critically, our democracy.

Alito's history represents a broader misogynist strategy to co-opt bodily autonomy via morality—a strategy he made plain in the first line of his opinion: "Abortion presents a profound moral issue." Indeed, this strategy—the aforementioned line is repeated in his conclusion—envelops his entire garbage-fire opinion. Not only does this framing mock the supposed constitutional value of "the separation of church and state," but, rooted in Christian morality, it locks abortion into the logic of equality. By situating abortion as a moral issue, Alito dehistoricized it, even though he tried to conceal this tactic through his repeated invocation of America's "deep roots and history." This maneuver also works to divorce abortion from its material and economic history and consequences—the health and financial burdens and dangers of carrying (and being forced to carry) a pregnancy that affect low-income women the most. In fact, the material and economic conditions of *actual* people—the real legal persons—affected by this judgment were almost entirely absent from the court's majority opinion, which offered more sympathy to a cluster of cells than real persons. As Justice Sotomayor, Justice Kagan, and Justice Breyer observed in their dissent: "'The most striking feature of the [majority] is the absence of any serious discussion' of how its ruling will affect women. . . . By characterizing *Casey*'s reliance arguments as 'generalized assertions about the national psyche,'" they wrote, "it reveals how little it knows or cares about women's lives or about the suffering its decision will cause."

It's absurd that we even have to consider what centuries-dead white men might have thought about abortion, as Ouija-boarded by constitutional originalists like Alito. The conservative majority said nothing about the effects of pregnancy on women or pregnant people—pregnancy, for the record, is not in the Constitution either. Unfortunately, because our bodily autonomy and control of our own reproductive lives have been interpreted through this originalist lens, we have been forced to negotiate our lives with these dead white men—of course, as anthropomorphized through still-living white men (and, thanks to Trump's third SCOTUS appointment, the devout patriarchal foot soldier Amy Coney Barrett, who is a member of People of Praise, a Christian faith group that believes in women's subservience to men and that pregnancy and childbirth are constitutive duties of womanhood).

Alito's calculated narrative sets him up to then argue that "a State's regulation of abortion is not a sex-based classification," and, therefore, abortion bans or restrictions are not, by definition, instances of sex discrimination against women. He cited the Supreme Court's 1974

Geduldig v. Aiello decision, which ruled that because only women can get pregnant, all pregnancy-related issues—in this particular case, the issue of insurance coverage—are distinctions between pregnant and nonpregnant people, not men and women. What this, in turn, means is that even if the ERA is certified, it does not constitutionally guarantee the legal right to an abortion, which the court does not consider to be a sex-based classification.

The underlying intention here is to more subtly assert that the Fourteenth Amendment—often heralded in sex equality jurisprudence as "the de facto ERA"—applies only to race. In a *New York Times* opinion piece, law professor Michele Goodwin dismantled Alito's racist interpretation of the Constitution by reminding him, and readers, of the real history of the Reconstruction Amendments. "Ending the forced sexual and reproductive servitude of Black girls and women was a critical part of the passage of the Thirteenth and Fourteenth Amendments," she wrote. Therefore, "mandated, forced, or compulsory pregnancy contravenes enumerated rights in the Constitution, namely the Thirteenth Amendment's prohibition against involuntary servitude and protection of bodily autonomy, as well as the Fourteenth Amendment's defense of privacy and freedom." As Goodwin makes clear, abortion law in the United States cannot be divorced from its history and specifically from chattel slavery—the use and abuse of Black women and girls for sex, breeding, and labor.

It was, in fact, the Fourteenth Amendment that the Supreme Court invoked to ground its decision in *Roe v. Wade* on privacy—not equality. And privacy, both in terms of bodily autonomy and secrecy, is integral to freedom. "The idea that there is a sphere of privacy around the home and one's familial, sexual, and domestic life is one long enshrined in American culture and jurisprudence," Jill Filipovic observed. "It's just that the privacy right was held by men." This was legally true until, she pointed out, verdicts in *Roe, Griswold v. Connecticut* (contraception), *Lawrence v. Texas* (oral and anal sex, no matter a person's gender), and *Obergefell v. Hodges* (gay marriage) expanded the right to privacy to more people than just straight white men. Overturning *Roe*, consequently, not only eliminated the constitutional right to an abortion but also repudiated our privacy rights. Filipovic further conjectured that the *Dobbs* decision represents a larger misogynistic agenda to restore "the patriarchal vision of privacy: that men have dominion over their wives, children, and households."

THREE CONSEQUENCES OF EQUALITY

In *Dobbs*, the court's conservative justices went to great lengths to emphasize their "judicial neutrality" to disguise their intentions. This included Justice Brett Kavanaugh's bewildering statement that "the Constitution is therefore neither pro-life nor pro-choice. The Constitution is neutral and leaves the issue for the people and their elected representatives to resolve through the democratic process in the States or Congress." As if the United States cares nothing for its citizens—which, arguably, is accurate when it comes to people who are not white and male.

The neutralizing effect of equality has three significant consequences. The first concerns voting and the court's decision that "the authority to regulate abortion must be returned to the people and their elected representatives." This argument blithely ignores the long and continuing history of racist voter discrimination, gerrymandering, and other barriers both preventing Black and brown people from voting and stymieing communities of color from amassing political power in the redistricting process. The premise of the court's assertion—audacious considering its own role in removing voting rights—is that everyone has the equal right to vote and can access and perform this right equally, sans state, political campaign, or armed vigilante interference.

Furthermore, the idyllic democratic voting process that these conservative justices repeatedly invoked is indirect and uncertain—if people can vote, their votes still do not guarantee policy outcomes. Elected representatives are more beholden to moneyed interests than to their constituencies, reflected in how often their votes—like the refusal to pass the FORMULA Act during a baby formula shortage in 2022 or the infuriating refusal to pass substantive gun control legislation—do not align with public opinion. Furthermore, the congressional filibuster—which is a rule, not a law—impedes the passage of any substantive bill.

It is pertinent to note that while sixty votes are needed to surpass the filibuster in the US Senate, only fifty-one votes are needed to confirm a Supreme Court justice. In a way, Supreme Court justices get an E-ZPass through our checks-and-balances system. Not to mention, they have lifetime appointments, so there is no mechanism in place that holds them accountable to the public.

The *Dobbs* decision is even more threatening when it comes to legal, antidiscriminatory protections for women, which brings us to the second consequence of equality: the argument that the voting power and electorate size of women demonstrate they have equal citizenship and participate equally to men in the United States. The underlying presumption is that all women experience the right to vote equally. Alito's claim is that women's voter turnout numbers prove they have significant political power: "It is noteworthy that the percentage of women who register to vote and cast ballots is consistently higher than the percentage of men who do so." Therefore, he wrote, "Our decision returns the issue of abortion to those legislative bodies, and it allows women on both sides of the abortion issue to seek to affect the legislative process by influencing public opinion, lobbying legislators, voting, and running for office."

By declaring that "women aren't a political minority and don't lack political power," Alito undermined court precedent on antidiscrimination laws and protections pertaining to women's constitutional equality. One consequence, already invoked by Alito, is that of interpreting the Fourteenth Amendment to apply only to race.

The third and arguably most devastating consequence of the logic of equality employed in *Dobbs* is the equation of fetal life to the lives of real persons—that is, autonomous, legal people existing outside of the womb, the cord cut. The equation of these two undeniably different life-forms lays the groundwork for the court to contend that abortion is a "profound moral issue" and that it is murder. It's clear what side the court stands on, as its majority opinion repeatedly used the language of "unborn child" and "unborn human being" to justify the false equivalence between a clump of cells and a person.

The logic of equality attempting to neutralize the differences between a zygote and a person was widely on display during the case's oral arguments, which is important to note because it was precisely this language that the court majority recited in its opinion. During the oral arguments, the lawyers defending Mississippi's restrictive law equated fetal life with legal personhood, primarily by repeatedly referring to a fetus as a child ("unborn child") and claiming that it "is fully human from a very early stage." Humanizing a fetus is imperative to asserting—as Scott G. Stewart, Mississippi's solicitor general arguing on behalf of the petitioner, did—that the state has an interest in protecting "the unborn child too, whose life is at stake in all these decisions." To further buttress his argument, he then asserted that "nowhere else does this court recognize the right to end a human life"—which is incorrect, since the Supreme Court has held that the death penalty is constitutional.

This equality strategy is roundly employed by antiabortionists—epitomized by the 2022 Right to Life March theme of "Equality Begins in the Womb"—and extends back decades. The roots can be traced to when abortion began to garner media attention in the late 1960s and early 1970s, concurrently with the rise of states' legalization of abortion (New York, Hawaii, Alaska, and Washington were the first, in 1970, although with varying restrictions) and the call to legalize it nationwide. In 1971, John Willke, who served as the president of the National Right to Life Committee, coauthored a handbook with his wife, Barbara, that established the template for decades of antiabortionist strategy and activism built on a simple argument: People must apply the "feminist credo" of the "right to her own body" to fetuses to win the abortion debate. This meant, in short, wresting control of language to take control of the cultural narrative.

"Words are important. Words are powerful," Willke asserted. "The words we or the abortion activists use very clearly and frequently shape the value system of those who listen." And he was right—words are powerful because, as I argue throughout this book, they don't just communicate our beliefs and actions but more fundamentally give form to them.

Willke recommended antiabortionists craft language guided by two intentions: to imbue a fetus with personhood and to decenter women—erase their personhood and physical and economic well-being—from the debate. The latter was accomplished with dehumanizing rhetoric aiming to redefine women exclusively as mothers so that women's existence was reduced to their reproductive function. "You should say: mother," Willke wrote. "You should not say: pregnant woman. Mother is a much softer word, calling for love and compassion by the reader. . . . You should say: womb. You should not say: uterus. Womb is a warmer, maternal term. Uterus is coldly medical."

The intention of this language tactic is to counter the feminist point that the value of women's existence is wholly distinct from their procreative abilities—that women have humanity and dignity, and that the purpose of their lives isn't only to make babies. This tactic also functions to create the "moral issue" Alito and his fellow justices were so eager to adjudicate by reimaging a pregnancy as a human relationship between mother and unborn child. All people have organs that perhaps generate growths or tumors. But only, according to Willke (and decades of antiabortionists after him), *mothers* have *babies*. In this dynamic, the humanity of the woman is subsumed, or consumed, by the fetus. This is another instance of how the patriarchal logic of the binary works to dehumanize women, because women are always positioned in negative relation to the other figure. Women are the object to the subject of men/fetuses. They are lesser than men/fetuses. What is important to note here is how this dynamic belies antiabortionists' claim that "all life is equal." The tactic of dehumanizing women exposes the lie of this—because "mothers" are not persons; they are patriarchy's vessels for social reproduction and, subsequently, social control.

The rhetorical device of apostrophe is the antiabortionists' tactic of choice. Usually, this materializes in imagery that illustrates a fetus alongside words in quotation marks or cutesy speech bubbles to suggest they can talk and are begging for their lives to be saved. This imagery depicts the fetus as fully agentic and independent of the person carrying it. The body of the pregnant person is, of course, cropped out of the image. As feminist writer Susan Faludi explained in *Backlash*: "In the movement's literature, photographs, films, and other props, the whole 'unborn child' floats in a disembodied womb. The fetus is a conscious, even rambunctious tyke, the mother a passive, formless, and inanimate 'environment.'"

The antiabortion movement even found a way to give fetuses voice in the courtroom through legal representatives known as "fetal attorneys," as part of their chipping away strategy. That's right. Attorneys who represent fetuses in court. And such performances are apostrophe writ large, as *The Daily Show* correspondent Jessica Williams exposed in a hilariously memorable 2015 interview with a fetal attorney in Alabama—a state that, in 2014, had just passed a law allocating state funds for the defense of fetuses in court. This exchange epitomizes the absurdity of these attorneys and their job:

<u>Williams</u>:

"You get a call from a fetus seeking legal representation. Then what happens?"

<u>Attorney</u>:

"I cannot get a call from a fetus for anything, much less legal representation."

<u>Williams</u>:

"So how do you mean, 'confidentiality with your client'?"

<u>Attorney</u>:

"Well, of course if you've got an unborn child in somebody else's

womb, I cannot communicate with them directly. You know
better than to ask the question."

Williams:
"Well, I dunno. You have a crazy-ass job, sir."

"I cannot communicate with them directly"—the attorney's response is so matter-of-fact to the point of being a confession. Of course he can't communicate with a fetus—it is not a person. It cannot speak with a real person or make informed choices, like a person. It is not autonomous or agentic, like a person. It has no history that can be invoked to speculate about its desires or wishes in case of a health emergency. It has no independence, no existence in the world outside of the uterus. A fetus may have life, but it has no sociality, or social life.

While Alito insisted that the court could not opine on the origins of personhood, the *Dobbs* verdict effectively negated the precedent established in *Roe* that the Equal Protection Clause does not apply to fetuses: "The word 'person,' as used in the Fourteenth Amendment, does not include the unborn." *Dobbs* paved the way for litigation in a handful of states, with fetal personhood clauses (tucked into antiabortion laws) already in place in Georgia and Alabama (and in Arizona, before a federal judge blocked the law in July 2022). In August 2022, Georgia even declared that fetuses can be claimed as dependents on tax returns. (Meanwhile, I still cannot claim my freeloading cats!)

"Fetal personhood" is the antiabortion movement's endgame because securing the legal personhood of a clump of cells means all constitutional rights apply to those cells.

The fetal personhood strategy explicitly calls upon the Equal Protection Clause to assert its constitutional validity, with advocates relying on originalism to contend that the legislators who penned the Fourteenth Amendment believed fetuses were people. "If the Constitution recognizes fetal personhood," legal historian Mary Ziegler explained in the *Atlantic*, "then unborn children would have the right to equal protection under and due process of the law. Abortion would be unconstitutional in New York as well as in Alabama."

Again, apostrophe is essential to the performative equality operating in this strategy. And it is, by all measures, trying to prove a simple argument: If, through a twisted originalist interpretation of the Fourteenth Amendment, fetuses are people, then abortion is unconstitutional.

State legislatures across the nation have been at work to emend the legal designation of all fetal life—whether zygote or embryo or fetus—to that of personhood. Alabama's Human Life Protection Act, enacted in 2019, bans abortion for "an unborn child in utero at any state of development" and criminalizes any doctor or provider for performing the procedure. In May 2022, Oklahoma passed a law banning abortion from the moment of fertilization, save for instances of rape or incest that—it is critical to note—are *reported to the police*, which puts an additional burden on victims to report the crime and places authority in the hands of the police.

Legislating pregnancy as a matter of fetal personhood, in turn, has abetted America's policing and surveillance state apparatus. And it has fed the capitalist prison industrial complex, as we've seen an increasing number of manslaughter charges brought against people who have suffered miscarriages. Oklahoma has invoked its felony child neglect law to penalize people who have experienced pregnancy loss, and, in tandem with a 2022 law that equates abortion with manslaughter, has charged dozens of women with child abuse or manslaughter. Fetal personhood enables the "full-scale criminalization of pregnancy," *New Yorker* writer Jia Tolentino said, "whereby women can be arrested, detained, and otherwise placed under state intervention for taking actions perceived to be potentially harmful to a fetus."

Fetal protection and personhood laws could even be applied to outlaw contraception, in vitro fertilization (IVF), and the interstate travel of pregnant people. So the fetal personhood strategy does not just seek to afford a clump of cells constitutional rights and protections; it seeks to criminalize pregnant people and anyone who aids and abets their abortion.* Antiabortionists have been transparent about this strategy. Bradley Pierce, leader of Foundation to Abolish Abortion, who helped to draft legislation in Louisiana that did just this, told the *New York Times*: "If the fetus is a person, then we should protect them with the same homicide laws that protect born persons. . . . That's what equal protections means." (Can we pause for a minute on the language of abolition used by this group? Conservatives have a clear and consistent strategy of appropriating progressive language centered on dignity and justice and applying it to their misogynistic and racist agendas.)

Rendering all life equal has profound consequences on our ability to make important life decisions, including the decision about how a person builds their family. As we've seen, the antiabortionist equal life argument operates upon a dynamic rooted in the dehumanization of women and pregnant people. And this serves to remind us that equality is always manufactured according to its patriarchal design. Here, the patriarchy is designed to control bodies by controlling procreation, and men stay in power by maintaining control of all modes of social reproduction.

SYSTEMIC ENTRAPMENT

The trend in jurisprudence and legislation of bestowing fetal life with legal personhood is just one facet of how equality is used *against* women, pregnant people, and anyone fighting for their basic civil rights.

Legislative and judicial equality efforts are barriers to justice because they ultimately rely on identity politics to determine our rights. From our nation's founding, rights have been granted based on identity—on race, gender, and ability status—which signifies how our political system is inherently discriminatory. At most, our racist and sexist institutions become diverse and inclusive, but the accession of equal rights will never

---

* In the weeks and months since *Dobbs*, the speed with which conservative legislators across the country have been writing and passing laws to ban and criminalize abortion has been nightmarish. It is materially impossible within the confines of this book to note every single action that has been taken thus far—a seemingly endless list that Jessica Valenti has been exhaustively documenting in her newsletter, *Abortion, Every Day*.

transform these institutions into levers of care and justice for the entire American public.

This reality represents the catch-22 of the feminist movement's identity-based strategy, grounded in the gender binary. Within the realm of the law, we have sought advancement by entrenching ourselves in a second-class status—which, on the surface, makes sense because women have been subjugated and treated as second-class citizens. The consequence, however, is that we've anchored our humanity to this binary dynamic: Are women fundamentally different from men, and therefore do we need protections in the form of antidiscrimination laws? Or are we the same as men—are we all human—and therefore should we be afforded the same rights and privileges?

"Yes, no . . . and what else?" This is one of my favorite lines, and lessons, from Barbara Johnson. What else other than equality? The binary has trapped us in a legal quagmire. But, what else? Why even imagine the rights we want and the supports we need in relation to men? If we aspire, for some asinine reason, to send people to Mars, can't we be innovative enough to think beyond the equality system? I don't give a flying fuck about launching rockets at asteroids when doctors are still using barbaric and medieval devices to examine my breasts and reproductive organs to check for cancer.

When it comes to equality, the image we often have in mind is of the scales of justice held by a woman. But the fact is that these scales are not held by a woman. They are in men's hands.

Equality is not, nor will it ever be, enough to change our world, eradicate structural racism, or smash the patriarchy. Even progressive legislation promising universality—from universal health care to a universal basic income—is based on the fallacy of inequality being experienced the same by everyone. Equality might exist in theory, but it is impossible in practice. Patriarchal systems and institutions, which are conservative by design because they work to maintain and preserve the status quo, can never truly realize equality.

Feminists' unwavering commitment to equality in principle—to the same goals, the same values, the same rights, the same desires, and the same capitalist measures of success as men—has only enlarged our systems of oppression. Equality has given us unethical billionaire "girl bosses," carceral feminism promoting policing and prisons as solutions to violence, and superficial gender representation in positions of power. When we rely on equality to improve the conditions of our lives, we place the responsibility for social change on systems and institutions built on white supremacist cis-heteropatriarchal values. This dependence makes us politically complacent, even as those laws often treat symptoms rather than causes.

Remaining wedded to the equality system forecloses substantive societal and institutional change. Instead of continuing to invest our time, energy, and resources into equality-driven efforts, feminists should rethink our logic, strategies, and tactics currently grounded in identity politics. Because it is identity politics that has hemmed us into what political theorist Wendy Brown has called the "wounded attachment" of *woman*—an identity defined by its exclusion, suffering, and subordination. Identity is, ultimately, a superficial way to connect and build a politics. Rather, we must imagine and devise the types of policies and laws that will rebuild our institutions so that their primary function is to care for us all. Our institutions should not be driven by profit motives that oppress, surveil, and criminalize the most marginalized among us. The rights of our citizenship should not be determined by identity. We need to imagine the kinds of institutions and supports that will help us thrive. Black and abolitionist feminists like Angela Davis and Ruth Wilson Gilmore have been doing this work for decades. They, in turn, have encouraged us to begin this work by reframing social issues on dignity, care, and justice: What institutions will provide us with safety and security, respect our human dignity, and nurture our self-determination? What institutions, what policies and laws, can we advocate for that do not rely on policing, surveillance, or violence to ensure our health and flourishing? What kinds of community and support services can help people through crisis without incarceration?

When we rely on systems to change us, we fail to realize that *we* make the systems. *We* make the values that we live by, and our actions communicate and realize our values. The systemic change that we crave begins at the individual level. This change demands *going to the root.* And the root—beyond systems—is us. The core of us. Who we are in terms of expressing our authentic selves, which demands the integrity of living our values. Of walking the talk, so to speak.

It is time for us to realize our freedom to make this change and catalyze this politics.

It is time for feminists to reclaim freedom.

CHAPTER 3

THE VISION OF FREEDOM

Step one to reclaiming freedom for feminism: Claim it.

Unlike with equality, we do not need to wait for men or their patriarchal institutions to patronizingly bestow us with freedom (and then send out dozens of press releases celebrating their beneficence). Freedom is not given. It is claimed. We have the power to choose it. We are not subject to men's impulses, nor do we have to petition them to lay claim to it.

But to be clear, freedom is not a thing that is claimed like a material possession. Rather, when I say we must claim our freedom, I mean we must *affirm* it. As an ideal, freedom is no more abstract than equality but is far more achievable because it is a continuous practice that begins within us. Whereas equality is imposed externally by institutions, in the form of rights and protections, freedom is a felt and shared experience created through our active *doing*. Therefore, it is claimed—actualized—in practice. We can express our freedom daily in how we choose to live our lives and by engaging with the world in a way that acknowledges and respects the dignity and freedom of all people.

Step two: Take back freedom from the white supremacist patriarchy. We can begin this effort by learning from and building upon the decades of Black, radical, lesbian, and freedom-centered feminists whose ideas and activism have shown us that freedom is not realized through the domination and oppression of others but through mutual relationships. Collective freedom depends on our mutual freedom.

Freedom is a lifelong practice of self-creation based in accountability and care and that endeavors to build a freer and more just world.

To level-set and define these terms: *Self-creation* is inspired by Black feminists like Patricia Hill Collins, bell hooks, and Audre Lorde who have theorized the importance of "self-determination" as a direct response to Black women's long-denied human dignity and bodily autonomy. "Black self-determination," hooks wrote in *Killing Rage: Ending Racism*, is how "African Americans, across class, create radical liberatory subjectivity even as we continue to live within a white supremacist capitalist patriarchal society." This creation is a collective process, she explained, "by which we learn to radicalize our thinking and habits of being in ways that enhance the quality of our lives despite racist domination" so that "we live lives of sustained well-being." The effort to determine oneself is nothing short of a willed survival for oneself as well as for one's community. As Lorde said in "Learning from the 60s," "If I didn't define myself for myself, I would be crunched into other people's fantasies for me and eaten alive."

Self-creation is a version of self-determination that elevates aesthetics as a constitutive element of our becoming, of how we design and give meaning to our lives. The process centers creativity as a driving force in manifesting our authenticity and imbuing our life with meaning.

Accountability is the deliberate choice to take responsibility for our choices and actions as well as for their impact. The significance of accountability is that it is an ethic that precedes and informs our actions, and it also compels us to ensure and increase the freedom of others by, for instance, taking action to repair harm when harm is done. Accountability is the lynchpin of freedom because it indicates how freedom is both relational and conditional. *Care* is not just about repair, restoration, preservation, and survival. A feminist ethic of care is much more expansive and includes our mutual pleasure, thriving, and satisfaction. Touch is care. Love is care. Sex is care.

A feminist freedom, therefore, is realized in *how* we intentionally design our lives *with* other people. Our lives are codesigned, cocreated. Self-creation is world-building—which is another way to interpret the famous feminist mantra that the personal is political. Because if we choose to center freedom and live by its values—dignity, authenticity, mutuality, justice, accountability, and care—we not only can liberate ourselves from oppressive systems but also can revolutionize those very systems. This includes liberation from the patriarchal gender binary and reductive identity politics. I agree with Linda Zerilli that "a freedom-centered feminism is concerned not with knowing (that there are women) as such, but with doing—with transforming, world-building, beginning anew." Our identities do not and should not prevent us from doing the work of freeing other people—which, according to Toni Morrison, is the very function of freedom.

With my definition, I engage with, honor, and build upon the decades of work by feminists who have fought for freedom, including Barbara Smith, who in a 1979 lecture said:

> Feminism is the political theory and practice that struggles to free all women: women of color, working-class women, poor women, disabled women, lesbians, old women—as well as white, economically privileged, heterosexual women. Anything less than this vision of total freedom is not feminism, but merely female self-aggrandizement.

Freedom is fundamentally a collective endeavor. The horizon of my freedom is not limited by yours but broadened by it. And feminists must challenge any rhetoric about freedom that suggests otherwise.

Whereas equality feminism measures its ultimate success in its obsolescence, freedom feminism maintains an opposite teleology, guided by the belief that freedom is not a one-time event or achievement but a commitment to live deliberately and with the intention to realize and affirm our freedom and the freedom of others. Because, as the steady chipping away of voting rights and the *Dobbs* decision have shown us, no right is guaranteed. The fight for freedom is not one and done—or, in the context of rights, won and done. It is enduring, and it must endure if we are to ever upend the stranglehold of the white supremacist patriarchy.

We can only surpass the current conditions of our lives through our relationships with people—those who raise us, teach us, mentor us, support us, inspire us, and love us, and whom we raise, teach, mentor, support, inspire, and love in turn. This is how my freedom is connected to your freedom. Freedom does not exist—it cannot be felt or experienced—in a silo.

Step three: Practice, practice, practice. Freedom is expressed and felt in action. Only through practice can we engender a culture that affirms a feminist understanding of freedom. The collective impact of this daily practice can produce societal change through rewriting the scripts about freedom and American values. A feminist politics can emerge that is not based on identities or the gender binary but in efforts to realize freedom for all—to secure and respect everyone's human dignity, to provide care specific to need, and to advocate for justice for all, no matter identity, no matter citizenship status. What is considered a feminist "victory," then, is no longer measured by profit or having what men have. Burning ourselves out and burning up the Earth so that a handful of women can become rich and powerful is not feminism. We don't seek a seat at the table. In fact, we don't want to even use the table that men built. Success, rather, if it is even the right word, is measured in terms of the collective well-being—the public good, public health (including housing), public education, and environmental health (biodiversity and ecosystems).

Freedom practice can be visualized as a continuous, enfolding relationship comprising internal work and external action. Our mindset and beliefs inform our actions, and our actions—and their effects—also inform our mindset and beliefs. We generally understand this process in terms of learning from experience over time. Of "not making that mistake again." The ongoing internal work also indicates that our actions should always be thoughtful, not thoughtless, and that we should lead with intention, care, and consideration for how our actions affect people we know and don't know, all species, and the Earth itself.

The internal work of freedom liberates us from the equality mindset. The cognitive process of breaking free from old ways of thinking and patriarchal conditioning entails an *awakening* that liberates the mind, producing an *awareness* of oneself and one's place in the world. From this awakening and awareness, one can develop a critical consciousness, which inspires the choice of *accountability* as an ethic that shapes one's *actions* to create a more free, caring, and just society.

The internal process of developing a critical consciousness also reveals how our lives are interconnected and interdependent, proving how my freedom is made possible by your freedom, and vice versa. The very fact that we exist in a world with multiple ecosystems and depend on those ecosystems for the continuation of our existence proves our inter-dependence and justifies a philosophy of freedom based on it. Beauvoir used the term *intersubjectivity* to describe how it is through our mutual recognition of each other's human dignity that freedom is possible.

Fundamental to this internal work is rest. The Nap Ministry founder Tricia Hersey explained that "rest is resistance" to white supremacy, capitalism, and the patriarchy because it provides us the dream space to imagine liberated futures and heal from systemic harm. Dreaming is powerful, Hersey noted in *Rest Is Resistance: A Manifesto*, because it disrupts the capitalist grind culture that demands we treat our bodies and each other like machines: "Dreaming is the way we move toward liberation because it is a direct disturbance to the collective reality of life under capitalism. Grind culture is violence." And the consequen-tial exhaustion, burnout, and isolation are not coincidental. They leave us depleted and alone, without the energy to imagine better, freer, and more caring ways to be in this world. We become disengaged, dispas-sionate, and even disembodied, zombie-like people. And who hasn't felt this way? I certainly did trying to write this book while holding down a demanding full-time job. There were days and weeks when I was just tapped out, without an idea, and without the creative reserves to write one word. Creativity, as I have experienced it, is sparked by engagement with the world—with friends, in group activities, and at events like book clubs and lectures, as well as by reading (which allows the reader to textually engage with the ideas of others, even those who may no longer be alive). But grind culture and, correlatively, the "having it all" of equality feminism, prevent such creativity from happening. The work of freedom demands that we rest, that we give our bodies the time to feel and think through—and even let go of—experiences so we can learn from them.

The internal work and external practice of freedom are mutually constitutive. We can think of freedom, therefore, as an ethics—a set of practices cultivated through our encounters and experiences intended to express our values. Integrity and authenticity come from living our values. And the final trio of chapters in this book explore this freedom work via an examination of the three most critical spheres of women's liberation from both the patriarchy and the equality mindset: the mind, the body, and movement.

The feminists—and specifically the Black feminists—who have done this freedom work not only knew that dignity, self-determination, and justice were impossible within the politics of equality feminism, they knew equality wasn't good enough. It wasn't real. It wasn't experienced. And their ideas resonated with me, because I have always craved the freedom to become my own person, to move freely, to think freely. That freedom, however momentary, has always made me feel powerful. Made me feel real, and really seen. And while I could intuit this truth about freedom from an early age, it was only by studying these feminists that I understood that freedom is about more than personal experience. It is about all of us, and, guided by freedom, we have the potential to liberate and lift up everyone—not just those who are already at the top—without losing sight of ourselves and the differences that make us who we are.

The fight for freedom, too, is about more than just feminism. It is about the future of this country. The conflicting philosophies of freedom—

the white supremacy masquerading as freedom and the feminist freedom I offer here—represent the tensions at play in America's culture wars. Yet, for our collective survival—and for the survival of this planet and all its life-forms (because if there is no Earth, no oxygen for your mortal body to stay alive, you can't abscond to your metaverse)—we must dismantle white freedom's cultural dominance, break down the logic of its parts and reveal its motivations.

It is time for feminists to reclaim freedom from the white supremacist cis-heteropatriarchy, reassert its true definition, and take control of the narratives that shape our lives and our society.

AMERICA'S WHITE FREEDOM

When I think of freedom as it is widely understood in America versus what it could become, I often think of the difference between guns and books, and specifically how the former, and not the latter, are cherished as an emblem of American freedom. In fact, books are considered by a disconcerting number of Americans to be more threatening than guns—dozens of states have implemented book bans but cannot even fathom gun control legislation.

Guns are weapons designed to kill or maim. Books are published to educate and enlighten. One is a barrier between the self and the world, representing aggression, aggressive defensiveness, and the belief in protection through violence. The other is a conduit between the self and the world, connecting the reader to people unlike themselves and fostering critical thinking and a self-awareness born from empathic connection.

Even though guns, and not books, are killing us and our children, US legislators and a vocal minority of the public would rather a teacher be armed with a gun than teach a book that has a gay character.

Freedom does not ring in America. It fires. It is a rhetorical gunshot.

This predominant understanding of freedom in America—a narrative that stretches back to the nation's founding in slavery and genocide—is what Tyler Stovall called "white freedom."

It is a freedom not intended for everyone, as Black scholars, activists, and freedom fighters have told us time and again (and to which, I am hoping, many of my readers will say, "no shit"). As Stovall put it, "To be free is to be white, and to be white is to be free." Coded in the language of individual rights, freedom has been utilized to preserve and defend white supremacy. Talk of freedom in America, especially when it comes out of white mouths, typically evokes ideas of unfettered autonomy, the entitled liberty to say and do whatever one thinks without consequence.

Today's popular notion of American freedom took shape during the Reconstruction era. The white backlash to Black liberation and enfranchisement, written into federal and constitutional laws endeavoring to make the nation a multiracial democracy after the Civil War, manifested in efforts to limit government and undermine Black freedom, dignity, and citizenship. The consequential rhetoric of limited government of, as Ronald Reagan later promised, "getting the government off our back," was a result of white supremacist efforts to prevent and derail the freedom and civil rights of Black and Indigenous people, as well as immigrants and women.

"Freedom today is a battering ram against democracy," historian Annelien de Dijn asserted in *Freedom: An Unruly History*. "The West's most ardent freedom fighters (who are now more likely to call themselves conservative than liberal) remain more concerned with limiting state power than with enhancing popular control over government."

It is not simply that white people controlled the scope of freedom through racist laws and terroristic violence. More fundamentally—and this is Stovall's argument—freedom signifies whiteness. This white freedom is "the belief (and practice) that freedom is central to white racial identity, and that only white people can or should be free," Stovall said. "As an ideology it argued that to be white meant having control of one's destiny, of being free from domination by others."

White people are possessive of freedom because they believe it signifies their racial superiority and, as their privileged possession, is theirs alone and theirs to give. The ideology of white freedom, therefore, morally justifies systemic racism, from slavery, to incarceration, to invading and colonizing other countries while chomping on their freedom fries. Yet without this white freedom, they are nothing. And they know this. As James Baldwin observed in "A Letter to Prisoners," the fragility of white freedom is palpable in how aggressively it is touted. Like being hit with a cudgel. Like a bombastic white man proudly donning his gun in an open carry state:

> It is impossible not to recognize that the people who are endlessly boasting of their freedom—*we're the best because we're free!*—loathe the very suggestion of such a possibility for anyone other than themselves. They are forever stitching flags, making and threatening and dropping bombs, creating instruments of torture and torture chambers and overseers and deputies and detention centers. Their notion of freedom is so strenuously calisthenic, not to say defensive, that freedom becomes a matter of keeping everybody else out of your backyard.

Baldwin wrote these words in 1982, yet they could've been written today, say, in response to people who decried mask or vaccine mandates during the pandemic. Or they could've been written to describe those people who feel personally injured at the thought of gun control legislation and yell, "No one is going to take my guns!" after yet another school mass shooting.

White freedom is the belief in one's entitlement—articulated as a God-given right for Christian Americans—to do whatever one wants, regardless of the impact of those actions, and regardless of, or *in spite of,* the fact that one lives in a world *with* billions of people. It is navel-gazing narcissism writ large: the inability, like a child, to understand the self in relation to other selves. From a white-freedom mindset, there aren't other people—there are just commodities, labor, bodies to use, pussies to grab.

The white-freedom mindset espouses "liberation from the dictates of the *we*," as Ta-Nehisi Coates wrote in the *Atlantic*. "Freedom without consequence, freedom without criticism, freedom to be proud and ignorant; freedom to profit off a people in one moment and abandon them in the next; a Stand Your Ground freedom, freedom without responsibility, without hard memory; a Monticello without slavery, a Confederate freedom."

The myth of rugged individualism at the heart of white male American identity is composed precisely of this willful ignorance, this cognitive dissonance that contends we don't need each other, that our lives are not dependent on each other for anything. It is Emersonian self-reliance filtered through a white supremacist mindset. And it is a mindset premised on hypocrisy because it maintains the belief of one's absolute authority while requiring a suspension of this belief to deny responsibility for one's actions—crucial to refusing accountability. It claims superiority while feigning complete powerlessness over one's actions: the insistence, we've all heard variously, that "I couldn't help it" or "She brought it on herself."

Equality is as critically important to white freedom as it is to white feminism. Its neutralizing effects on centuries of discrimination project the illusion of an equal playing field, where all people are the same and have the same rights. The underlying intention is to give license to the idea that we are all free to do as we please. This lie is integral to the continued domination of white freedom as American freedom.

White freedom has established a society of opposition and oppression, a society where individual rights trump collective welfare and where the two are believed to be antithetical to each other. This freedom is narrow-minded—one of limited government, limited perspective, and limited understanding of what it means to be a citizen of the world. White freedom is action without accountability. And so the unwavering belief of entitlement—to act without thought, consideration, or consequence—is a defining feature not only of white supremacy but also of white freedom. And this entitlement reinforces and is reinforced by the gender binary, the gender hierarchy, and women's oppression, such that men believe they are entitled to women's bodies, *and* women are conditioned to believe their fundamental role is to be men's caretakers.

Given the prevalence of white freedom in America, it is no wonder that freedom has been sidelined by the mainstream feminist movement. Black feminists, who have done this freedom work for generations, have had to go against the tide of not only white freedom but also white feminism. Alongside Indigenous, lesbian, and radical feminists, and other feminists of color, they have argued that freedom is not an individual possession but a collective experience. These feminists have understood how dignity and self-determination were made unfree by colonialism and slavery, how consciousness was colonized, and how Christian patriarchal societies imposed artificial racial, gender, and sexual binaries onto people to enforce white supremacy.

FREEDOM AS AN ETHICS

Centering freedom in feminism allows us to understand how feminism is not just a politics but more precisely an ethics from which a politics emerges. This shift to freedom pivots us away from the equality mindset that demands rights based on *who we are*—identities set by the patriarchal gender binary—toward a mindset that conceives of a politics built on not just what we do but *how* we do it. Equality feminism's origins in religious egalitarianism moralized the movement in a way that dispossessed women of our power and authority. It established a politics that demanded equality rights from men based on identity, which, over time, resulted in the superficial forms of representation we see today. We have conceived of and justified a politics rooted in oppression rather than in our power.

A mindset shift toward freedom allows us to more fully comprehend how the personal is political. It is no small thing, because it demands we change our perspective and perceptions of ourselves and each other. It reveals to us that the power to change society is in our hands, as we are responsible for our actions and accountable to others for them. The politics of a freedom-centered feminism resides in people power—the power of relationships and especially of relationships between women—and not in reactive relation to the patriarchy.

When we attribute discrimination and violence to "the system," we do so because we have cultivated a politics that situates the problem beyond our control. And it *is* beyond our individual control. But together, our efforts become movements and can and do change the systems, institutions, and society. The question of why freedom—why freedom for feminism—finds its answer in this potential. Freedom puts the power to change society in the hands of the people.

If freedom comes from action, from critical engagement in the world, then it is imperative that feminism be understood as both an ethics and a politics. Ethics are *how* we live: how we create, design, and cobble together our lives based on our specific material conditions (from economic status to place of residence to ability status). An ethics is not a morality that prescribes our actions. Rather, the process is dynamic and enfolding. The values you live by emerge from how you act and with whom you interact. They can be affirmed, challenged, and/or negated over time; they guide us but are not inflexible.

Morality and ethics are often believed to be synonymous and as such are used interchangeably, but there is a clear difference between them. Whereas morality is a system of values that people *should* live by, ethics refers to how we have chosen to live, act, define ourselves, and design our lives. Ethics consists of the daily practices we have cultivated because they are forms of self- and community care. There is an intentionality and artistry to these practices, which remind us that the power of and responsibility for our actions is ours.

Put slightly differently, morality is the *shoulds* and *shalts*—rules written by men, let's be clear—that women must submit to if they want to maintain their safety and privilege. These rules acquire power through their institutionalization. Originally crafted by and for men, they become moral truths ordained by God. In religious systems, *good* and *evil* are dictated by the people in power. And, across time and cultures, those people have overwhelmingly been men. In the United States, white Christian nationalists—always extremely powerful and more emboldened in recent years—invoke morality to authorize their supremacist behavior (e.g., the belief that the Christian God ordained Trump to rule the United States was used to justify attacking the US Capitol on January 6, 2021) and to condemn any behavior that subverts their authority (e.g., homosexuality is "immoral," women who wear pants are "immoral," and interracial marriage is "immoral").

My definition of ethics borrows from materialist philosophy—for my fellow nerds out there, from the Stoics to Spinoza, Nietzsche to Bergson, Beauvoir to Deleuze—and is adopted specifically from Elizabeth Grosz. "Ethics," she wrote in *The Incorporeal*, "is an attempt to live in accordance with the principles one has chosen for oneself by which to regulate one's life, according to the goals and ideals that are also those life takes from the world." The individual, in other words, creates the principles, or values, they live by in relation to their situatedness. In this way, ethics doesn't describe what we *must* do; it describes the things we do to try to create a good and happy life. (*Happy* in the ancient Greek sense of *eudaimonia*, or flourishing, which for Beauvoir is a product of our freedom work, what she called the "projects" of surpassing our situatedness through our encounters.) Those values become feminist when they make possible and expand not only a person's individual freedom but the freedom of others as well. This is why Grosz regards ethics as the "capacity for the enhancement of life."

We express our freedom through our ethics—through how we live in the world, stylize our lives, and engage with others. The word *stylize* here is deliberate, as materialist philosophers have referred to ethics as a kind of self-stylization or self-fashioning. Think about the creative flourishes and personal touches that make you feel like *you* and communicate who *you* are to the world, from the way you cut and style your hair to how you speak (language, accent, and pronunciation) to how you edit your social media posts. (I was very deliberate about my tattoos—the design, the color, the message—as signals to the lesbian community. Like, *Hey, lesbians, I'm over here!*) The French philosopher Gilles Deleuze believed *ethics* and *aesthetics* are inextricable from each other. "It's the styles of life involved in everything that makes us this or that," he said in a 1986 interview. We are not blank slates or passive, inert subjects. We are the primary agents of our self-creation.

The components of how we stylize our lives—from cultural influences to chosen social communities—comprise the narrative of us, the story of who we are and are becoming over time, with the past informing the present and carving possibilities for the future. What self-creation demonstrates is that an authentic self is never a fixed thing. There is no truth to reveal, only creation. "We don't discover ourselves, we make ourselves," philosopher Skye C. Cleary said. "Creating ourselves is an art form—the act of intentionally choosing who we become." This lack of fixity, of there being no *there* there, should not scare us but excite us. Make us feel alive, full of potential, and free.

In their art and activism, Alok Vaid-Menon has championed the idea that creativity, and specifically creativity as the cultivation of beauty, is a practice of freedom. And just as freedom is a collective practice, they told *Allure* magazine, "beauty and glamor are collective projects. . . . We have to help one another be able to express each other, express ourselves." In this spirit, Alok has campaigned around the world to liberate beauty and fashion from gender norms. "I'm fighting for a world where all people can creatively self-express, where creativity belongs to all of us," they said.

The power of self-creation is especially important for women who have been conditioned for centuries to be ashamed of their power, sexuality, and desires. Perhaps this is why I adore lesbians who have deliberately tailored their lives to their own desires despite normative societal pressures to, say, cohabitate with a long-term partner, or marry, or have children. The iconoclastic wit, proud New Yorker, and perennial angry homosexual Fran Lebowitz is one of my favorite examples. She has often described her life in terms of diligent and conscientious choice making. "I'm aware that I've had a lot of choices that a lot of people don't have. So, I mean, you can have a lot of privilege without having a lot of money, you know, you just have to insist upon it. Or, avoid certain things, or be willing to give up certain things, or not care about certain things," she said in a 2021 podcast interview. "The most important thing to me always in my life was freedom. I think, like, the big, lucky thing for me is I always kinda knew what was important to me."

In a 2020 interview, Lebowitz connected lesbianism to this freedom and the ability to create a life that has allowed her to live alone and skirt women's traditional domain of domesticity: "I loathe domestic life; probably one of the greatest accomplishments for any lesbian is to live by themselves their entire life."

Understanding freedom as an ethics allows us to feel that freedom is in our grasp if we claim it. The practices we cultivate reveal the power we have in our choices and actions and, as such, in our ability to find meaning in our existence. Cleary refers to "freedom as a tool to shape ourselves" to remind us that authenticity manifests from acts of self-creation: "to realize and accept that we are free; to be lucid about what we can and can't choose about ourselves, our situation, and others." And when we understand our capacity to be free and the intentional effort it takes, we are able to comprehend how we matter in the world, even if we are just one person among billions. Our actions have impact, create ripple effects in ways we cannot foresee. Oceans may feel incomprehensible in their vastness, but, remember, they are made of drops of water. So, the collective impact of our actions can change the world.

A LIBERATORY TOOL

The internal work of freedom is responsible for cultivating our critical consciousness, a tool of self-awareness and self-examination of our situatedness—our power, privilege, advantages, and disadvantages—in the world.

Critical consciousness has always been an important tool in women's liberation efforts, which is why feminists have always advocated for women's education. Of course, women who are critical thinkers and who ask questions are perceived as threats to society—some were even burned at the stake. Yes, knowledge *is* power, and the patriarchy has gone to great lengths to prevent women not only from acquiring knowledge but also from speaking, reading, writing, learning, and sharing their knowledge with each other.

Ignorance serves the status quo and keeps women in their place. In *The Second Sex*, Beauvoir examined how women have been conditioned to accept their inferior position as the "second sex." She unpacked the myths of womanhood in order to awaken women to this social conditioning that produces their ignorance, subservience, and weakness to maintain the patriarchal social order. This conditioning is as much mental as it is physical, training women to believe that they are inferior and that their limitations are a result of their gender. What women think to be their available capacities or choices—let's just say, for the sake of this argument, the whole equality thing—is a belief created by men and ingrained in our minds over generations. This is how ideology becomes "truth."

This conditioning concurrently elevates men and teaches women to believe men are innately superior to women and therefore entitled to social and economic privileges as well as to women's bodies. Beauvoir believed this conditioning encouraged women "to ardently want to please men." We know these women today as white supremacist foot soldiers. The consequence of this conditioning is that women's sense of self is based on men. It is one thing to be subject to the male gaze and entirely another to understand our personhood to be rooted in men's approval. Beauvoir called constructing an existence entirely for men "being-for-men": "*It follows that woman knows and chooses herself not as she exists for herself but as man defines her.* She thus has to be described first as men dream of her since her being-for-men is one of the essential factors of her concrete condition" (emphasis mine). In a political context, this "being-for-men" aptly describes the equality mindset, where an entire politics has been constructed in response to men.

Women's historical conditioning is our historical conundrum: How can women liberate our minds so that, while we don't control the conditions in which we live, we can choose *how* to live the choices we make within those conditions? How does woman *choose herself*? How does she *exist for herself* or put herself first in her life? (Because, as RuPaul has told us, you can't love or take care of others if you don't love or take care of yourself first.)

Women awakening to their patriarchal social conditioning is a form of liberation. And it is from this liberated state, Beauvoir contended, that women's freedom can flourish, because they can begin to design their lives, if not on their own terms, then at the very least with an awareness of how the patriarchy enforces sexist strictures and stereotypes. One way to better understand Beauvoir's argument in *The Second Sex* is to reveal the source of its most famous sentence: "One is not born, but rather becomes, a woman." This sentence was adapted from the philosopher Alfred Fouillée's "One is not born, but rather becomes, free." The source material is enlightening because it establishes a critical connection between freedom and self-creation. Beauvoir held a steadfast belief that the meaning we find in our lives comes from our freedom to choose *how* we live them, including the choice of how to become a woman. A freedom-centered feminism, therefore, encourages us to find freedom, power, dignity, and joy in how we fashion our gender and how we choose to live as women.

As a tool of self-examination, a critical consciousness allows us to locate and think critically about our place in the world and the forces, factors, and conditions that have shaped us. This tool helps us comprehend what Beauvoir referred to as our "situated freedom," or how our freedom is contingent upon our circumstances. The conditions of one's situation are historical (the economic class or racial caste you're born into, for instance), material (where you are born; your physical and cognitive abilities), and economic (intergenerational and personal wealth). Another integral factor to our freedom, Beauvoir noted, is other people, including our social circles, families, friends, and other personal and professional networks. The people in our lives—from those we interact with daily to authority figures whose incredible power directly affects us but who we most likely will never meet—both determine our situatedness and help us surpass it.

Situated freedom might seem like an incredibly abstract idea, but it is the reality of all our lives. We take our situatedness into consideration when, for example, making decisions about our lives; whether we think of decisions in terms of their future potential or frame them as a kind of cost-benefit analysis. We ask, From where I am right now and what I have, what kind of choices can I make? Can a public schoolteacher who is a single parent to three children buy a mansion on the Amalfi Coast without a trust fund or winning the lottery? Probably not. Or, from a macro angle: Do women in America have the freedom to receive the health care they need and desire, given all the conditions (Supreme Court decisions, exorbitant costs, antiquated medical machines and devices that are torturous and inaccurate, institutionalized racism and misogyny that ignore and discredit our pain) that situate them?

I would add values to the list of conditions that situate our freedom because they guide our decision-making processes and actions. I would label them as ethical conditions of our freedom, and, ideally, they should augment rather than restrict our freedom. At times, our values are palpable to us as gut feelings—they're so deeply inculcated into the fibers of our being that acting on them feels automatic. We intuit them more clearly when we are confronted with something new or unexpected, or when engaging with someone who holds an opposite opinion or belief. If we become aware of the ethical conditions of our freedom, we can better understand ourselves and our values and, in turn, decide where we each locate our integrity—what some might call their moral compass. To make this more concrete: I know I would never take a job at an oil company because of the myriad harms the industry inflicts upon people, our biodiversity and species, and the planet are too egregious for me to stomach. The work—the devastation they produce for profit—frees no one. And no amount of life-altering money would ever change my decision. For me, these ethical conditions actualize rather than constrain my freedom because they put my values into action. The power of values is in their *doing*, and I find my dignity and integrity by living my values.

As a woman who lived and moved within the male-dominated worlds of academia, literature, and journalism, Beauvoir personally understood how freedom is situated by the conditions of a person's life, from their gender to their race to their wealth. This distinguished her from other existentialists—most notably, her life partner Jean-Paul Sartre—who believed, as only the most privileged of white men could believe, we are all born with the same limitless freedom. Beauvoir, rather, contended that freedom is contingent on the conditions of our life and only expressed and felt through our engagement with the world and encounters with other people. Because of this contingency, we are, in fact, not created equal, nor do we begin or go through life being treated equally or with equal opportunities. Even within the same family, the order in which children are born produces tangible differences. (Solidarity with the first-born children out there—our childhoods were the hardest! We had to walk uphill both ways and were expected to get straight As and take care of our younger siblings, who, to our consternation, could do whatever they wanted and were praised for it.)

For Beauvoir, then, becoming free is more like a cultivation of freedom from the unique standpoint of one's life. I think of it as assessing my resources and networks—from my own vantage point and with what I have available to me, what am I capable of doing? What choices can I make that improve my situation and entail risk I can bear? What kind of choices can I make to advance my career that, in this capitalist world, do not compromise my values to the extent that I lose my integrity and no longer recognize myself? Freedom is always conditional, always situated, depending on one's resources and advantages. I often think of it as I can be free *in* a situation, but not always *from* a situation.

Feminists dedicated to the pursuit of freedom also have done the work of thinking through how women have been constrained by oppressive structures and forces. The Combahee River Collective's idea of "interlocking oppressions," I think, is the clearest interpretation of the concept of situated freedom from the specific lens of the multisituatedness of Black women's lives. The power of understanding our situatedness is found in recognizing and claiming the agency we do have, no matter how limited. From our situation, there is always a choice, even if it doesn't feel like one.

Having a critical consciousness means we understand that our personal actions have impact beyond us—that there is a world fully outside of our ego. (This might seem silly to mention, like something you'd say to a toddler, and yet there are full-grown men who seem to not understand this.) From this knowledge of our situated freedom, we can build a considered life, in which our choices and actions are not made carelessly but with care-fullness. And the self-examination that informs such a considered life also serves as a catalyst for political action. For Audre Lorde, the internal work of developing a critical consciousness is foundational to feminist movement building and social transformation. "For as we open ourselves more and more to the genuine conditions of our lives," she observed in *The Cancer Journals*, "women become less and less willing to tolerate those conditions unaltered, or to passively accept external and destructive controls over our lives and our identities." That is, this tool activates our sense of responsibility to ourselves and others.

With a critical consciousness, we have the ability not just to identify a societal problem but to comprehend *how* that problem is a product of society and its systems and *how* it intersects with other problems, systemically and over time, to better address the root causes of those problems. We can understand how, for example, state-sanctioned police violence against Black people is not a new problem but has its origins in slave patrols. And, similarly, how the (technical) end of plantation slavery connects to the rise of the prison industrial complex as part of a deliberate systemic effort to keep Black people unfree, as Michelle Alexander and countless Black abolitionists have shown us. In many ways, the work of developing a critical consciousness demands a knowledge of history. It also demands, if it is to be feminist, capaciousness. As Angela Davis told us in *Freedom Is a Constant Struggle*, "Feminism must involve a consciousness of capitalism . . . and racism, and colonialism, and post-colonialities, and ability, and more genders than we can even imagine, and more sexualities than we ever thought we could name." The tool, therefore, is both ethical and political, because in our self-examination we discover that we are part of the world, part of communities, institutions, and cultures.

Feminists have long understood the power of critical consciousness for women's liberation. In the nineteenth century, Black women writers and activists—such as Sojourner Truth, Frances E. W. Harper, Ida B. Wells Barnett, and Mary Church Terrell—wrote, lectured, and published their ideas about how racism and misogyny frame Black women's double consciousness about their unique situation in America. This rich intellectual tradition is what writer and professor Brittney C. Cooper has called the "embodied discourse" of Black women. Decades later, in 1969, Black feminist Frances M. Beal conceptualized "double jeopardy" to describe Black women's situatedness and how it informs their double consciousness of how racism not only intersects with but, more fundamentally, *shapes* gender oppression and discrimination. And, nearly twenty years later, Chicana feminist Gloria Anzaldúa conceptualized the "mestiza consciousness" as an anticolonialist, antiracist framework through which Chicanas and multiracial people more broadly could reinterpret their situatedness outside the colonizer's gaze and center themselves as the subjects of their lives.

While consciousness is a tool at work in the mind, it is imperative to remember that it "comes into being through collective dialogue," as Barbara Smith noted. Engagement with others is essential to the formation of a *critical* consciousness. Just as our ideas acquire depth and validity through back-and-forth exchange, so too does our awareness gain shape through those who challenge us and question our ways of thinking. Consciousness-building is continuously evolving and regularly negotiated. As freedom work, then, cultivating a critical consciousness is collective consciousness-raising: an ever-changing, ever-enfolding process of internal thinking, self-reflection, and external dialogue with others.

Developing this tool in practice in the form of collective consciousness-raising was popularized by women's liberation groups—

notably the Chicago-based West Side Group and the New York City–based New York Radical Women (NYRW)—in the late 1960s. The term *consciousness-raising*, attributed to NYRW member Kathie Sarachild, refers to the practice of women collectively identifying patterns of shared experience—say, about consent during sex (or lack thereof), sexual pleasure and orgasm (or lack thereof), and domestic labor. These patterns served as source material for analyses about gender discrimination and oppression, from which these women could then build theories of change and strategize plans of action to fight against misogyny. Consciousness-raising groups weren't the only places where consciousness-raising and knowledge sharing happened. For example, what was in part revolutionary about underground abortion networks like the Jane Collective in Chicago was their mission to provide holistic services to women beyond abortion care, including sexual and reproductive health education, so women had the knowledge to take care of not only themselves but other women.

These groups, it must be noted, perpetrated the same racism that pervaded the mainstream feminist movement. This critique is not new. Even white women participating in these groups in the 1960s and 1970s perceived how women of color, and the issues more acutely or specifically relevant to their lives, were excluded from these consciousness-raising discussions. As journalist Ellen Willis—a white woman who was an NYRW member—acknowledged, "We were acting on the unconscious racist assumption that our experience was representative, along with the impulse to gloss over racial specificities so as to keep the 'complication of racism' from marring our vision of female unity."

In the 1980s, consciousness-raising was an integral component of general meetings of the AIDS Coalition to Unleash Power (ACT UP), where issue-oriented committees, caucuses, and affinity groups would raise awareness and petition the larger group—such as in 1990, when the Women's Caucus asked ACT UP to protest the Centers for Disease Control and Prevention (CDC) to change its definition of AIDS to include women.

While the heyday of formal consciousness-raising groups has passed, this work continues today, in both physical and virtual spaces. Coming together to raise consciousness about women's conditions, experiences, and the systemic intricacies of interlocking oppressions takes place in book clubs, women's circles, and school groups, as well as in Zoom meetings, on Instagram Live, and in other types of asynchronistic exchange on social media platforms, even cooperative gaming. No matter the forum, dialogue is crucial. What is important for a freedom feminism is that we continue to value the tool of a critical consciousness and commit to refining it so we stay sharp and ready to dismantle any barrier to our freedom.

OUR FREEDOMS ARE LINKED

If a critical consciousness helps us understand our interconnectedness—our mutual coexistence—with each other and the planet, then we can understand how our freedom, too, is interconnected. Freedom is activated through our connections with each other.

Countless feminists and freedom fighters have stated this point—the same as Beauvoir's: Other people are "the condition of my own freedom." A genealogy of freedom feminism can be forged from these visionaries. In 1883, Sephardic Jewish American poet Emma Lazarus wrote, "Until we are all free, we are none of us free." In 1971, civil rights organizer Fannie Lou Hamer said, "You are not free whether you are white or black, until I am free. Because no man is an island to himself. And until I am free in Mississippi, you are not free in Washington; you are not free in New York." Between the declarations of Lazarus and Hamer there exists approximately ninety years of freedom practice and freedom work. And what of the years before Lazarus? And the years after Hamer? It is amazing to consider just how many women fought for freedom.

That my freedom is inextricable from your freedom, and vice versa, means that to become free I must want the freedom of other people. Freedom is *conditional* because it is *relational*. Like Beauvoir, philosopher

Hannah Arendt understood that even our awareness of our own freedom is produced through engagement with others. "We first become aware of freedom and its opposite in our intercourse with others, not in intercourse with ourselves," Arendt asserted. "People can only be free in relation to one another."

That freedom is both *relational* and *conditional* is what critically distinguishes feminist freedom from white freedom. For the latter, freedom is relational but not conditional, such that through a white-freedom mindset, freedom is exacted through acts of domination that subjugate or terrorize other people. It is a mindset rooted in deep insecurity and fear, as it seemingly equates freedom with untouchability—by other people, as well as by the government and its institutions. To challenge America's culture of white freedom by proving that freedom is also conditional, therefore, threatens the very mindset of the nation's white supremacy.

Beauvoir was extremely vocal in her criticism of this supremacist interpretation of freedom. In *The Ambiguity of Ethics*, she argued that we must endeavor to discredit and eliminate this thinking from our culture by revealing it for what it is:

> A freedom which is interested only in denying freedom must be denied. And it is not true that the recognition of the freedom of others limits my own freedom: to be free is not to have the power to do anything you like. . . . I am oppressed if I am thrown into prison, but not if I am kept from throwing my neighbor in prison.

We see here the categorial distinction between white freedom and feminist freedom. The white-freedom mindset perceives others as a threat to one's freedom; the latter mindset understands that others are fundamental to one's freedom. And we can observe how these mindsets play out in the world, in how people understand the role of government, for example. The former wants limited to no government, especially no regulation, while the latter believes government has a significant role in caring for its citizens.

The crucial point of Beauvoir's final sentence is that you are not oppressed if you are prevented from oppressing—or violating, or threatening, or harming—other people. *"To be free is not to have the power to do anything you like."* Supremacist actions—like aggressively coughing in other people's faces during a global pandemic; or emailing women death threats if they don't want to date you; or openly, flagrantly carrying guns in public; or calling the cops on Black people because they are having a fun family BBQ in the park—are the antithesis of freedom. These actions are done to intimidate and/or harm. They are nothing less than acts of terrorism.

For feminism, the power of freedom is found not in domination but in connection. *Conditional and relational.* Our capacity for freedom—our collective capacity—is contingent upon our choice to care for and hold ourselves accountable to others.

ACCOUNTABILITY AND CARE

Accountability and care are essential components of freedom feminism.

To hold oneself accountable is not just a momentary or reactionary decision but an intentional lifestyle choice, a guiding ethic and practice. Accountability entails taking ownership of our actions and holding ourselves responsible for their impact, which includes repairing any harm that might result from them.

A critical consciousness makes accountability a possible, and even desirable, practice. For DePaul University professor Ann Russo, cultivating accountability is a practice of awareness, both of how our choices and actions affect others and of how our choices and actions are socially conditioned and situated.

Practicing accountability takes time, because it takes time to learn why, how, and to whom you've caused harm; to make amends and repair that harm; and to unlearn behaviors and recalibrate your mindset to prevent further harm. This requires commitment, sustained effort, self-reflection, and engagement with people who support and foster your growth. And nurturing this accountability, in the spirit of creating a culture of accountability, is the opposite of shunning or silencing people. Not all practices of accountability need to take the form of removing someone from their social and occupational settings, particularly if social interactions and dialogue are conducive to not just the individual's but the collective organization's learning. Unless a person continues to be a threat to society, instead of putting them on administrative leave (inevitably, paid leave), what if we cultivated a space for dialogue and learning, not only for that individual but for the entire community affected by both that harm and the mindset that enabled that harm?

Accountability is a form of care. It is the choice to take care when making decisions and taking action. It is the key to establishing the trust necessary to deepen relationships, and, at the same time, relationships make accountability work possible. Different accountability frameworks exist that pertain to types and scales of relationships. Writer and organizer Piper Anderson, for example, has proposed three types of accountability based on a scale of engagement: self-accountability, or the personal choice to hold oneself responsible for one's choices and actions; mutual accountability, which consists of a shared agenda within specific relationships, like between friends, family, and coworkers; and community accountability, which is the broader cultivation of community values and norms. For the activist organization INCITE! Women of Color Against Violence, community accountability involves a variety of practices, including developing "sustainable strategies to address community members' abusive behaviors [and] creating a process for them to account for their actions and transform their behavior" and committing to "ongoing development of all members of the community, and the community itself, to transform the political conditions that reinforce oppression and violence." What is crucial for any form of accountability work is that the guidelines be proactively, rather than reactively, established.

When accountability becomes a part of a culture, people feel supported, they are more willing to be open and vulnerable with each other, and they feel encouraged to help and care for each other. A culture of accountability is possible when people feel safe, which is a significant objective of accountability work. Accountability repairs and rebuilds. In contrast, punishment inflicts harm and isolates. "The difference between accountability and punishment has to do with relationships," Anderson explained. "Punishment breaks a relationship; it's rooted in isolation, shame, and disconnection. Accountability, by contrast, requires communication, negotiation of needs, the opportunity to repair harm, and the chance to prove that we can change and be worthy of trust again."

Unfortunately, American society has not established the tools, mechanisms, or culture to make accountability easy or desirable. This is because accountability jeopardizes the systems and institutions upholding white supremacy.

We haven't created a culture that, as prison abolition activist and organizer Mariame Kaba said, "allows for people to feel like they can take responsibility and that they can be accountable." And this willingness is crucial because *accountability is a choice.* You cannot force someone to take responsibility for their actions and commit to analyzing the behavior that led to harmful actions. "People have to take accountability for things that they actually do wrong," Kaba explained. "They have to say, 'This is wrong and I want to be part of making some sort of amends or repairing this or not doing it again.'"

Instead, when there is violence, our society craves justice in the form of punishment, in the form of incarceration. We have been conditioned to believe that more suffering is the answer to suffering, and for some reason believe that this twisted sense of equality is justice. Who among us, for instance, didn't celebrate when former Minneapolis police officer Derek Chauvin was convicted of murdering George Floyd? I jumped off my couch and cried. I sighed with relief. But what exactly was I relieved about? George Floyd is still dead. His family, friends, and community still grieve his loss. During his federal sentencing in July 2022, Chauvin expressed no remorse for murdering Floyd. He refused to take accountability for killing Floyd. And cops are still killing Black people—the very day the Chauvin verdict was announced, on April 20, 2021, a cop shot and killed Ma'Khia Bryant, a sixteen-year-old Black child, in Columbus, Ohio. And unlike Chauvin but like so many other officers, this cop was cleared of committing any wrongdoing. So, what has changed? What changes within us—what changes how we think, act, and regard other people—when the solution is punishment? What does this form of so-called justice actually resolve or improve? What future does it lead to? We all know what happens in Shakespeare when murder is met with murder—we're left with a stage filled with dead bodies. Absolute tragedy.

A freedom-centered feminism is directly committed to challenging and repairing the harms caused by gender violence, gender oppression, and all forms of systemic oppression—including that which is perpetrated by the state and the police. This challenge does not find an answer in the carceral system—accountability is not punishment.

"The current criminal punishment system," Kaba and lawyer and organizer Andrea Ritchie wrote in *No More Police: A Case for Abolition*, "actually discourages people from accepting responsibility and taking action toward repair, because to do so would expose them to harsh punishment." As such, accountability work entails abdicating our reliance on the state, police, and criminal punishment system for solutions to violence and violations. We need care, not incarceration. Accountability seeks recuperation, regeneration, and flourishing.

What this requires of feminism is a change of strategy and endgame—from seeking solutions within the criminal punishment system to abolishing the system.

FEMINISM IS ABOLITION WORK

Why is our gut reaction to call the police when something bad happens? This is the question lawyer and organizer Derecka Purnell asked herself (and, in turn, her readers) in *Becoming Abolitionists*. It's like we've been hardwired to seek assistance outside the communities that can best facilitate repair, accountability, and justice—communities that can even prevent violence from happening, because community members know and have relationships with each other. Police, however, are not care workers. In fact, "police failure to stop, interrupt, or transform violence is no accident," Kaba and Ritchie explained. "It has always been about fabricating and maintaining 'order' by using violence—directly or indirectly—to control and contain racialized and gendered populations of people in the service of a capitalist economic order."

According to the nonprofit Mapping Police Violence, US police killed at least 1,239 people in 2022—a number that keeps rising as data rolls in—making it the deadliest year for police violence in America. The nonprofit reported that Black people are "three times more likely to be killed by police than white people." And the *Washington Post*'s database on fatal police shootings reported that more than one in five people killed by police are neurodivergent and/or have a mental illness. Data on police violence repeatedly shows that society's most marginalized communities—those which need the most care—are the ones that suffer the most at the hands of the police state. Furthermore, most police who have killed people—more than 98 percent, according to Mapping Police Violence data—are not charged.

Ending gender violence is impossible when the police also commit that violence. Based on reported data, domestic violence occurs in police officers' families at four times the rate it occurs in the general population. Similarly, "police sexual misconduct," a 2014 national study of arrested officers reported, "is often considered a hidden crime that routinely goes unreported"—not surprising, since our criminal justice system demands that victims report their experience to the police. Despite this underreporting, the smattering of data on the subject suggests its prevalence. A 2020 study of police crime found that between 2005 and 2012 there were 669 reported cases of police sexual violence—663 of which were perpetrated by male officers. The authors of the study identified three primary types of victims: female drivers ("driving while female"), children, and sex workers. Recall former Oklahoma City police officer Daniel Holtzclaw, who, in 2015, was convicted on eighteen out of thirty-six charges of rape and sexual assault. He deliberately targeted poor Black women, whom he would stop or pull over on suspicion of drugs or prostitution—people he assumed he could assault because society has shown them so little care. This example raises another critical point about which lives seem to matter: What about all the women and girls society has shown so little care for? What about, for instance, the estimated thousands of missing and murdered Indigenous women and girls who go unreported in the media?

Prisons, furthermore, aren't correctives to the problem, especially when data shows that prison employees themselves commit this violence while on the job. In December 2022, a Senate investigation of federal prisons reported that "over the past decade, female inmates in at least two-thirds (19 of 29) federal prisons that held women were sexually abused by male [Federal Bureau of Prisons] employees." The nonprofit Freedom for Immigrants registered more than 3,300 complaints of sexual abuse in US Department of Homeland Security agencies, including immigration detention centers. Again, the most marginalized and oppressed—migrants, people of color, queer and trans people—continue to experience significant violence at the hands of the state.

Just as more guns do not prevent gun violence, systems designed to punish do not prevent violence from happening. Equality feminism, seeking inclusion within existing systems and institutions, cannot adequately address gender or sexual violence when it works to expand the carceral system. And infusing the system with more money only feeds the problem. The more than $2 billion that the 1994 Violence Against Women Act (VAWA) allocated to law enforcement (specifically the Services, Training, Officers, and Prosecutors Grant Program) between fiscal years 1995 and 2012, for example, has not stopped this violence from happening. In fact, statistics indicate gender and sexual violence are getting worse.

VAWA, reauthorized in 2022, is institutionalized carceral feminism because it establishes a direct connection between gender violence and state violence. Increases in policing and incarceration, however, do not prevent gender violence, and VAWA and similar arrest laws do not address the root causes of this violence. "Turning to punishment agencies and tactics of social control will not protect women and others harmed by gender violence," Angela Davis, Gina Dent, Erica R. Meiners, and Beth E. Richie wrote in *Abolition. Feminism. Now.* Instead, they maintained,

> Survivors of violence would be much more likely to benefit if the over eight billion dollars spent on VAWA between 1995 and 2018 supported free and subsidized services like safe permanent housing, education, accessible health and mental health care, high-quality childcare, and job training and employment placement, in addition to collective and environmental assets such as neighborhood services that promote health and well-being, safe parks, healthy food options, cultural and arts activism, and mutual aid projects.

Abolition, as the Movement for Black Lives (M4BL) policy platform states, means *divesting* resources from policing and the carceral state and *investing* in people, communities, and institutions that can ensure safety and care. If the police receive more than $100 billion a year, think of the real, positive impact that money could have if instead it was invested in our care and safety—in education, health care, and housing.

Abolition feminism, therefore, contends that gender oppression cannot be eradicated through state violence or incarceration. To recall Beauvoir, we cannot find freedom by throwing someone else in prison.

Social change begins within us, begins with the liberatory process of changing our mindset. "The true focus of revolutionary change is never merely the oppressive situations that we seek to escape," Lorde explained, "but that piece of the oppressor which is planted deep within each of us." As such, she added, "we must move against not only those forces which dehumanize us from the outside, but also against those oppressive values which we have been forced to take into ourselves."

To change society requires first and foremost a change of mindset. We must develop a critical consciousness in the spirit of what feminist poet Adrienne Rich referred to as a "keen lens of empathy" to become aware of our privileges and advantages and how they affect other people. Rather than placing demands on systems to implement equality or exact justice, we need to learn how to recognize and respect the dignity of all people. Baldwin, in "A Letter to Prisoners," described this effort as developing "a real recognition of, and respect for, the other and for the condition of the other. The other is no longer and is indeed . . . closer than a brother—the other is oneself." We must stop seeing people as objects and start seeing their humanity. Respecting the dignity and unique situation of each human being, and recognizing our mutual coexistence, is the opposite of equality.

The work of changing one's mindset—one's beliefs, routines, and behaviors—is an arduous process. But this change, what Beal in "Double Jeopardy" referred to as "a certain transformation," is a vital component of liberating society from all forms of oppression:

> We must begin to understand that a revolution entails not only the willingness to lay our lives on the firing line and get killed. In some ways, this is an easy commitment to make. To die for the revolution is a one-shot deal; to live for the revolution means taking on the more difficult commitment of changing our day-to-day life patterns. This will mean changing the traditional routines that we have established as a result of living in a totally corrupt society. It means changing how you relate to your wife, your husband, your parents, and your coworkers.

Developing a freedom mindset occurs over time. And so much of this work depends on the ideas and feelings that take form as language—both words and imagery—in our mind. Because language not only shapes our actions but also how we think and, in turn, how we engage with each other. Words are the tools that can transform our personal ethics and our feminist politics.

CHAPTER 4

FREE YOUR MIND

"My body, my choice!"

These days, we're just as likely to hear this popular feminist refrain from the mouths of anti-vaxxers and, when COVID-19 mandates were in place, anti-maskers as we are from feminists.

It is what my youngest brother vociferously spat at me when I asked him why he refused to get the coronavirus vaccine. In the summer of 2021, after receiving my two rounds of vaccinations, I traveled home to the East Coast to see friends and family. My mother was delighted that I made it home in time to celebrate his birthday because it would mark the first time in years that all three of her children were with her at the same time. The moment I saw him in the parking lot of the strip mall—the location of New Jersey's finest restaurants—I asked him if he was vaccinated. I did so somewhat jokingly because I assumed he would be, since we had always been on the same wavelength as the outsiders of the family.

"Nooooo!" he said, getting, what we call in Jersey-speak, "real loud." He laughed, and I was shocked. And then I got furious. A lot of cursing happened, accompanied by a lot of exaggerated hand gestures; whenever my feet touch the Jersey earth, I get real Jersey—real Italian Jersey—real quick. And then he barked the line that made me dizzy with rage:

"Cuz it's my body, my choice! Ha!"

More cursing. More hand gestures. All of which attracted the eyes of restaurant patrons seated at tables along the windows. I hope they got a good show. My mother ran outside to break us up. He went inside the restaurant, and I walked circles around the parking lot for nearly two hours, staying on the phone with a friend who calmed me down and validated my feelings. He made his choice, and I made mine.

Throughout the pandemic, I thought a lot about how the appropriation of this feminist mantra worked. I even wrote about it for NBC. The act of appropriation collapses the difference between two distinct issues: a global public health crisis and a personal medical decision. The decision to have a medical procedure is not equivalent to catching and spreading a deadly virus, I argued in that article. "Simply put, I cannot 'catch' an abortion because a friend of mine has one. And, guess what? Neither can you."

Several things at stake in this co-opting of the language of choice reflect broader distinctions between white freedom and feminist freedom, including the ongoing erosion of the meaning of *public* in how we understand the role and obligations of government (in providing public goods and services) as well as of its citizens. The noticeable disappearance of *public* from our discourse and our politics is in large part due to the decades-long conservative effort to disempower and discredit government—not coincidentally, a trend that aligns with the Civil Rights movement's efforts to expand massive post–World War II government investments in infrastructure, education, and housing to include Black and other racially marginalized people. That is, government investments in the *public* dwindled when the *public* no longer just meant white people. (The hatred of government has become the *Real Housewives* tagline of GOP candidates every campaign season: "Vote for me, a person who hates the government, because I want to DRAIN THE SWAMP!" has for some idiotic reason captivated their respective electorates. As if politics and policymaking require no expertise. It's akin to you want-ing me, someone with a PhD in Renaissance drama, to perform brain surgery on you.) In post–New Deal America, we have witnessed the dis-integration of government departments and programs through system-atic underfunding to the point where they lack basic operating budgets to function. Consequently, and in no small part a result of capitalism, Americans have turned to the private sector—corporations—and phil-anthropic foundations for support. These entities are incentivized to do the work the government should be doing with tax breaks for provid-ing benefits to employees and making charitable donations and grants to communities and nonprofits. Our society's increasing lack of knowl-edge about the meaning of *public* has even found its way into debates about free speech on social media, with conservatives obfuscating the difference between *public* and *social* to claim that their First Amend-ment rights are being denied when social media companies restrict their content. Social media is not public media. Twitter is not the town square. These so-called free speech advocates seem to conveniently forget this.

The critical difference between white freedom and feminist freedom is accountability, which is why what unites both uses of the phrase *my body, my choice*—bodily autonomy—is conceived in disparate ways. Bodily autonomy is sovereignty over one's body, meaning that we each possess authority over our own body and determine the future of our own body. A white-freedom mindset interprets bodily autonomy as a kind of abso-lute independence—not just autonomy but categorical detachment from other people. Therefore, to someone with a white-freedom mindset, any consideration of others and any form of external regulation are perceived as infringements upon their freedom. In contrast, a feminist-freedom mindset accepts the obvious fact that we live in the world with other peo-ple, and that bodily autonomy is a *political* concept that only has mean-ing in relation to other people. Bodily autonomy is socially constructed and socially contingent. My sense of bodily autonomy, in other words, is a product of my existence in a world with billions of other people and life-forms. If bodily autonomy is one form that freedom takes, and if our freedoms are relational and conditional, then bodily autonomy, too, must be understood in terms of being relational and conditional.

The COVID-19 pandemic demonstrates how people who possess a white-freedom mindset believe their bodily autonomy permits the disregard of and disrespect for other people. We have failed as a society to hold ourselves accountable to each other by refusing to adhere to safety protocols, especially mask mandates and getting vaccinated. And so we have continued to be frustrated, years into the pandemic, by the ever-growing number of virus variants and the waves and spikes in infections, hospitalizations, and death rates, as if we are completely oblivious to the fact that we have been doing this to ourselves.

We haven't learned that accountability determines our freedom.

The anti-vaxxer and anti-masker appropriation of *my body, my choice* signifies a perennial problem with equality feminism: the potential of false equivalences born from an equality mindset seeking to neutralize difference to assert sameness. *My body, my choice* is a futile slogan—frankly, I cringe every time I hear this smooth-brained phrase, designed to be universally appealing—because it subscribes to an understanding of bodily autonomy through the white-supremacist-patriarchal lens of "doing what I want, when I want." It is no surprise that it's been so easily appropriated by anti-maskers and anti-vaxxers. It is in perfect alignment with supremacist thinking.

Self-determination—the inalienable right to determine the course of one's life—cannot be the only factor framing the freedom to choose. Rather, from a feminist-freedom mindset, the power of choice inheres in our *creative* capacity to determine the course of our lives, and the integrity of choice lies in making choices from a place of critical consciousness that requires holding ourselves accountable for them. Choice is socially situated and socially determined, and if we are to make choices based in freedom, then a freedom feminism offers a reconceptualization of choice in terms of the collective.

Instead of interpreting choice through the reductive—capitalist and patriarchal—lens of individualism, we can reconceive its power based in freedom by recognizing how it is collective in its production and impact. Freedom feminism allows us to define choice as a *collective endeavor* because it is *collectively determined*. We do not make our choices in a vacuum but within our given situatedness, and with a consideration of multiple perspectives and multiple potential outcomes. Reenvisioning choice as such presents us with the opportunity to rethink the settled language, logic, and frameworks of some of feminism's most significant issues—especially abortion. It allows us to understand that choice is not binary, or ahistorical, or without context or consequence. That even what seems to be a binary, either/or choice to have an abortion is informed by one's own life circumstances, personal and financial supports, age, and desires and aspirations, particularly in terms of how one wants to build their own family. And furthermore, that the factors informing this choice play out for months during a pregnancy and for years, if not a lifetime, after giving birth. That is, one choice—always situated within multiple factors and conditions, within multiple contexts and personal and professional relationships— invariably ushers forth a plurality of potential future choices.

Yet even in situations that feel like matters of life or death, some degree of agency exists in the space of the possible choices available to us. Within the parameters of the space of those possibilities lie our agency, our power, and our freedom.

The liberatory power of choice comes from this agency as well as from accountability, because, in holding ourselves accountable for our choices, we secure our dignity and integrity. Choice communicates intentionality, and to take accountability means we both affirm and actively stand in our choices and agree to take action to repair any consequential harm. Even a "thoughtless" choice is a choice.

The language and logic of equality feminism, however, have produced the lie that women's ability to make choices for themselves, and for their benefit alone, is a feminist victory. We know this kind of feminism under the banner of "choice feminism."

HOW EQUALITY GAVE US CHOICE FEMINISM

Choice feminism is the theory that any choice any woman makes is by definition a feminist act. The logic being that she is asserting her agency and power in a man's world. Jessa Crispin depicted choice feminism as an allergic reaction to the historical accumulation of choices denied to women: "So simply by choosing anything at all, you are bucking the patriarchy." She rightly identified choice feminism as a "problem of white feminism," whereby the popular mantra of "the personal is political" has been misconstrued "to mean that [women's] own personal victories are political victories."

The modern origins of choice feminism are found in the mainstreaming of the reproductive rights movement, which championed a "woman's right to choose" (as code for abortion) to the exclusion of almost every other issue concerned with reproductive health. Stripped of its parts, we know this as the pro-choice movement. Pro-choice language is so innocuous as to have become ubiquitous—it's the, let's say, language of choice for Democrats who seem incapable of saying the word *abortion*. Because it is so vague and inoffensive, over time, pro-choice language has expanded to apply to any choice made by a woman. Choice feminism, therefore, overlaps with white feminism: Both assent to asocial and ahistorical individualism, and a gendered but apolitical perspective.

In a consumer-capitalist-driven society like ours, personal choice is primarily rendered in terms of purchasing power, which was historically denied to women—who, until the passage of the Equal Credit Opportunity Act in 1974, could only get a credit card or bank loan if they had a husband willing to cosign for them. The power of being able to buy something for yourself—hell, even Mrs. Dalloway felt it—made it easy to mistake consumerism for feminism and therefore to frame women's freedom primarily in terms of economic freedom. Media celebrations of women's equality, too, overwhelmingly point to women having credit cards, bank accounts, and the right to sue people as feminist victories.

Capitalism has lulled Americans into believing consumerism is freedom. We don't have clean air or water, free health care or medicine, free elections without gerrymandering or voting restrictions, or even the freedom to walk outside without fear of being gunned down. Instead, American freedom has meant having a million cereals to choose from and the free and largely unregulated ability to purchase as many guns as possible. White freedom represents the juncture between supremacy and materialism—where having more is always better, a sign of success, and, as evinced by the hero-worship of billionaires as humanity's saviors, somehow proof of genius.

Purchasing a tote bag printed with the clever phrase "Totes Feminist" or with an image of a uterus gesturing a middle-finger salute with one of its fallopian tubes is, of course, not wrong. Rather, the problem is when consumerism is understood as feminism, effectively reducing the latter to a kind of vapid advertorial campaign—something easily performed, commodified, or purchased. This "marketplace feminism," to use *Bitch Media* cofounder Andi Zeisler's phrase, has mutated a politics into an aesthetic posture. Consequently, the labor-intensive, less glamorous work that deserves our attention and resources—fighting gender-based violence and discrimination with political organizing and activism—is overlooked by the mainstream media, which opts for snide coverage or an equivocal op-ed when they want to point to fractures within feminism as illustrative of the infighting that keeps it "in crisis" or results in its "failure." People like their feminism the way they like their women: defanged and neutered so as not to disrupt the status quo. Feminism is pleasing to the mainstream media and culture when it smiles.

Equality is the bedrock of choice feminism, as the fixation on equality has sanctioned the lie that all women's choices are equal and democratic. Similar to the fallacy that free-market capitalism is democratic and enables fair and equal participation and wealth accumulation, choice feminism assumes that every person makes choices from the same standpoint, regardless of the specific conditions framing the choices available to us and the choices we can make—or the risks we can take. But this assumption is completely divorced from how and why choices are made.

THE GAME OF CHOICE

No two people make the same two choices, because each person makes their choice from the conditions specific to their own lives—conditions that are historically, politically, and socially determined. In Barbara Johnson's words, "I have not chosen the conditions under which I must choose." Johnson's insight reflects Beauvoir's idea of situated freedom. No one has absolute freedom over the choices they make; the range of possible choices that lie in front of us are delimited by the particularities of our lives.

The situatedness of our lives means our choices, too, are situated, in that how we make them depends on a complex set of factors. Political theorist Nancy J. Hirschmann described this process as a negotiation of internal factors, like desires and preferences, and the external factors of our situatedness "that not only inhibit or enable the realization of such desires but also contribute to or influence the formation of these desires." For example, I may personally have a desire to stop the billion-dollar federal financing of policing—funded by our tax dollars—but this desire is foreclosed by the fact that I am not the president of the United States or an elected official with the political power to make this happen. The political situation of my life delimits my ability to defund the police.

Situations of domestic violence exemplify how internal (e.g., mental state, emotional well-being, and desire) and external (e.g., physical safety, wealth, dependents) factors influence a woman's choice to stay or leave. The point is that choices are rarely simple or easy. For women, centuries of gender oppression have entangled the factors of negotiation; systemic discrimination and sexual violence have restricted not only the field of play but the field of vision when it comes to the choices we make.

"Being oppressed," bell hooks reminded us in *Feminist Theory: From Margin to Center*, "means the *absence of choices*." Law, religion, and tradition have denied women choices about our education, health care, and ability to travel and move through public and private spaces. Such restrictions have placed control of women's bodies in men's hands.

Denying women their bodily autonomy in terms of making choices is just one part of a bigger picture. At the same time men claim authority over women's bodies, they also divorce themselves from their own choices and actions. It is an amazing sleight of hand—what I call Patriarchal Strategy 101—to simultaneously refuse women their bodily autonomy and blame them for everything that happens to them. This patriarchal strategy aims to sever action—and actor—from accountability. The strategic severance keeps the patriarchy intact by subjugating women and asserting that men's choices are not choices at all but ontological truths. Their *subjectivity* rendered as *objectivity*.

Do you know whose choices are interpreted not as choices at all but as destiny, morally right, natural, and unassailable? Who is accountable to no one?

God.

When one person holds all the cards, they dictate the entire game. Or, when men make all the choices and women make none, the concept of choice disappears. The field of play appears as a mirage of objectivity and fairness disguising the white supremacist patriarchal forces that have shaped it. The game unfolds, then, not with the game's participants making intentional choices but with women and girls being told they just have to suck up and accept what appear to be predetermined outcomes, because "that's how the world works" or "there are just some bad apples" or "God says so." Actions *happen*, but, amazingly, no one seems to have caused them. *Thoughts and prayers.*

The media notoriously reifies this white supremacist patriarchal strategy in confusingly circuitous, passively constructed headlines. In the United States, we've witnessed this manipulation in abundance, for example, in news stories that suggest Black and brown Americans are just randomly falling down dead in the proximity of police. On social media, these passive constructions are particularly egregious. Here's a *New York Times* tweet from August 2020: "3 people were shot and one of them died, law enforcement officials said, during a chaotic night of demonstrations in Kenosha, Wisconsin, over the shooting of Jacob

Blake, a Black resident who was shot by a white police officer." Many of these stories use the language of "officer-involved shooting" to obscure responsibility while feigning standards of professionalism—despite the Associated Press's update to its *Stylebook* in August 2020 directing journalists to "avoid the vague 'officer-involved' for shootings and other cases involving the police." According to *Columbia Journalism Review*, the media's use of the phrase has proliferated in the past two decades. *Officer-involved* and other passive-voice constructions epitomize what writer Vijith Assar, in a piece about ambiguous grammar for *McSweeney's*, called "the past exonerative tense, so named because culpability is impossible when actions no longer exist."

WHEN CHOICE BECOMES ENTITLEMENT

"Men fear responsibilities above all," Beauvoir remarked in "Existentialism and Popular Wisdom," because to accept responsibility is to acknowledge one's fallibility, which would be a sign of weakness. Instead, inviolable authority is strengthened by refusing accountability for one's actions.

Religion enables severance from accountability through the logic of determinism, whereby a religious authority (a god) is understood to cause all events, thereby annulling people's responsibility for their actions because, this logic holds, determinism disavows free will. People need their god because, Beauvoir argued in *The Ethics of Ambiguity*, "if God does not exist, man's faults are inexpiable. If it is claimed that, whatever the case may be, this earthly stake has no importance, this is precisely because one invokes that inhuman objectivity which we declined at the start."

God serves as a convenient alibi for peoples' actions. Beauvoir's slicing invective offers a jaw-dropping shot about what religion, and specifically Christianity, condones and enables: thoughtlessness. Thoughtless choices and actions. This is the root of the banality of evil.

Religious institutions are accomplices in the patriarchal strategy of establishing man as God. They provide moral justification—or what I would more accurately call an excuse—for violence perpetrated by men, especially when that violence is directed at "evil," "sinful" people. In the United States, Christianity has functioned as the moral arm of the white supremacist patriarchy. For centuries, it has asserted its dominance through terroristic acts, from bombings at mosques to mass shootings at Sikh temples and Jewish synagogues, to more covert efforts like advocating for school voucher policies to offset racial integration in public schools after *Brown*. The increasing political power of white Christian nationalism is apparent in the rise of religious freedom laws (which, oddly, are available only to Christians) and in prosecuting abortion as a crime more punishable than rape. Several conservative politicians, emboldened by the Supreme Court's *Dobbs* decision, have reversed their position that abortion should be legal in cases of rape or incest. In an April 2022 Ohio House Government Oversight Committee meeting during which she introduced a trigger-ban measure on abortion, state representative Jean Schmidt even declared that rape presents "an opportunity for that woman, no matter how young or old she is." This is yet another example of how the logic of equality—here, in the form of bothsidesism—operates to neutralize the issue, which is that forcing a person to gestate a pregnancy resulting from rape is nothing less than committing violence upon violence. Sexual assault followed by state-sanctioned assault.

The patriarchal strategy of evading accountability, as in cases of rape and sexual violence, occurs through tactics of displacement and projection. It is a godlike slip of hand that successfully divorces the actors from responsibility by giving the appearance that they were not the agents of those actions. Women's oppression is reinforced by this strategy, because the tactics of displacement and projection also serve as justification not only for the actions themselves but for the displacement of consequences *onto women.*

We know this tactic by another name: victim blaming.

The fact that victim blaming has been deployed for centuries makes it much more than a tactic. It has become endemic to our society, materializing in cultural symptoms we see in the actions of a range of players, from Jeffrey Epstein and his sex-trafficking associates to the Proud Boys to incels.

Incels, or so-called involuntary celibates, are perhaps the most nefarious example of how the strategy and tactic combine to justify violence against women. Their argument is that men are the real victims—victims of "involuntary" celibacy—and women are to blame because, they believe, women owe them sex. In 2014, their hero Elliot Rodger published his manifesto online shortly before his murderous rampage, killing six and injuring fourteen, in Isla Vista, California. "My orchestration of the Day of Retribution is my attempt to do everything, in my power, to destroy everything I cannot have," he wrote. "All of those beautiful girls I've desired so much in my life, but can never have because they despise and loathe me, I will destroy. . . . Their behavior towards me has only earned my hatred, and rightfully so! I am the true victim in all of this. I am the good guy."

Rodger blamed women for his own feelings of gender insecurity and his own fear of emasculation. Instead of taking responsibility for his feelings and actions, he held women responsible and, thus, believed it was his right to "destroy" them.

This is how the patriarchy works.

Patriarchal entitlement also manifests as the choice to rape and violate women. Enculturated to believe in their own entitlement, perpetrators make the choice to commit sexual violence. Yet, while they make the choice, they are not responsible alone, because our patriarchal society has told them it is right to believe they are sexually entitled to women's bodies. Their choice to commit sexual violence, in other words, is culturally green-lit. And then it is institutionally sanctioned by the courts, which end up harassing the victims on the witness stand (about what they were wearing or about dancing and socializing at a party) more than they hold the perpetrators accountable.

Sexual violence is an act of domination. And sexual violence against women and feminine people is a form of policing and punishment intended to regulate their movement in public and private spaces, as well as their joy and pleasure. Statistics indicate that sexual violence is primarily an expression of male supremacy. Data from a 2016/2017 CDC survey reported that 94 percent of female victims "reported having only male perpetrators in their life—2.4 percent had both male and female perpetrators." Any kind of systemic redress to this violence, furthermore, is incredibly difficult when victims are encumbered with the burden of having to report their sexual assault to the police or authorities (from college administrations to HR departments)—retraumatizing work that undoubtedly results in many people not reporting the crime.

The codification and legal and cultural permissibility of rape and sexual assault have systematically oppressed women for centuries. Rape has been used to condition women's fear to preserve patriarchal domination. (A consequence of this social conditioning, as Black feminists like bell hooks and Angela Davis pointed out, is that it has contributed to the racist stereotyping of Black boys and men as predators.) In the United States, marital rape wasn't outlawed in all fifty states until 1993. Until the mid-1970s, it was not considered a crime because the legal contract of marriage made women their husbands' possessions. The origins of this jurisprudence come from the mouth of seventeenth-century jurist Sir Matthew Hale—fondly quoted by Alito in his *Dobbs* opinion on how abortion is a "great crime." In *The History of the Pleas of the Crown*, Hale wrote, "The husband cannot be guilty of rape committed by himself upon his lawful wife for by their mutual matrimonial consent and contract the wife hath given herself in this kind unto her husband, which she cannot retract." This one quote, from a text published in 1847, has guided American jurisprudence on marital rape for decades. Even today, several states still have marital rape loopholes and statutory exemptions. It wasn't until October 2021 that California—one of the most progressive states in the nation—eliminated its spousal rape exemption.

The many failures of the criminal punishment system—from police malpractice to the failure to test rape kits, to victim blaming, misgendering, and legal loopholes and exemptions—have meant not only that victims of sexual violence rarely if ever receive the justice they seek but also that perpetrators are rarely if ever held responsible for their crimes. And statistics suggest that "rarely if ever" is more like "never." According to the US Census Bureau's 2018 National Crime Victimization Survey, only about 25 percent of rapes were reported to police that year. And according to 2010–2014 Department of Justice data, fewer than 1 percent of rapes lead to felony convictions.

The maliciousness of victim blaming has also materialized in the pervasive violence against trans and gender-nonconforming people. Trans people, according to a 2021 study by UCLA's Williams Institute, are four times more likely to experience violent victimization, including rape and sexual assault, than cisgender people. Trans women, and especially Black and brown trans women, are murdered at alarming rates. From March 2020 to March 2021, the murder rate of trans women jumped 266 percent in the United States. And then it jumped again: 2021 was the world's deadliest year on record for trans and gender-nonconforming people. According to the Transrespect versus Transphobia Worldwide research project, 95 percent of the 327 trans people murdered globally between October 1, 2021, and September 30, 2022, were trans women or trans feminine people. More than one in four were killed in their own homes, and half were sex workers.

The murderers' line of defense, steeped in trans misogyny and victim blaming, is so common that it has come to be known as the "trans panic defense." The logic of this defense epitomizes the patriarchal strategy to evade accountability by victim blaming and claiming the perpetrators had no agency in the sexual encounter. The perpetrators thus maintain they were the real victims—they were the ones harmed because, they claim, they were "deceived" by trans women. This supposed gender deception, their passively constructed narrative goes, causes them to panic, which, for some incomprehensible reason, then causes them to commit murder. The glaring inconsistency in logic is apparent: On the one hand, these men assert that they lack agency in the situation, as if they are being puppeteered by trans people, but then, on the other, they clearly have enough agency to murder another person.

The word *panic* conveys a primal fear and a sense of urgency. The word is used to intentionally misconstrue the agent and victim as well as the level and urgency of the threat. In instances where the murder takes place during or after a sexual encounter, panic signifies not the emotional reaction to an external threat but the emotional reaction to an internal fear of emasculation. *Panic* is code for shame and the fear of being seen.* The trans panic defense deliberately obfuscates an *internal fear* with an *external threat* to argue that the perpetrator is the real victim. It egregiously blames trans people for existing. And the obfuscation is a symptom of a patriarchal culture that has conditioned cisgender men to believe that their gender identity and expression—their sense of their manhood and masculinity—are somehow jeopardized by having sexual relations with a trans person. And little is deadlier to women—trans or cis—than a man who feels emasculated.

The violent reinforcement of men's entitlement has socially conditioned us to believe that this violence is normal, expected, and acceptable male behavior, such that entitlement itself is considered a defining trait of masculinity, and we have tacitly accepted it as such—*Oh those boys!* Or, *Men will be men!* Entitlement fortifies men's authority over choice as a birthright without consequence. It operates not just on an individual level but on a systemic level to reinforce the oppression of women and other marginalized groups. The ubiquity of entitlement demonstrates how deeply entrenched white freedom is in our society.

Furthermore, our society systemically and culturally reinforces white male entitlement by insisting that the effects of systemic oppression are just personal failures. The phrase *to pull themselves up by the*

---

* The panic defense is not new. The gay panic defense of the 1950s justified violence against gays because, the argument went, they were sexual deviants and therefore the real sexual predators. According to the Movement Advancement Project, as of January 2023, fifteen states and Washington, DC, prohibit the use of the gay/trans panic legal defense.

bootstraps is a racist dog whistle suggesting that racially marginalized people struggle not because of centuries of racism but because they are "lazy." Equality as a logic of whiteness is employed here to neutralize the compounding intergenerational effects of racism in order to render one's situatedness as a personal choice—as if people of color have willingly chosen poverty, chosen incarceration, and chosen death. This line of thinking asserts that Black, brown, and Indigenous people suffer because of their own moral failure.

Our situations are not products of our own making but of generations of choices—all made within their own set of conditions—beyond our individual control. Intergenerational poverty is not a personal choice but a systemic failure *and* a systemic design of racism. In a viral video made during the antiracism protests in 2020, author and activist Kimberly Latrice Jones used a Monopoly analogy to depict how the design of systemic racism has economically devastated Black Americans for generations:

> If I right now decided that I wanted to play Monopoly with you, and for four hundred rounds of playing Monopoly, I didn't allow you to have any money, I didn't allow you to have anything on the board, I didn't allow for you to have anything, and then we played another fifty rounds of Monopoly and everything that you gained and you earned . . . was taken from you, that was Tulsa. That was Rosewood. Those are places where we built Black economic wealth, where we were self-sufficient, where we owned our stores, where we owned our property, and they burned them to the ground. . . .
>
> You can't win. The game is fixed. So when they say, "Why do you burn down the community? Why do you burn down your own neighborhood?" It's not ours. We don't own anything. . . . The social contract is broken. . . .
>
> You broke the contract when you killed us in the streets and didn't give a fuck. You broke the contract when, for four hundred years, we played your game and built your wealth. You broke the contract when we built our wealth again on our own, by our bootstraps, in Tulsa,

and you dropped bombs on us, when we built it in Rosewood, and you came in and you slaughtered us. You broke the contract.

Jones is right. White people—and I include myself—are responsible for breaking this nation's social contract. But while we cannot change the horrors of the past, we can hold ourselves accountable for its continued effects on communities of color through active repair—through, that is, *reparations*, directed to these communities to make them safer, more secure, and healthier. Accountability is not a blame game but an active choice to improve the collective conditions and situations of our lives.

CHOICE AS BODY CONTROL

Men's historical entitlement to women's bodies has meant that the choices women make about their bodies have never been theirs alone. Even in *Roe*, Supreme Court justices declared that a woman's choice to have an abortion rested in the hands of "the attending physician, in consultation with *his* patient" (emphasis mine). The institutionalization of men's entitlement has rendered women's bodies as sites of oppression. Authority over women's bodies is conferred to whoever gets to choose what's on the menu—whoever legislates, regulates, and polices those bodies. And the patriarchy has always had a vested interest in ownership of the bodies that can grow and birth other bodies, because controlling the means of reproduction is to control life itself.

The patriarchal need to control all life by controlling reproduction has intensified in the decades since *Roe*. And the overturning of *Roe* has opened more avenues for states to pass legislation that deputizes citizens to sue anyone they suspect is enabling an abortion and charges abortion-care seekers, as well as their providers, with homicide. The goal of the antiabortion movement, former NARAL Pro-Choice America president Ilyse Hogue explained in *The Lie That Binds*, is "the maintenance of a social order in which men have control over women and white Americans have control over people of color with a concentration on economic wealth that reinforces order." For white supremacists, procreation is essential to ensuring the continuation of the so-called white race. To compel white people to join their cause, they have fabricated the "great replacement theory," which alleges that there is an agenda to eliminate white people. The media has fed this racist narrative through its framing of America's changing racial demographics: "White population aging rapidly in US, dying faster than babies are born, data show," stated one Fox News headline from 2018. This paranoid theory, in turn, has been cited by racists as justification for multiple mass shootings in communities of color—the murder of ten Black people at a grocery store in Buffalo, New York, in May 2022 is just one among several recent examples.

Unfortunately for these racists, data disproves not only their theory but also their correlative argument that outlawing abortion will help replenish the white race. According to 2019 data from the Kaiser Family Foundation, roughly 33 percent of legal abortions in the United States are performed on white women—meaning that a majority of abortions are performed on Black (39 percent), Hispanic (21 percent), and other racially marginalized women (7 percent).

Framing the control of reproduction as an agenda to preserve white supremacy by regulating populations provides essential context for understanding how and why the state and its institutions have inflicted racist violence on Black and racially marginalized women. Starting in the early twentieth century, the United States institutionalized this racist population control through eugenics. Thousands of Black, Latina, and Indigenous women—as well as queer and disabled women—were sterilized against their will or without their knowledge and consent in order to limit the population size of their respective communities. Civil rights organizer and activist Fannie Lou Hamer, who in 1961 had surgery to remove a noncancerous uterine tumor and was sterilized by doctors without her consent, made it part of her purpose to bring national attention to this state-sanctioned violence to help end its practice.

A consequence of white supremacist patriarchal body politics is that women's bodily autonomy has been conscripted into a false ultimatum:

They can choose themselves or choose children. They can decide to contravene their "God-given" purpose or procreate "as God intended." This ultimatum is inculcated in women—making me wonder if the so-called biological clock is really just a centuries-old patriarchal clock. "When I had to have a baby before I was ready to," writer Merritt Tierce reflected in the *New York Times*, "it felt as if my family was saying to me: *Your time's up. On to the next. Be the vessel, open your body and give us something more valuable than you.* No one asked me if I was ready to be a mother or a wife. No one asked if I was ready to disappear."

Women, furthermore, who choose to be child-free are condemned as selfish, immoral, or—even worse—lesbians. Even childless women, who for medical or other reasons cannot carry a pregnancy to term, face societal judgment, as if they have failed to live up to the standards and expectations of their gender.

It is not wrong for women to center themselves in their own lives. It is not immoral for women to have minds of their own or to make themselves the subjects of their own stories. And women and nonbinary, trans, and transmasculine people—anyone who can become pregnant—must always factor the *possibility* of pregnancy into their dreams and aspirations. That is, the possibility of pregnancy in conjunction with misogynistic laws situates us and conditions our freedom. Abortion bans and restrictions encapsulate the landmine of gender oppressions laid to control women, to box them into a world of don'ts: If you don't want to get pregnant, don't have sex. Don't want to get raped? Don't wear that. And definitely don't dance like that. Don't do anything that men might find too alluring, but also don't be too direct about your disinterest or unavailability because then they might retaliate and violently remind you that you exist for their pleasure. Women do a lot of cognitive labor to not upset fragile male egos.

Of course, "parenthood can only be a choice if abortion is allowed," reproductive health researcher Abigail Aiken said in an interview with the *New Yorker*. Enforced pregnancy under threat of criminalization is nothing less than turning pregnant people into chattel, as possessions of men and the patriarchal state.

We can further see how the false ultimatum affects the language and binary framing of abortion. What is at stake is not just control over women's bodies but control over entire populations. Reproduction is power, and choice is control.

The fatuous notion of "having it all" made women believe they could focus on cultivating their own lives *and* have children. Equality feminists touted the phrase as the full realization of gender equality—women making choices about their lives, just like men, understood largely in economic terms. Interestingly, this individual-focused, economic-driven messaging of equality feminism has been recently co-opted by young antiabortionists. Their version aims to convince women that they are liberated from the ultimatum by claiming that women don't have to choose at all. "This is 2022, not 1962," Students for Life of America president Kristan Hawkins told *New York Times* correspondent Ruth Graham in a story about young antiabortionist activists. "If feminism tells young women they need to be able to end their pregnancies in order to achieve their educational and career goals," Graham summarized the prevailing sentiment, "the anti-abortion movement tells them they can have it all."

Have. It. All.

As one twenty-six-year-old female antiabortionist commented in the same article: "I just reject the idea that as a woman I need abortion to be successful or to be as thriving as a man in my career."

Supreme Court Justice Amy Coney Barrett parroted this same language during the oral arguments in *Dobbs*, asserting that pregnant people can just willy-nilly give up their babies for adoption and resume their professional lives—with no physical, emotional, or economic costs during or after their pregnancy. The notion completely dehumanizes pregnant people and ignores their experience—as if they are just baby-making machines.

Abortion, of course, is not just about career success but more fundamentally about health, human dignity, and self-creation. Decades of pro-choice messaging, however, have emphasized career and wealth to the point of excluding other factors. This messaging thus reflects the centrality of capitalism in equality feminism. Certainly money is a significant factor in the choice to have a baby—those things are expensive, especially considering that the government does little to nothing to support them after birth, when, ironically, they become legitimate people. But, while framing abortion as a choice might have made it more palatable to the mainstream, doing so undermined the effort to protect abortion under the right to privacy as a constitutive element of human dignity and bodily autonomy.

Outlawing abortion, of course, doesn't always stop it from happening; it just makes getting one exponentially more dangerous. Even deadly. Women and people capable of pregnancy die when abortion is illegal. The 2020 *Turnaway Study*—the largest study of abortion and unwanted pregnancy in the United States to date—reported that women who are denied abortions suffer psychological and physical effects, are more likely to remain with abusive partners, and are more likely to experience economic hardship. Any children they already have suffer poorer child development compared to children of women who are permitted abortions, and children born as a result of denied abortions are more likely to live below the federal poverty line. While the patriarchy cannot actually prevent people from making choices about their own bodies, it can criminalize, terrorize, and punish people who assert authority over their own reproductive lives.

In this context, it is worth noting that the United States has the highest rate of maternal mortality among high-income nations in the world, and, according to 2021 national vital statistics data from the CDC's National Center for Health Statistics, this rate is worsening. The overall maternal morality rate was 17.4 per 100,000 live births in 2018 and rose to 32.9 in 2021. Non-Hispanic Black women's maternal mortality rate was 69.9 per 100,000 live births—2.6 times the rate of white women. For women under 25, the rate was 20.4 per 100,000 live births; that rate rises to 138.5 for women over 40. These data are supported by a 2020 longitudinal study of nearly five decades of national vital statistics data, which found that "unmarried status, US-born status, lower education, and rural residence were associated with 50–114 percent higher maternal mortality risks, [and] mothers in the most-deprived areas had a 120 percent higher risk of mortality than those in the most-affluent areas."

If data collected between 1998 and 2005 indicated that women were fourteen times more likely to die carrying a pregnancy to term than having an abortion, then the longitudinal study showing that the maternal mortality rate has significantly worsened in recent years is undeniable proof that it is more life-threatening for people to carry and deliver a pregnancy than it is to have an abortion.

REFRAMING ABORTION AS CARE

Abortion is about a person's freedom of self-creation: their ability to determine their life's trajectory and their autonomy over the reproductive capacity of their own body. However, when the argument for abortion is presented in terms of equality—the line of thinking being that women can only fully and equally participate in society if they have a right to choose—the logic and language of equality are activated in ways that thwart our dignity, bodily autonomy, and broader reproductive justice efforts. Equality neutralizes critical differences between real, autonomous, legal humans and fetal life, effectively serving up a binary choice: pregnant lives or fetal lives? The logic, rooted in the equality mindset's architecture of the gender binary, is that because men can't have abortions, no one can.

If we refuse to upend the conservative narrative that has eliminated the very real and very clear differences between a woman and a fetus in the name of equality, then we will never invalidate antiabortionists' argument. If feminists refuse to engage in the debate about life, then we will continue to witness the use of equality against us, especially as medical advancements in the hands of misogynists have been refined to pinpoint the moment a clump of cells—the tiniest of floofs arguably the size of a cat booger—have an electrical charge, egregiously called a "heartbeat" in order to anthropomorphize it.

Espousing that all life is equal, furthermore, has given antiabortionists control of the terms of the debate. The statement that "all life is equal" is the essential foundation for the binary framing of life versus choice. And when the issue becomes a debate of "pro-life vs. pro-choice," they automatically win. I mean, who would claim to be against life?

The oppositional framing answers the question: Pro-choice women, by this binary logic, are against life. The logic works to erase the real lives of women and people capable of pregnancy—you know, the people in the position to decide if they want or medically need an abortion to save their own lives. For example, an ectopic pregnancy, which is by definition unviable because the fertilized egg attaches to the ovary or fallopian tube instead of the uterus, can lead to death without an abortion. As Adrienne Rich wrote in *Of Woman Born*, "An antiabortion morality that does not respect women's intrinsic human value is hypocrisy."

When I talk about abortion as lifesaving health care, I think of *save* in several ways. Carrying and delivering a pregnancy and raising a child present monumental life changes and challenges. Pregnancy changes people's bodies, literally shifts bones and squashes organs. "There is almost no part of the human body that does not transform in pregnancy," wrote *New York Magazine* senior correspondent Irin Carmon. "One way or another, your flesh will be torn asunder . . . your gums swell and bleed; sores can mushroom in your mouth; your teeth can loosen or erode," she continued. "You know about the vomit and the constant peeing, but did you know the shape of your eyeballs and the size of your feet might change? These are the minor signs, however much their accumulation can estrange you from the person you once were."

And this is just a description of what happens during a pregnancy—not during birth or after birth. "Giving birth is violent; pregnancy is violent," writer Jude Ellison S. Doyle observed. "If you do not consent to be pregnant, then these experiences are so violent that the [United Nations] has classified forced pregnancy and birth as a form of torture." By overturning *Roe*, the United States has sanctioned the torture of women and people capable of pregnancy.

Feminists must separate abortion from the language and logic of equality, which have locked us into an ethical quandary about which life matters more. To break free of the binary pro-choice/pro-life framework, we need to first admit that, yes, all stages of pregnancy are stages of life. We should not be afraid to admit that fetuses do have life. But we also need to acknowledge that not all life is equal. And that the life of a zygote is in no way equal to the life of a real, legal person. We need to refute the antiabortionist rhetoric that fetal lives are autonomous persons by pointing out that they are actually a material part of pregnant people. As writer Charlotte Shane explained in *Harper's Magazine*, "My pregnancies were not separate from me—they were not in me but of me. My physical form marked where the phenomenon began and ended. The growth would be impossible without my organic matter; nothing about it occurred without incorporating the material of me."

Feminists have shied away from admitting that life is unequal perhaps out of a concern that doing so would be interpreted as a pro-eugenics argument. But this interpretation misconstrues life as personhood. My understanding of life is informed by the philosopher Henri Bergson, who defined life as anything with duration, or that is affected by time. Life consists of dynamism, not stasis. So a fetus has life because it has duration.

In contrast, a plastic bag, sitting in a landfill for centuries, does not. Objects do not have life. The items on my desk—a turquoise ceramic jar filled with black-ink pens, a black metal lamp, a picture of Bette Davis in *Front Page Woman* that I tore out of a magazine—do not have life. They do not accrue experiences with time that change the very materiality of their existence. They are not mortal.

A blade of grass, however, does have life. It grows, is nourished by sunlight and rain. It is sensate. Did you know that? Did you know that the smell of freshly cut grass is actually the scent of chemicals grass emits upon being whacked by a lawnmower as a lifesaving distress signal to other blades of grass? What we humans smell are the organic compounds, called green leaf volatiles, that notify surrounding grass of imminent harm and also repair the injured blades.

So, like a blade of grass, a fertilized egg develops over time through nourishment—here, instead of sunlight and water, the nourishment comes from the person carrying that egg. That fertilized egg is entirely dependent on the host body nourishing it and giving it life; "my organic matter," as Shane said. The host's body determines the life of that egg, if and how it becomes a zygote, then an embryo, and then a fetus. That fetus absolutely has life. But, like a blade of grass, it is not a legal person.

This comparison might offend some people, who scoff: "A fetus and a blade of grass are not the same thing!" And, yes, you're absolutely right. No two life-forms are the same. No two life-forms are equal. This is a factual reality of our daily lives, and it is up to us to accept this fact. Every time we eat a meal, buy flowers, menstruate, or ejaculate—discriminating against life inheres in staying alive and, dare I say it, even our pleasure. We don't even need to do an apples-to-apples comparison with antiabortionists who demand fetal life be protected yet staunchly oppose gun legislation that protects actual, real, legal children from being murdered in school. Just ask them: Do you eat food? Do you eat meat? Do you eat fruit? Do you cut down and/or purchase Christmas trees? Do you swat at flies and kill mosquitoes? They discriminate against life every day. We all do. By denying the basic facticity of our lives, we refuse to hold ourselves accountable to life, and to living. A careless consumption of life—of animals and the land and its resources—results from this denial. Instead of only taking or using as much as we need and can nurture and care for, we signpost power and prestige by the number of cars, homes, and boats we own. The acme of our gross consumer capitalism is epitomized by the equation between the amount of stuff we own and our human worth.

A related point is that antiabortionists assert that people seeking an abortion or who believe it should be a safe and legal right are careless, thoughtless people. That is, they concoct the idea that the decision to have an abortion is a frivolous one that takes place at fantastical abortion parties. Conservatives employ this line of reasoning when they claim girls are too immature to have an abortion—while believing these same girls are mature enough, both physically and psychologically, to give birth and become parents—or when they repeat the prevailing myth that people willy-nilly have abortions as a form of birth control. This is not only wrong but cruel. Separating abortion from the humanity of the pregnant person and from the historical stigma associated with having an abortion is a terrible ethical failure in compassion. Every person having an abortion deliberates that choice. It is a choice made with care and consideration and, as such, is fundamentally always a collective choice.

Equality is the lynchpin of the pro-choice/pro-life binary that frames the issue of abortion. Only by breaking free of this binary can we extricate abortion from it and resituate it as a health care issue. From a freedom mindset, we can connect our self-creation to care—to our health care. Reframing abortion in this way harkens back to its earlier framing by the women's liberation movement that rooted abortion in freedom. Laura Kaplan, a member of the Jane Collective, wrote in *The Story of Jane* that the movement "framed the issue, not in terms of privacy of sexual relations, and not in the neutral language of choice, but in terms of a woman's freedom to determine her own destiny as she defined it, not as others defined it. Abortion was a touchstone," she elaborated. "If she did not have the right to control her own body, which included freedom from forced sterilizations and unnecessary hysterectomies, gains in other areas were meaningless."

With an eye toward freedom, we can unequivocally assert, as Shane contended, that "every impregnatable person has the right not to be pregnant." From a freedom mindset, we can make care the framework for not only abortion care but all health care. That all life is unequal is a given. Rather, it is by the mutual recognition and care for our human dignity that we can begin to imagine structural and systemic change. This work begins by asking: What does care mean and look like? Whose bodies, historically, have been cared for and receive the care they need? How can we provide the care people need to not just keep them alive but allow them to live meaningful, satisfied, and joyful lives?

For decades, Black feminists and feminists of color have contextualized abortion as a health care issue. They also criticized white feminists' exclusive focus on abortion. In 1979, the women-of-color-led Committee for Abortion Rights and Against Sterilization Abuse (CARASA) published the pamphlet *Women Under Attack*, which situated care at the center of reproductive freedom. CARASA asserted that women's reproductive health must include "other aspects of reproductive freedom, such as contraception, child-care, prenatal and maternal care, sexual freedom—particularly for homosexuals and lesbians—and sterilization abuse," in addition to abortion. The committee's emphasis on freedom is crucial to understanding that care—here, reproductive care, health care, and abortion care—determines our freedom, including our sexual freedom. And their language of *reproductive freedom*, in lieu of pro-choice rhetoric, has been increasingly adopted into the mission statements of nationwide organizations like NARAL, suggesting a critical cultural shift to the framework of care and an understanding that care is essential to our freedom.

We don't have to look far back in history to observe that there are plenty of examples of care centered in women's reproductive health. In the late 1960s and early 1970s, for example, the Jane Collective made care the organizational principle in its abortion work, telling women they were doing the procedure *with* rather than *to* them. "They were so detailed in care," noted Doris, a woman interviewed in the 2022 HBO Max documentary *The Janes*. The experience was a noticeable departure from her first abortion, at the hands of the Italian Mafia. "The assurance, the trust, the respect I got—when I tell you they changed my life, they changed my life."

She added, "When I saw women caring about women . . . it was a whole new world for me."

This care work is the focus of numerous nonprofit and grassroots organizations, including SisterSong Women of Color Reproductive Justice Collective, a women-of-color-led reproductive justice organization formed in 1997. For SisterSong, reproductive justice is "about access, not choice," because "there is no choice when there is no access." And this access—this freedom—is about much more than abortion. The collective advocates for greater access to all forms of reproductive care, including "contraception, comprehensive sex education, STI prevention and care, alternative birth options, adequate prenatal and pregnancy care, domestic violence assistance, adequate wages to support our families, safe homes, and so much more."

Situating abortion within a broader framework of care expands feminist politics to include all people. Care is, fundamentally, a collective choice. So the politics of the movement broadens and becomes stronger, pivoting from the single-issue focus on abortion as an individual choice to care as a collective choice and endeavor to attain reproductive freedom for all. It is in this regard, as sociologist Dorothy E. Roberts wrote in *Killing the Black Body*, that "reproductive freedom is a matter of social justice, not individual choice." And this political revisioning forces us to reckon with the history of misogyny, racism, homophobia, transphobia, and ableism of the health care system by asking, again, who has been cared for and how.

Listening is an essential component of care. It is a form of empathy. One way we can collectively begin to care for each other, even if we are not certified medical professionals, is to *listen deeply* to each other, to attune ourselves to each other's needs and to what we might be telling each other between the lines. The choice to listen deeply is intentional and requires practice, particularly as the institutions we live and work in—the many facets of our burnout culture—devalue and destroy this attentive care work.

Serena Williams's struggle to receive the lifesaving care she needed after giving birth to her daughter in 2017 brought much-needed media attention to the longstanding issues of the health care system's misogyny and racism. In an April 2022 feature story for *Elle*, Williams detailed her harrowing experience after giving birth. She had to repeatedly advocate for herself when medical professionals dismissed her pain, which was later revealed to be caused by a pulmonary embolism. Those responsible for her care might have *heard* her, but they certainly were not *listening* to her. "Being heard and appropriately treated was the difference between life or death for me," Williams wrote. "I know those statistics would be different if the medical establishment listened to every Black woman's experience." Women, especially Black and other racially marginalized women, are not listened to when it comes to our own bodies. Our concerns and our pain are written off as paranoia or anxiety or depression. Williams's story is far from unique. But if this particular Black woman was not listened to about her own body—Serena Williams, GOAT of all GOATS*—what does this imply about the experiences of Black women who have less power, wealth, and influence? What does it say about how deeply misogyny and racism are baked into the foundations of medical institutions? Take, just as one example: A 2016 University of Virginia study of 222 white medical students found that nearly half of them believed in at least one dehumanizing myth about Black people, such as the myth that Black skin is thicker than white skin and therefore Black people have higher tolerances for pain. What kind of medical care do you think these white people are giving to Black people?

Without care, without caring, we can never be free. We can only experience and expand our freedom if we care for each other. Care work dignifies people's humanity and builds trust, which, in turn, builds relationships that serve as the connective tissue for our collective freedom. We can reimagine care work not as an individual burden but, as writer Angela Garbes said about raising children in *Essential Labor*, as "a social responsibility, one that requires robust community support." When it

---

* Serena Williams won a two-week-long tennis grand slam tournament while pregnant, folks. Her GOAT of all GOATS status is just facts.

comes to childcare, we can also turn to Black feminist and community activist Dorothy Pitman Hughes, who demonstrated what this care work looks like. In 1966, she founded a daycare center that functioned much like a community care center because she knew that adult education, housing, and job training factored into childcare and raising a family. Feminists like Hughes who have come before us have already shown us how to center care.

And, importantly, we do not need professional degrees or licenses to do this care work ourselves, with each other, and within our communities. The Jane Collective is case in point—not one single member had a license to practice medicine. Disability justice activists have devised the idea of "care webs" to provide the collective access and mutual aid necessary to honor the dignity of people with disabilities. In *Care Work*, Leah Lakshmi Piepzna-Samarasinha explained that care webs operate on "a model of *solidarity not charity*" and "are controlled by the needs and desires of the disabled people running them." Care webs are collective care models that step in when the system refuses or fails. They nurture friendships and communities while also, Piepzna-Samarasinha pointed out, building political power.

If we establish a vision of feminism based in freedom, we can begin to address how we envision care specific to individual and community needs. Dedicated to the pursuit of freedom, we can cultivate forms of care that encompass all stages of life, from beginning to end.

THE CHOICE OF DEATH

"There must be some way to integrate death into living," Audre Lorde wrote in a 1979 diary entry later published in *The Cancer Journals*. "Once I accept the existence of dying, as a life process, who can ever have power over me again?"

Death with dignity is the freedom to choose death with the care and compassion one needs to determine the end of one's life—as Lorde said, as a part of life. Not everyone, of course, has the ability or opportunity to make this decision. A freedom-centered feminism includes death with dignity as a feminist issue, connected to values of care, accountability, and self-creation.

For Lorde, this issue is particularly relevant to the Black community and other racially marginalized communities in the United States that historically have had little to no say in their deaths. "Even in the face of our own deaths and dignity," she observed, "we are not allowed to define our needs nor our feelings nor our lives." In the context of the systemic dehumanization of Black people, then, Lorde found something liberating in being able to have agency in her cancer experience, being able to encounter death on her own terms—rather than, say, at the hands of the police or another racist with a gun.

In addition, the American health care system is an injustice unto itself. In our capitalist society, our health care and access depend not on the government but on the private sector. Our health insurance is tied to our employer. And even if you have insurance, you can be denied lifesaving treatments and/or social security if your illness or disability doesn't qualify for coverage. So let me be abundantly clear: The freedom to choose death is systemically restricted, mired in spiteful bureaucracy, such that the health care many of us can access and afford not only does not improve our health but actually contributes to our decline and untimely death. The choice of death is one most of us do not have—rather, the health care system decides for us.

This is especially true for people with disabilities, who encounter a health care system rife with ableist prejudices that negatively affect their medical treatment and care. Research by disability ethics scholar Heidi Janz published in 2019 documented health care professionals' biases, primarily about disabled people's mental competency. This particular bias, Janz observed, leads them to significantly underestimate the quality of life of people with disabilities, which can "result in treatment options for people with disabilities being either limited, or altogether eliminated."

To choose death with dignity is the final act of our self-creation. Understanding death as a part of life informs our critical consciousness about our situatedness and how we choose to hold ourselves accountable to ourselves and others. Lorde reflected upon how this consciousness influenced her ethics:

> Living a self-conscious life, under the pressure of time, I work with the consciousness of death at my shoulder, not constantly, but often enough to leave a mark upon all my life's decisions and actions. And it does not matter whether this death comes next week or thirty years from now; this consciousness gives my life another breath. It helps me shape the words I speak, the ways I love, my politic of action, the strength of my vision and purpose, the depth of my appreciation of living.

With finite time in this life, how do you choose to live it? For Lorde, this consciousness inspired what she referred to as living a "considered life"—to live deliberately, much like Thoreau said, "to front only the essential facts of life . . . to live deep and suck out all the marrow of life."

One doesn't necessarily need to live in the woods like Thoreau to cultivate such a considered life. Yet to live with consideration means to make choices from a standpoint of care and accountability. It means that, even though we don't all have the same ability to determine when or how we die, we incorporate discussions about how to approach death into our feminist politics.

Such discussions have been absent from mainstream culture until fairly recently. The media and cultural visibility of death with dignity has increased with the rise of the death positive movement: books like Atul Gawande's *Being Mortal: Medicine and What Matters in the End* and Katie Engelhart's *The Inevitable: Dispatches on the Right to Die*; documentaries like Ondi Timoner's *Last Flight Home*; and, during the height of the COVID-19 pandemic, the rising demand for death educators like the late Shatzi Weisberger, who taught the art of dying, and death doulas, who help people and their loved ones go through this inescapable life transition.

A memorable storyline in season 2 of *Grace and Frankie*, in 2016, brought the issue to my attention. Grace and Frankie's friend, Babe, asks them to assist her with suicide after a party celebrating her life. Babe's cancer, she has just learned, has returned and is terminal. Grace vehemently opposes Babe's plans and refuses to help her. "It's not her choice to make!" she tells Frankie, adding that "only God can make that decision." Frankie, however, responds from a place of care and respect for Babe's freedom to determine the course of her own life: "Of course it is. Her life. Her death. Her choice. . . . If Babe wants to end her life tonight, then, yes, I would help her. I will help her do anything that supports her decision."

As someone who has panic attacks when thinking about death (my own death and the death of the sun and universe), I understand how uncomfortable these conversations can be, because they force us to confront our mortality and consider the meaning of life. "The intensity of it, the mystery, all of the unknowns," Francesca Arnoldy, the lead instructor of the University of Vermont's End-of-Life program told the *New York Times*. "You have to relinquish your sense of control and agenda and ride it out."

However, in the United States we still lack a caring culture of death—indeed, we still have not collectively processed the million-plus deaths caused by the coronavirus. Instead, we charge ahead with a puritanical Protestant ethic of productivity, growth, and wealth accumulation—no matter the consequence, no matter the destruction or harm we inflict. Mark Zuckerberg's tossed-off line—"move fast and break things"—has become the mantra of Silicon Valley and beyond. In many ways, capitalism denies us the ability to think about death while driving us to death.

Yet, it is only by having conversations about death and building a culture of death that we can begin to imagine ways to provide and practice the care people need to die with dignity and help their loved ones live through and after their deaths. (The fact is that we cannot grieve our own death because we do not live through it—only our loved ones do.)

And our collective, continued failure as a society to discuss death as a process of life has foreclosed our ability to radically reconceive care, and health care specifically, in ways that honor our personal dignity and facilitate collective justice. According to the nonprofit, Order of the Good Death, this is what the death positive movement strives for: "Death positive means you should be given support during and after a death, including the ability to speak freely about your grief and experiences [to] push back and engage with systems and conditions that lead to 'unacceptable' deaths resulting from violence, a lack of access to care, etc."—again, dying is not an equal experience. Founded by mortician Caitlin Doughty in 2011, the Order is part of the movement to "[shift] our cultural and national beliefs surrounding death" to allow us to cultivate "a good *end* of life"—not simply for the dying but for "those affected by it."

Despite a 2018 Gallup poll finding that 72 percent of Americans support physician-assisted suicide, as of 2022, only ten states and Washington, DC, legally allow it. However, to be eligible for physician-assisted suicide in most of these jurisdictions, a physician must certify that a person is terminally ill with no more than six months to live, and that person must reside in one of these states (or DC) and be able to express both verbally and in writing the desire to die to two local doctors. The exact legal parameters vary per state, with some states even demanding that people must be physically capable of administering and ingesting the medication that ends their life. These requirements indicate that the right to die with dignity is less accessible than it appears—as writer Amy Bloom and her husband, Brian, realized shortly after his Alzheimer's diagnosis, which she chronicled in her memoir, *In Love*. "People who wish to end their lives and shorten their period of great suffering and loss—those people are out of luck in the United States of America," Bloom wrote. Within a week, Brian knew "the long good-bye of Alzheimer's was not for him," and, soon after that decision, they found "the only place in the world for painless, peaceful, and legal suicide[,] Dignitas, in the suburbs of Zurich."

Death with dignity demonstrates how death—and choice, more generally—is never an individual issue, despite it feeling so singular. As the final act of care, it is a collective choice. The story of Brittany Maynard, who was twenty-nine years old when she decided to end her life after being diagnosed with an aggressive type of terminal brain cancer, shows us how feminism can claim this issue as integral to our freedom.

"I am dying, and I refuse to lose my dignity. I refuse to subject myself and my family to purposeless, prolonged pain and suffering at the hands of an incurable disease," Maynard stated. "Knowing that I can leave this life with dignity allows me to focus on living. It has provided me enormous peace of mind." She recorded this statement in a video message for California lawmakers just eighteen days prior to taking legal medication that ended her life on November 1, 2014, in Portland, Oregon—one of only five states at the time with legal physician-assisted death laws. At the time, death with dignity was not a legal option in her home state of California. Her story received nationwide media attention, and her message had impact. California passed its End of Life Option Act in September 2015, and it went into effect the following June.

In several blogs, videos, and op-eds, Maynard repeated her message, emphasizing that choosing death was an assertion of her bodily autonomy and a choice made not only for herself but for her loved ones as well. The choice, echoing the sentiments of Lorde, was made from a place of considered care.

If oppression is the lack of choice, then freedom is the ability to make choices, no matter whether we avail ourselves of them or not. The power that comes from self-sovereignty, the feeling of authority over one's life, comes from taking ownership of our choices and holding ourselves accountable for them. This expression of freedom is as true for abortion as it is for death. Maynard described these exact feelings in her writings. There is always a choice, no matter how situated one's life is. Maynard's knowledge of this filled her with a feeling of power from a powerless place. "I have been in charge of this choice, gaining control of a terrifying terminal disease through the application of my own humane logic," she wrote in an October 2014 blog post. And in an opinion piece for CNN, she asked, "Who has the right to tell me that I don't deserve this choice? That I deserve to suffer for weeks or months in tremendous amounts of physical and emotional pain? Why should anyone have the right to make that choice for me?" As Maynard said in a YouTube video released that month, "The worst thing that could happen to me is that I wait too long because I'm trying to seize each day, but that I somehow have my autonomy taken away from me by my disease."

Maynard further elaborated on the feelings of strength and solace she got from the knowledge that her choice would also mitigate her family's suffering by shortening the length of time they would have to witness her body deteriorating from the cancer. She believed to force herself to continue living would otherwise be irresponsible and cruel. "Because the rest of my body is young and healthy, I am likely to physically hang on for a long time even though cancer is eating my mind," she explained. "I probably would have suffered in hospice care for weeks or even months. And my family would have had to watch that. I quickly decided that death with dignity was the best option for me and my family."

In this way, Maynard recast what has long been stigmatized as a selfish act as a selfless one. Her choice of death was made from the place of a freedom mindset that situated it within the collective, centered on care. "Death with dignity is an American health care choice," she said at the conclusion of her statement to lawmakers. "Every one of us will die. We should not have to suffer excruciating pain, shame, or a prolonged dying process. . . . Let the movement begin here, now."

THE CHOICE OF SEX(UALITY)

Sex—it gives us life and gives us (a little) death. The freedom to choose the act of sex and, relatedly, our sexuality, is a reclamation from the patriarchy, which has historically denied women our bodily autonomy, criminalized and moralized our sexual desires out of existence, and reduced the meaning of sex and women's worth to reproduction.

The freedom to choose sex, to give one's consent, puts us in control of our bodies and, crucially for women, *our pleasure.* "Who we can desire, how we can express that desire, who has the right to desire, and our right to determine for ourselves whose desire we can and cannot accept or reject," Mona Eltahawy declared, "go to the heart of defying, disobeying, and disrupting the patriarchy." The social conditioning of women has led us to believe that our pleasure is shameful and sinful—another dirty thing. As such, the noticeable reluctance of the mainstream feminist movement to apply the mantra of *my body, my choice* to sex and sexual pleasure intimates a deep cultural shame about sexuality, as if linking sexuality to abortion, under the auspices of reproductive health care, would hinder political efforts to secure and protect the right to an abortion. (In the late nineteenth century, the radical Free Love movement was largely divorced from the movement for women's rights, save for a few brave souls, like Victoria Woodhull. Better known as the first woman to run for president of the United States (with Frederick Douglass as her running mate), Woodhull was an extremely vocal proponent of women's sexual liberation. She opined frequently about it in *Woodhull & Claflin's Weekly,* a newsletter she wrote with her sister, Tennessee Claflin. "Women must vindicate their right to an absolute freedom in their own conduct," the pair wrote in an article on virtue, "except that they shall have no right to encroach on others." In the year of her presidential campaign, she gave a speech declaring that women were "plotting a revolution" before shouting, "I am a free lover!")

To control women's bodies, the patriarchy had to control their relations—especially their sexual ones. "Compulsory heterosexuality," as Adrienne Rich defined it, is the ideology that has conditioned us into heterosexuality, which, she claimed, is the political institution that exerts, enforces, and justifies men's domination over women. In the United States, Christianity, as the moral arm of the white supremacist cis-heteropatriarchy, instantiated heterosexuality as God-ordained and therefore natural and right. For white supremacists, the right way to be heterosexual has included the racist agenda outlawing interracial relationships and marriage. Rape and incel culture, too, are manifestations of compulsory heterosexuality—also verbalized in the threat heard around the world by lesbians and bisexual women that we can be "fucked straight."

Freedom is expressed in the choice to fuck. And it is this freedom—and the independence and power that fucking confers to women—that makes women's sexuality so threatening to men. (As one very obvious example, just recall how conservative pundits at Fox News went ballistic—for months in 2020 and 2021—over Cardi B and Megan Thee Stallion's "WAP.") Women's sexuality challenges the patriarchal belief that women's primary purpose is to serve as caretakers, wives, and baby-makers who fulfill men's every need.

Sexual freedom means having an awareness and knowledge of your desires and being able to make the choice to say yes or no—or what else?—to sexual experiences.

Sex is an act. Sexuality is a social identity one chooses based on their sexual acts and behaviors. Every person writes their own story of their sexuality throughout the course of their life. So, when I say my sexuality is a choice, I am owning it: My freedom and my power are in taking authority over and accountability for my choices and actions.

One of my favorite lines to convey this is, "I don't just fall into a vagina and stay there." Whenever I have a chance to drop this gem in person, as opposed to dashing it off in a tweet, I add a little performative stumble, as if I have literally tripped and fallen, gleefully, mouth first, into a great big vagina. (I know, I know! *Vulva*.)

My intention is not just to get a rise out of people or to provocatively communicate my sexuality—admittedly, I am doing these things. But I also say it to make a larger point about my sexuality as a choice. Because it is my choice whom I have sex with (on the condition that they also choose to have sex with me), how I have sex, when, where, and why I have sex. These choices are within my control. And affirming this makes me feel independent, strong, and powerful.

That idea of sexuality as a choice is often perceived to be more controversial than my "falling into a vagina" framing. This is because homosexuality has been—thank you, Christianity—historically portrayed as a kind of moral affliction. And instead of breaking the frame of morality that has binarized sexuality in terms of good (hetero) and evil (homo), gays have largely adopted this patriarchal Christian ideology, claiming "God made me this way" to protect themselves from theologically based bigotry. But the assertion that it is not a choice both conveys an acceptance of the belief that homosexuality is immoral and divorces accountability from the act of sex.

But I'm not sorry for who I am. Neither am I ashamed of my sexuality. So no one can make me feel guilty about it, which means I don't feel compelled to justify it in biology. (It's certainly not genetic, if my extremely stereotypical heterosexual parents are any indication.) Again, why would I apologize for something I choose every day? If it's my choice, it means I desire it. I find it pleasing and pleasurable.

So I choose what my sex life looks like, how I express my desires, and how I define my sex life through language, especially the language of identity. And I choose how I design or style my life to represent those desires and align myself with a particular culture in order to communicate to people, *Hey, Big Dyke Energy right here!*

So, no, baby, I was not born this way.

Claiming that sexuality is a choice has always been very important to me, because with choice comes both power and responsibility. These in turn function as the basis for holding myself accountable in all my sexual experiences. I didn't *whoops!* fall into a giant, warm vagina (okay, vulva). No, I am responsible for the choices I make.

And so are you.

To choose is an act of freedom. And freedom is found in the power and responsibility of making a choice. I choose to honor my desires. I choose my lifestyle. To not be awash in gay shame feels immensely freeing. If you take pride and find joy in how you love and whom you love, then no one can ever make you feel shame about it.

So what would happen if, instead of feeling the need to justify our sex lives with *It's not a choice!*, we were to understand that there is always a choice? That while we cannot choose the conditions we are born into, we *can* choose *how* to live within those conditions? And that while our desires—those swirling, amorphous, libidinal forces inside our bodies—are beyond our control, we can control *how* we act on them? And, furthermore, we can choose the language—the identity—we use to represent the totality of those desires and actions?

The process of developing our critical consciousness includes the work of assessing and understanding our desires. Having a critical consciousness means we choose how we express those desires in language and action. The quest for the origins of homosexuality is both a fool's errand and, more insidiously, a biopolitical mandate to condemn lifestyles that do not prop up the white supremacist patriarchy. Whether you attribute your gayness to a gay gene or, in my case, Michelle Pfeiffer straddling a ladder while singing "Cool Rider" in *Grease 2*, what actually matters in terms of an ethics is *how* we live those desires in the world with other people. Meaning is not found in the *why* but in the *how*. Because it is the *how* that affects other people—how I respect the people I am involved with and how others respect me.

From a very early age, we observe, take in, and affectively respond to whom and what we see in the world; for example, on television, in the media, at the market, and at school. We may desire what we see, but we may also see what we desire. (RIP to our favorite mistakes.) To make sense of these desires, we use language—*a social tool*. We put a name on these desires, filter them through understood social narratives to not just help them make sense to us but to help communicate them to other people. For example, I have chosen to label myself *lesbian* based on my sexual preferences for women, but I certainly wouldn't say that all my desires are lesbian. This sexual identity then communicates my chosen sexuality to the world. The point is that the desires that affect and stimulate us exist prior to the words we give to them.

At the same time, the productive social work of naming and giving language to our desires is a form of visibility that allows people to know that a life other than heterosexuality exists and is possible. This is the power of LGBTQ+ visibility—evident in greater numbers of people identifying as part of the LGBTQ+ community from an earlier age. (I think, to their credit, younger generations know binaries are bullshit.) This also corresponds to why the language we use to describe our sexuality—especially the identities we feel best represent how we express our desires—changes over time. New experiences may connect to previously explored or unexamined desires, completely changing someone's life. As such, if that person chooses to live authentically, they may choose new identities to reflect those newly perceived desires.

Declaring the choice of one's sexuality is a sex-positive standpoint, and an important one for feminism. To stand in one's intentionality is powerful, as it confers authority and signals the acceptance of accountability. I am responsible for my sexuality not only in terms of social identity but in terms of the older understanding of the word: the sexual expression of self, through behavior, gesture, and language.

Cynthia Nixon, who has also asserted that her sexuality is a choice, said in a 2012 interview in the *New York Times Magazine*, "People think I was walking around in a cloud and didn't realize I was gay, which I find really offensive," adding, "I find it offensive to me, but I also find it offensive to all the men I've been out with." It's offensive because the assumption is that Nixon and the men she dated and had relationships with were either oblivious or liars. Furthermore, it implies that choosing a new identity that best reflects one's current lifestyle is nothing but a sign of a personal crisis.

Nixon has also made similar arguments about her *Sex and the City* character, Miranda Hobbes, who in the first season of the spin-off, *And*

Just Like That . . . , chooses to leave her straight marriage and pursue a relationship with Che, the show's first nonbinary character. Critics who dismissed Miranda's affair as a midlife crisis were missing the point, Nixon told Drew Barrymore in a 2022 appearance on *The Drew Barrymore Show*, adding that it's sexist to criticize a woman for making radical changes in her life when she's not happy. "When you put a negative spin on it, you can call it a midlife crisis, right? But out of crises come really productive things, and it's like you're not young anymore, but you're not old either, and you still have time to make sure that your life is the way you want it to be," she said. "If you're deeply unhappy in your career choices, and you're really deeply unhappy in your marriage, you should look at it and demand more."

Demanding more of ourselves and our relationships is not wrong. A freedom-centered feminism encourages us to make hard choices and explore our desires and needs, despite the patriarchal strictures imposed upon us. Indeed, to cultivate one's own life and live authentically means that sometimes even our stable careers and loving relationships aren't enough.

OUR CHOICES MATTER

When it comes to choices we make about our lives and bodies—choices that have been historically denied to women—it is essential that we actively and deliberately take ownership of those choices. That we stand firmly in them, and that we hold ourselves accountable for them and are willing to be held accountable by others.

We can make choice a practice of freedom when we anchor it to accountability. The power of this freedom practice is experienced through creative self-determination—what I call *self-creation*—in which we break free of artificial, misogynistic, and racist binaries to design our own lives. If we make our choices from this position, we can confidently stand in them, and this is a position of strength rooted in integrity.

This definition of choice does not demand moral purity or absolutism. Our freedom to choose is situated, so what is required of us is an awareness of ourselves and of others when we make our choices. We live together in various ecosystems small and large—from families and communities to nations and the world.

In this vein, I heed the words of writer Roxane Gay, who in a 2022 *New York Times* opinion piece wrote: "Every day, I try to make the best decisions possible about what I create, what I consume, and who I collaborate with—but living in the world, participating in capitalism, requires moral compromise. I am not looking for purity; it doesn't exist. Instead, I'm trying to do the best I can, and take a stand when I think I can have an impact."

Gay's words evoke those of Maya Angelou: "Do the best you can until you know better. Then when you know better, do better."

It has been a bit of a feminist taboo to focus on individual choice rather than, say, a collectivist politics. But this perspective fails to see how the two are inextricably connected. Contrary to that thinking, I believe we must examine how we make our choices and consider their impact because individual choices inform our collectivist politics. I agree with Princeton University professor Ruha Benjamin that social change begins *within* the individual. "It's in our daily actions and shifts in thinking that new worlds are first conceived," she wrote in *Viral Justice*. Her call to action is "for individuals to reclaim power over how our thoughts, habits, actions shape—as much as they are shaped by—the larger environment." Our choices absolutely matter because we matter. Our choices matter not only because they are practices of freedom but because they can inspire the choices of others. Only by reimagining choice from a freedom mindset can we understand both our individual and collective capacity for change.

Reconceptualizing choice as a constitutive element of freedom, we can better advance a politics that begins with the understanding that there is, in a way, no such thing as a purely individual choice.

That choice, through a feminist lens of freedom, is always a collective endeavor. Indeed, it is the world in which we live, our relationships and encounters with others, that establishes the scope—or the situatedness—of the choices we make. And, if choice is collective, it must include accountability.

Freedom feminism breaks free of the belief that the individual and the collective are two separate and distinct standpoints. It means understanding that the collective always figures into the choices we make. This is especially true not only when it comes to the choices we make but in how those choices contribute to our self-creation, which, we will see, is never achieved by the self alone.

CHAPTER 5

FREE YOUR BODY

"Margo will not only never refuse sex, but also allow me to be as violent as I want, which turns me on," Yuri Tolochko said of his then wife in a 2021 interview with *Vice*. "I like that I can fully control her. I also like to have sex with Margo's head off in the shower. But I may have overdone it after our wedding. Maybe that's why Margo broke down just before Christmas."

If you're concerned about Margo, don't be—Tolochko sent her to a repair shop to get fixed.

Margo is a robot. And Tolochko is no aberration. Rudimentary sex dolls date back to the late 1960s, and silicone sex dolls have been on the market since the launch of Abyss Creation's RealDoll in 1996. The 2018 documentary *Silicone Soul* shared the stories of men and women—called iDollators—who have sexual relationships with dolls. There are even sex doll brothels speckled throughout Asia, Europe, and North America.

Technological innovations in artificial intelligence (AI) have made an everyman of Pygmalion, the mythical Cypriot sculptor in Ovid's

Metamorphoses, whose female statue came to life (and, thanks to Venus's divine intervention, delivered him a child).

"You can pick her nipples, you can pick her eyelashes, their eyebrows, their colors, their lipstick, their makeup, their fingernail polish, everything. You can create the doll that is most arousing for you," sex doll beta-tester Brick Dollbanger said in a 2018 interview with *Forbes*. (Yes, "Brick Dollbanger" is a pseudonym. A bit on the nose, for my liking.) People who purchase a Harmony doll can choose from forty-two nipple colors and fourteen different labia. These Pygmalions even get to choose six among ten personality traits for their doll, from "sexy" and "smart" to "jealous" and "angry." The woman of their dreams is just a few clicks away.

That verisimilitude is the goal suggests that what is going on here is more than just a sexual kink. As writer Jeanette Winterson argued in *12 Bytes: How We Got Here. Where We Might Go Next*, "Doll-world likes to paint itself as a daring challenge to convention. In reality, doll-world reinforces the [female] gender at its most oppressive and unimaginative." No matter how advanced the AI programming—predominantly done by the minds of men, for the record—sex dolls are "perfect" women because they are objects. They have no agency independent of their programmer; they have no autonomy, and so they can never question or threaten their owner's authority.

"Usually, there are certain obligations where you enter into a relationship," Tolochko said of human relationships. "But Margo is different. Margo never reproaches me when I'm busy, or when I'm not home for three days. So it's very convenient for me, because I am very busy. She gives me sex whenever I want, no matter the day or time. Margo can get into positions no normal girl can, and the greatest charm in our relationship is that she can give me the freakiest, most unusual sex."

This Pygmalion fantasy is part of a larger tapestry of storytelling, from Adam and Eve to *Weird Science* and beyond, which has established man as the godlike protagonist who is the creator of all life. Women are supporting characters of man's design, written into *his* story. They play the role of subservient "giver," as philosopher Kate Manne noted, who attends to man's needs—their labor, ironically, makes his story possible.

As the sex doll market booms, the increasing demand for life-like female dolls points to human women's fatal flaw: being alive. Our humanity—from our aging to our agency—has proven a real downer for men.

Despite the patriarchy's unending efforts to control women, the insurmountable gulf between being *objectified* and being an *object* points to its impossibility. And men know this. "Often, it's not a sense of women's humanity that is lacking," Manne observed in *Down Girl: The Logic of Misogyny*. "Her humanity is precisely the problem," specifically when she gives herself, her love, her care, and her attention to "the wrong people—including herself and other women." It is women's very humanity, as we have discussed, that is erased in debates about abortion. Consequently, advances in technology have enabled men to pivot their strategy from turning women into objects to turning objects into women, not only through dolls but also through AI chatbot innovations like Replika, which is designed to mimic its owner in speech style and patterns over time. (Another example of woman fashioned by the man in the mirror.)

Yet, whether idealized as men's complement or perfect match, or denigrated as their subordinate, women will never be free to design our *own* lives if we continue our allegiance to the gender binary, which circumscribes our existence in a contingent, fixed relation to men. As bell hooks told us, women's liberation means we must "destroy dualisms." I think, most critically, this applies to the dualism of the gender binary, which situates women into a subservient, inferior position to men.

Life, however, doesn't happen in binaries. Women are not created by men or for men, and we do not have to limit ourselves to becoming what men tell us to be. We can refuse to be conceived of as Galateas sculpted by Pygmalions, Eves born from Adam's rib.

Women can toss out the limiting scripts written for us by men through the practice of self-creation. We can be intentional about the choices we make and govern our own lives according to our own desires.

In practicing this kind of freedom—the freedom of self-creation—we can realize our dignity and authenticity. This practice is one of self-cultivation and considered design framed by the values of care and accountability. It means developing habits, establishing our values, and fashioning our aesthetics—an ethics of the self.

Aesthetics is central to designing our own lives. Its role in living authentically is why I call this freedom practice *self-creation* rather than self-determination. Creativity—how we render and express our imaginations and ideas—is fundamental to self-creation. Indebted to Black feminists' notion of self-determination, self-creation emphasizes creativity, because the imagination's limitless capacity is integral to cultivating authenticity and finding moments of joy despite society's oppressive constraints. Furthermore, expressions of creativity in art and storytelling create spaces of visibility—a critical first, but not final, step in a politics, as visibility enables awareness and facilitates belonging. These expressions also give us the tools—inspirations of language, imagery, narratives, and ideas—for our own self-creation.

A freedom feminism advocates for the creative potential of self-determination as the cornerstone of bodily autonomy. We experience freedom through creating our own lives, the authenticity of which exists outside of binaries, and outside of identities. Liberating *woman* from the gender binary, and from the equality mindset, presents the radical potential to transform the feminist movement away from an identity politics and toward a politics fighting for freedom, dignity, care, and justice.

THE CATCH-22 OF IDENTITY

Self-creation takes its form in action—extensions of ourselves into the world, outside of ourselves—and so language is a constitutive medium of this practice. Language is communicative and performative—it performs an action and makes what is spoken real, as in the marriage vow of "I do" or the judgment of "the defendant is guilty." Or, even, "No!"

Language informs our actions, their meaning, and how they are interpreted. It has assumed even greater significance in the practice of self-creation as our lives have become increasingly virtual. Many interactions today are not physical (IRL) but rather take place on social media, where we primarily encounter each other visually, through text, images, and video.

Because language is the social system of making and communicating meaning, people rely on the language of identity to communicate both who they are to others and to describe who others are to them. In thinking about how we create ourselves, we often turn to identity both to make ourselves visible and to represent and give ourselves meaning in society. Identity primarily functions as shorthand to make sense of others and to get a landscape view of the diversity of our social fabric. It is, thus, also a double-sided shortcut—helpful in providing quick, bite-size information about people. But this information is generic and overly simplistic, and it lends easily to stereotypes. We are more than our identities, and yet the catch-22 is that they are fundamental to our self-creation.

What complicates self-creation is the sociality of language. Meaning is made socially, among and by people, rather than by one person. We express ourselves through language in society, not just as a declaration of autonomy but as a means of recognition of our existence. Language is viral: It flows. It's fluid. Not only does it move without obstruction—trigger warnings be damned—it can infect us with ideas, catalyze new ways of thinking about ourselves and each other. (Which is precisely a goal of this book!) So the practice of self-creation is always prefigured by existing language—we enter and encounter a world already filled with language, with meaning, and with other people who are also trying to define themselves. In effect, the very tool we use in self-creation is the same one that inscribes us, binds us to the political, cultural, and historical baggage that a word or phrase has accrued.

We have the freedom to choose our identities and to embody them in ways that feel authentic to us, which is why people place such importance on the precision of the words they use to represent themselves. Within one of my own communities, some people prefer *lesbian*, some use *dyke*, others opt for *queer*, and younger ones have brought back *sapphic*, to my absolute delight. Some people adamantly believe these words have fixed and distinct meanings, while others, believing these concepts are porous, use them interchangeably, employing them variously, perhaps in different contexts among different groups of people, or perhaps simultaneously.

Yet, while identities may feel extremely *personal*, they are, by definition, *social*. As socially constructed language, identities always exist in negotiation. This is the insurmountable caveat to the notion of self-creation. If identities play a critical role in our self-creation, our lives may come to feel like an endless negotiation between who we say we are and who society labels us to be. And, in a supremacist society, this negotiation operates as a power struggle for domination. Will people respect our dignity by respecting the language we give to ourselves? Or do they feel compelled to use language to pin us down, categorize us to criminalize and ostracize us for their own benefit?

In this regard, identity is political because it is social—it is a continual negotiation between the *freedom to* identify oneself and the *freedom from* being identified by others. In other words, we select our identities to make sense of who we are or would like to be, and, at the same time, people we encounter try to make sense of who we are by matching our appearance or identities. As such, identities are used to make sense of differences, but they are also used to make snap judgments, or prejudgments, which, in a white supremacist cis-heteropatriarchy, are in turn used to codify power imbalances, justify discrimination, and moralize violence.

Hatred is rationalized through the categorization of people as deviant or criminal. If you dig a little into the etymology of identity categories, you'll notice a tendency for differences considered atypical, or not "normal," to be classified before that which is considered "normal." For example, the word *homosexual* was coined by German psychologists and psychiatrists to designate sexual perversion in the mid-nineteenth century. But *heterosexual* didn't emerge until decades later, in 1892, only gaining traction as the so-called normal and correct sexual identity at the turn of the twentieth century. This terminology was then deployed by various institutions to pathologize and criminalize all people who exhibited or were perceived as harboring tendencies that were identified as homosexual. This pattern of identifying "otherness" as a threat to the status quo is a supremacist strategy to point the finger, label, and oppress a group of people in order to figuratively step on and step above them.

For historically marginalized groups, identities have been tools of their oppression. The n-word, James Baldwin explained in a series of essays published in the mid-1960s, was created to condone and codify the dehumanization of Black people.* Baldwin perceived the origins of the word to be rooted in a kind of psychological projection: that the word itself was a crystallization of the purpose of and motivation for white supremacy. "White people will have to ask themselves precisely why they found it necessary to invent the [n-word]," he wrote in "The White Problem," "for the [n-word] is a white invention, and white people invented him out of terrible necessities of their own."

Baldwin then unpacks the identity as a site of negotiation—as a racist, psychological projection and as an emblem of whiteness itself:

It is the American Republic—repeat, the American Republic—which created something which they call a "[n-word]." They created it out of necessities of their own. The nature of the crisis is that I am not a "[n-word]"—I never was. I am a man. The question with which the country is confronted is this: Why do you need a "[n-word]" in the first

---

* In this book, I cite the work of Elizabeth Stordeur Pryor, a Black historian, and James Baldwin, a Black writer and one of America's greatest public intellectuals. Both include the explicit, racist word in their texts—the potency of Baldwin's use, in particular, is performative, because by deconstructing the word's etymology, he projects its dehumanizing function onto the creator of that word. I, however, as a white person, have chosen to substitute it with "the n-word." Doing so, I acknowledge, both mitigates the affective power of their respective points and results in me, again, a white person, changing their language, which is its own kind of erasure of Black voices. But because I am quoting their words in my book, I have chosen not to repeat that word in order not to offend or harm my readers.

place, and what are you going to do about him now that he's moved out of his place? Because I am not what you said I was. And if my place, as it turns out, is not my place, then you are not what you said you were, and where's your place? There has never been in this country a Negro problem. I have never been upset by the fact that I have a broad nose, big lips, and kinky hair. *You* got upset. And now you must ask yourself why. I, for example, do not bring down property values when I move in. You bring them down when you move out.

If you watch video footage of Baldwin, you'll notice his full-bodied rejection of this identity when he speaks about it. He refuses the box, refuses to be shackled to its meaning, and refuses to become what white supremacist society demands him to be. And, in this deft sidestepping, he exposes all sides of the box, reveals its artifice, and shows how the identity was a necessary invention for people to be able to claim white identity and therefore their superiority based on the color of their skin. What Baldwin sought was accountability. He wanted white people to acknowledge that this identity was their own creation—because only by holding themselves accountable for this creation *and its repercussions* can they liberate not just Black people but also themselves from the harmful, supremacist binary of this linguistic construction.

Differentiation is not discrimination, of course, but it is—and certainly has been—a conduit for it. Here, I think of Ta-Nehisi Coates's concise explanation of the causality between race and racism in the United States: "American notions of race are the product of racism, not the other way around." White supremacy is achieved by codifying race in the law, the sciences, and culture. White supremacy operates by discriminating against difference, which is why it utilizes identities to establish and fix its hierarchy, segmenting people by caste, race, class, gender, sexuality, ability, and citizenship status. It is invested in maintaining the boundaries of those categories—the tighter the box, the less porous the identity. Without fixed and impermeable categories based on the meanings ascribed to those categories, the system would collapse. And so white supremacy polices identities to maintain its power *precisely because* identities—as social constructions and sites of negotiation—are porous and permeable.

Historian Elizabeth Stordeur Pryor has examined how the increasing freedom of African Americans in the northern states after the Civil War correlated with the proliferation of the n-word as a kind of verbal manifestation of the white backlash to Black freedom. The force of the n-word, she wrote in an essay on the word's etymology, exacted lacerating and intimidating effects intended to limit Black people's physical, spiritual, and economic mobility:

> Going out in public meant confronting the verbal assault "[n-word]." This single word—[n-word]—captured the magnitude of anti-Black feeling and was unleashed upon free people as they moved through urban space, rode public vehicles, and even ventured abroad. . . . The ubiquity of the word [n-word] illuminates the limits of their freedom. . . . As African Americans became free in the North . . . [n-word] latched on like a shackle. White Americans of all classes and ages hissed out the word, branding free Black people as foul smelling, unproductive, licentious, and unfit for self-rule. . . . Most significantly, the word [n-word] became a slur in conversation with Black social aspiration. To prevent such freedom of mobility, [n-word] emerged as a weapon of racial containment, a barometer against which to measure the increasingly rigid boundaries of whiteness and a mechanism used to police and cleanse public space.

Pryor's account shows how the proliferation of this word "as a weapon of racial containment" occurred simultaneously and in response to Black freedom. That identities are leaky containers, furthermore, explains the n-word's proliferation, as if repeating the word over and over again seals the cracks, functions to make the identity real and true. This effort points to the lie of identity—identities are not fixed, or certain, or biological, or true. And *this* is why they are so highly policed. Because their permeability means we have the power to push back against them, eradicate them from discourse, and appropriate and redefine them.

Coincidentally, it is also because identities are permeable that generations of immigrants have been able to claim white identity. Baldwin's reflections on the work people do to claim whiteness, largely in the language of social uplift made possible by colorism, often makes me think of my own Italian family's assumption of whiteness. My father was born in 1957, not long after my grandparents—from adjacent villages in Calabria (aka the toe of the boot)—arrived on Ellis Island (at different times; my grandmother arrived earlier than my grandfather). Not unlike many first-generation Americans, my father's first language was not English. In post–World War II America, his language marked his inferiority, his otherness, and, given that Italy had just been in a fascist, Axis alliance with Germany, his evilness. Consequently, he was mercilessly bullied and beaten up by other children in the South Jersey town the family settled in. "Get back on the boat and go home" was a daily assault.

By the time I was born, in 1980, my father had disavowed his language and his culture. He refused to speak Italian with me or to teach me anything about Italy. As a child, I remember watching my grandparents yell at him for his refusal to speak Italian, which, to them, amounted to a familial rejection. His dissociation with his ethnicity, it seems, initially was necessary for his safety and survival. Over time, his actions arguably reflected his choice to embrace whiteness—a choice available to him because of the lightness of his skin color—and become American. "The Italian immigrant arriving from Italy . . . makes a great point of not speaking Italian," Baldwin noted, "because he's going to become an American." And the choice of whiteness, Baldwin added, is "a moral one" because it functions to reinforce, through complicity and acquiescence, America's white supremacist society. Assimilation is so deeply coveted by the ideological right because it is the process of consumption by subsuming foreign "otherness" into the status quo to preserve the status quo.

What is shortchanged in this fixation on identity is the richness and complexity and messiness of our humanity, which no box can contain.

Perhaps having dozens of gender identity options to choose from on social media platforms is a sign of a gender revolution as well as a cultural symptom of late-stage capitalism, where we have been conditioned to categorize and reduce even the most personal and private aspects of our lives into consumable brands—these social media companies, remember, are businesses with profit motives for offering us "free" platforms from which they can sell our personal data. While the creation of more and more gender identities can feel liberatory by allowing us to choose more precise language to represent our authentic selves, it also reflects our social, even supremacist, desire to define, pin down—and, consequently, limit—our humanity.

Our lives are more abundant than can ever be represented by any identity. While identities help to anchor us in social meaning and build communities, they also run the risk of essentializing who we are into a stereotype or a commodity. And I'm not sure which is worse—living without a sense of self or being scripted into a role to which we haven't consented. Marginalized people lose the most in this scenario, as they rarely are given the opportunity to define themselves and share their own stories.

Relatedly, opting out of socially acceptable identities is a choice situated by one's privilege. For many people there is often too high a risk to make choices that allow them to live their lives openly and authentically. In many nations around the world, for example, it is still illegal to be gay, queer, and/or transgender; in some countries, it is even punishable by death. When encumbered by such life-threatening risks, self-creation is restrained by the need for self-preservation.

THE BATTLEGROUND OF *WOMAN*

The identity of *woman* has been a site of endless policing and regulation, because the gender binary—the organizational principle keeping the patriarchy in power—is imperiled without a fixed definition of it. This policing has materialized in debates about who is a "real" woman, and such debates are not new; variations have emerged in battlegrounds differentiated only by their players. Feminists, lesbians, queer women, masculine-presenting women, and trans women all have been accused of not being real women at various and often intersecting points in time. These women have faced scrutiny and persecution for refusing to conform to the gender roles and behaviors that men have assigned to them—ways that men need them to be so men can feel like men. We have heard or read stories about these women: They are the ones who have sought knowledge, who have been outspoken or disobedient, who have formed their primary relationships with other women, or whose bodies subverted men's demands for what a female body should look like and, therefore, have threatened men's sense of masculinity. These are the women who have, for one reason or another, broken man's mold of an acceptable woman. They refused the con of the gender binary and all its misogynistic strictures.

The categorical confinement of *woman*, consequently, has afforded women little space and even less mobility to determine their own lives. The centuries of social conditioning that have indoctrinated the belief that women are inferior to men have produced a scarcity mindset in women: the breadcrumb thinking that women should cherish what the patriarchal authority figure (God, father, husband) has graciously bestowed upon them, which results in a fierce possessiveness that they translate into the source of their power. (Feminists, of course, established an entire political agenda from this second-sex position.)

This scarcity mindset plagues the identity of *woman* and has resulted in the belligerent patrolling of its fictitious borders by some very strange bedfellows. Men first took up the defense of *woman* to reinforce the gender binary—again, without the gender binary, men's superiority has no structure upon which to stand. They accomplished this with their authority over the institutions of religion, government, law, education, and the medical sciences—where they crafted laws, scientific studies, and religious doctrines declaring the morality, legality, and biological facticity of the two genders.

In recent decades, cisgender women have joined men in patrolling the identity of *woman*. These puppets of the patriarchy have appropriated the very same gender essentialist argument that feminists have fought against for decades to make claims about who is and who is not a real woman. They are so blinded by their fear and hatred of trans women that they cannot see the hypocrisy of their own thinking or how policing *woman* effectively gives *them* less room to move in that identity box. The patriarchy has trained these women to patrol themselves, offloading the work of gender policing onto them and making them feel like superstars. Good girls with Daddy's approval. Pretty ingenious, you must admit.

Flying the flag of gender essentialism allows cisgender women to shield themselves from reflecting upon the constructedness of their own gender. By asserting that womanhood is biological, they conveniently sidestep examining the extent to which they have, deliberately or not, molded themselves to fit into the acceptable man-made box of *woman*. Essentialism permits ignorance and the abdication of responsibility for the choices these women have made in fashioning their own womanhood—from taking hormones like birth control pills to consuming diet pills, from body modification like cosmetic and plastic surgery to shaving their body hair, piercing their ears, and gluing synthetic fibers and animal fur to their eyelashes—to conform to men's expectations of a desirable and appropriate woman.

It's almost like, to return to an earlier idea, women are too afraid to look at themselves because they might see the man in the mirror. And to throw into question something believed to be the quintessential core of their being, the guiding light for understanding their place in the patriarchal world, would be to shatter the very ground of their reality. Gender essentialist thinking is rooted in a deep commitment to the gender binary, so without the gender binary—without *man* defining *woman* and *woman* defining *man*—they would have to reckon with what their own womanhood actually means. And it is, indeed, jarring for cisgender, heterosexual women to realize that the person they are and believe they *have made all by themselves* is, in fact, a product of the choices the patriarchy has laid out for them. (Yes, just like Andy's cerulean sweater in *The Devil Wears Prada*.) Again, individual choices are collective choices.

I wonder, then, if the hatred of trans women is really a projection of the fear cisgender women have of examining their agency in their self-creation, of the disgust they might feel when they become aware of their complicity in how they have created their womanhood. Well, really, I don't wonder—I believe this to be true. Because trans women are just trying to live their lives. Like, I don't wake up in the morning and think to myself, *OMG, I can't be a woman today because there is a trans woman in Philadelphia out there living her life!* I simply can't get over how fucking ridiculous this thinking is. Only if one harbors a scarcity mindset do they believe that trans women "steal" womanhood from cisgender women. A product of the patriarchal gender binary, this mindset dictates that cisgender women advocate the exclusion of trans women or any other female-, femme-, or feminine-identifying persons whose very existence threaten the *perceived* facticity of their gender.

It is because gender is socially constructed and socially conditioned that we've seen, time and again, the absolute failure of every attempt to lay claim to *woman* through biology or physiology. Sex, like gender, is much more complex than the male-female binary allows for—it is certainly much more complex than how it is assigned at birth, which is based on the very meticulous and not at all egregiously misogynistic science of <*checks notes*> what our junk looks like. (Countless medical documents and stories of intersex people have reported that if a newborn's junk doesn't fit the white supremacist patriarchal standard of so-called male or female parts, then that newborn's body is barbarically, surgically altered so that its junk looks like the sex the doctors have assigned to that baby.)

Forcing both sex and gender into binaries is dehumanizing and ignorant of the science proving that not all chromosomes are identical or manifest internally (organs) or externally (characteristics) in the same ways. The essentialist argument for the biological facticity of *woman* is further undermined by the fact that not all cisgender women—especially prepubescent girls, menopausal, and post-menopausal women—menstruate, and not all cisgender women have a uterus or breasts.

For centuries, certain body parts—breasts, vulva, uterus, and vagina—have been sexualized, medicalized, and codified as female. We have been conditioned to interpret these body parts as female, or, at least, as a sign of femininity. But their meanings have been established by centuries of Western philosophy and religion determined to prove women to be irrational and unintelligent creatures—lesser than men in all ways—because of these body parts. Philosophers, doctors, and other male authorities would point to these parts as the cause, for instance, of women's "hysteria" and the reason why women were too incompetent to receive an education or to participate in civil society. Just take, as part of the long history of rendering woman as a mutilated male (thanks, Aristotle!), the notion of the "wandering womb"—the notion that wombs jauntily traveled around women's bodies and made them too emotional to be in charge of themselves. Men, of course, devised a solution to keep the wandering womb in place: Fuck it into submission. That's right, the argument was that man's virile penis was the most effective tool to hammer this itinerant, unruly creature into submission.

To colonize *woman*, gender essentialists draw a line in the proverbial sand, carving a boundary that separates "us" from "them," real women from fake women. But the line always shifts—because the distinctions and definitions are arbitrary and artificial. This is nothing less than tribalism proclaimed as feminism. Often, we witness transphobic attacks launched through a power play of victimhood. From a scarcity mindset, these transphobic people argue that the history of cisgender women's discrimination at the hands of the patriarchy is being silenced and erased by trans women's existence. (A cognitive dissonance operates here, since these women complain they are being silenced and erased while appearing on nationwide talk shows and broadcasting their feelings to their thousands of social media followers.)

Everyone, including me, has to unlearn this essentialist thinking if we are to liberate *woman* from the patriarchy. Just a decade ago, I still clung to the belief that sex was biological. Over time, I realized I had held on to this belief because I resented my period—about every three weeks, the burning pain of my ovaries, the numbness from my gut through my thighs, the exhaustion, and the intensity of how much and how heavily I bled for nearly a week. I hated it. I still do. But back then I felt it was *unfair* that I had to experience this pain, which I believed was constitutive of womanhood. I admit that I believed *woman* was defined by this pain, and that, if you didn't experience it, you were not a woman at all.

I am not proud of this past, but I share it to show that everyone—perhaps save the younger generations—has been deeply conditioned by the patriarchy, and that its principle architecture of the gender binary has been etched into our minds. And, true to how freedom is realized, what liberated me from this transphobic thinking and my own internalized misogyny was other people. Gracious and patient queer and trans folks who didn't set out to correct my thinking had conversations with me and asked me questions and encouraged me to think critically about sex and gender identity—and myself. I had been so angry and defensive about my pain that I refused to acknowledge that I was wrong to assume all women experienced this pain, and that this pain was somehow the defining feature of womanhood. In addition, I reflected on the extent to which my scarcity mindset affected my understanding of being a woman—why was it so negative and based in pain? And why did I feel offended by the idea that *woman* could represent more than one way of being? That *woman* was not a monolith? Why did I think that someone whose experience of womanhood was different from mine somehow undermined or negated my experience of it? The sum of my internal work of self-reflection and my discussions with other people helped me to unlearn this reductive thinking, which, in turn, helped me feel less resentful of my gender identity.

This internal work of building a critical consciousness is foundational to a feminism that champions the freedom to become or not become a woman according to one's desires. Over the years, my internal work has led me to wonder what exactly is being held on to when one clings so desperately to the identity of *woman*. Historically, the identity has been defined by its oppression, aligned with victimhood, inhumanity, and inferiority to man. I mean, I even confessed to defining womanhood by pain—how depressing is that? I also find the anger directed at the inclusive language of *people*—as in *pregnant people*, which simply indicates the obvious fact that anyone with a functional uterus can carry a pregnancy to term—quite baffling. No one is denying that abortion has been so fiercely opposed by the patriarchy because women needed it. How does the language of *person* erase the identity of *woman*? As if exclusion or erasure inheres in the act of inclusion. As if one could not be a woman and a person at the same time. Wouldn't that be precisely the human dignity that women have fought for, for generations? To be respected as *people*?

And isn't it a bit ironic that women decrying the use of *people* and gender-neutral pronouns are some of the very same women who, just decades ago, fought to make professional identities gender neutral? That we should say *firefighter*, not *fireman*, and *mail carrier*, not *mailman*, to account for the women who do these jobs?

In the context of feminist politics, women have been conditioned to fall in love with their oppression as a symbol of moral fortitude and righteousness not distinct from the sentiment Elizabeth Cady Stanton championed more than a century ago. It bespeaks that strange martyrdom that Christianity demands of women. The sentiment is also expressed in oft-heard phrases like *Women persist!* and *Women can do it backwards and in heels!* This is the standpoint from which equality feminism operates, the politics of which necessitates chaining *woman* to the gender binary to locate and build its credibility and currency. The refusal to liberate *woman* from the gender binary is in part a refusal to recognize the gender oppression of others—the thinking being that this recognition would erase women's historical oppression and thus their political power. The equality mindset, therefore, enforces a zero-sum game of womanhood.

However, we can begin to change our thinking if we understand that our freedom includes the freedom to choose and express one's gender. Guided by freedom, women—cis, trans, and anyone within the social constellation of genders—share the same goals: to have the freedom to create authentic lives and control our own bodies; to recognize and respect the differences among us; to be able to create ourselves as the women we want to become (and not who men tell us to be); and to understand that this becoming is not a finite, singular act but a process that continues throughout one's life.

My intention is to assert the mutual interdependence of our respective freedoms, while respecting the dignity of people's self-creation. My freedom is bound to yours, and yours to mine. We can only liberate *woman* by allowing each and every one of us to determine our own path of womanhood—if we want it—which means we also have to let go of the social expectations and policing and cultural scripts tied to the gender binary. People have the freedom to create and express themselves within and without gender identities. Gender is a choice that can change over time to better represent the person we are becoming. My freedom to choose my own gender identity acquires meaning socially, but its sociality does not pose a threat to another person's gender. Breaking free of the socially conditioned scarcity mindset of *woman*, we can realize that women—*all* women—can mutually coexist without jeopardizing anyone's identity.

FREE *WOMAN*

If we each have the potential to become our own version of *woman*, then what meaning does the word really have? What is an identity without an essence? Without a clear, unquestionable definition? If we liberate *woman* from the gender binary, then what is a woman?

It is here that we must remember that our bodies—our flesh and blood, fat and muscle and organs—all exist independently of identity, the language given to what is perceived and experienced. Bodies are material; identities are immaterial. Where the confusion, or debate, about *woman* lies is in mistaking cultural signification for biological fact.

It's not the body part that makes a woman. It's not her oppression or pain. It's not her desire or ability to become a mother, or her choice to be a good wife to a man.

The answer to *What is a woman?* isn't found in biology but sociology—the study of social relationships. The identity of *woman* has been traditionally defined as a complementary relation to *man*. As countless male storytellers, thinkers, and authorities have asserted, women are the lesser sex, "the second sex," to quote the German philosopher Arthur Schopenhauer, "inferior in every respect to the first." (Simone de Beauvoir borrowed this line for her book's title.) The identity, by definition, has been attributed no autonomy or independence—the gender binary has established women's dependence on men. *Woman* as *not man.* A woman has been reduced to her biological reproductive abilities *as determined by the needs of men.* This distinction underlies the power dynamic that reinforces women's dependence upon and subservience to men. This system of belief that this relation produces is known as heterosexism.

This definition of *woman* has also been deeply conditioned by racism. That gender is a racial construct is something Black women in the nineteenth and early twentieth centuries like Anna Julia Cooper, Frances E. W. Harper, and Sojourner Truth knew and shared in their lectures and writings. They analyzed how Black women were excluded from discussions about sexism and women's rights, and how Black women's dehumanization was in part a product of the denial of their womanhood. "The colored woman of to-day occupies . . . a unique position in this country," Cooper wrote in "The Status of Women." "She is confronted by both a woman question and a race problem." Perceived whiteness conferred one's femininity and status as a woman. A rejoinder to this racialization of gender is most famously epitomized by Sojourner Truth's "Ain't I a Woman?" speech, which she delivered at the 1851 Ohio

Women's Rights Convention.* Her point was that she was simultaneously Black and a woman, and that her Blackness did not disqualify her
womanhood.

Beauvoir's *The Second Sex*, first published in French in 1949, ushered
in a broader societal examination of how beliefs about gender became
accepted as truths. A few decades later, in *Ain't I a Woman*, bell hooks
analyzed why, out of necessity, Black women and men adopted white
gender roles. Yet, she wrote of the consequences, when Black women
"accept[ed] the female role as defined by the patriarchy, [they] embraced
and upheld an oppressive sexist social order and became (along with
their white sisters) both accomplices in the crimes perpetrated against
women and the victims of those crimes." This social conditioning recalls
Beauvoir's "one is not born, but rather becomes a woman." It's a seismic
shift in thinking to recognize that what has long been considered truth
is, in fact, a very elaborate, intentional design to sanction the categorical
oppression of women and people of color.

In recent decades, the definition of *woman* has expanded to
encompass both gender *identity* and gender *expression*—here, a body's
expression of femininity or femaleness. Gender expression—a person's
movement, mannerisms, posture, and gait, in addition to their style or
fashion sensibility, including how they sculpt or design their physical
bodies—is what is perceived and evaluated by the outside world. How
one identifies and how one expresses oneself, furthermore, do not necessarily align with each other. (Masculine-presenting women as case in
point.)

What happens if we fully break free of the gender binary? How can
we define *woman* not as the opposite of *man*, but as an identity situated
within a broader spectrum of gender identities?

---

* Truth, in fact, never said the words "Ain't I a woman?" As researched and first proven by Princeton
University professor Nell Irvin Painter and later documented by the Sojourner Truth Project, Truth
spoke in a "distinct New York State low-Dutch accent." Twelve years after Truth delivered her speech,
Frances Dana Barker Gage reinterpreted Truth's speech in a racist interpretation of a Black southern
accent and had it published in 1863. According to the Sojourner Truth Project, Gage admitted having "given a faint sketch" to Truth's original speech.

And, if we free *woman*, what can she become?

She can become anything she wants to within her situatedness.

What makes a woman?

A woman makes a woman.

It's really as simple as that.

By breaking free from the artificial confines of the gender binary, by rewriting the stories and scripts that established, as French feminist Monique Wittig argued, the political concepts of *man* and *woman* as ontological truths, we can free ourselves from the oppressive structures and narratives that have conditioned us to devalue, discount, and discredit women. Through this liberation—by demonstrating that the identity is not a monolith but capacious—we can reinvent *woman*. From a freedom mindset, then, we understand *woman* as nonbinary.

Feminism is a "liberation struggle," hooks said. "The oppressed struggle in language to recover ourselves—to rewrite, to reconcile, to renew." And what better way to liberate *woman* than by blowing up the box it was put into, such that *woman* no longer represents one way of living, but contains multitudes?

As Patricia Hill Collins said, "Identity is not the goal but rather the point of departure in the process of self-definition." It is a launchpad for our self-creation.

CREATING OURSELVES TOGETHER

Within the white supremacist cis-heteropatriarchy, identity has been a site of negotiation—a power struggle. But what would happen if we reconceived identity as a site of mutual creative self-expression, even cocreation, that took us beyond the limitations of identity itself?

We might think of this cocreation using University of Wisconsin-Madison professor Ramzi Fawaz's terms of "shapeshifting," or "taking shape," to understand the process of self-creation within collective society. "This is the freedom to become something else in concert with others," he explained in *Queer Forms*, because "we grant one another the opportunity to appear and be perceived as an evolving form, not only to claim our visibility, but to be better understood in all our dimensions." Shapeshifting frees us from the restraints of identity, but, he emphasized, it does not mean "dissolv[ing] into pure fluidity." Here is the critical difference: Identities are launchpads for expressing ourselves in the world. They have social and political meaning we rely on to build communities. Yet the language of fluidity suggests our bodies do not matter, when, in fact, they do. We are not fluid because our bodies are made of *matter.* We live in these material bodies, and so who we choose to become in the world is *materially* situated by them. To disregard this fact, furthermore, is to also ignore the historical and economic conditions of these bodies.

The freedom of self-creation is conditioned by other people. "We can only be who we are because of the others in our lives," Beauvoir maintained. Parents, teachers, friends, relatives, mentors, even strangers on the subway—the list is endless when it comes to who guides us, educates us, inspires and stimulates us. The affects can be positive (*I want to be just like her!*) or negative (*Oh my god! I do NOT want to be like her!*) or somewhere in between. Importantly, creation entails not moral but ethical judgments, as the choices we make are acts of discrimination defined by our tastes and preferences.

There are many people in my own life who have clearly influenced the paths I have taken, my values and ethics, my dreams and aspirations. Similar to many kids, I dreamed of being president of the United States, and—my depression be damned—set out in college to realize this dream. But after my political experience interning on Capitol Hill and working for Al Gore's 2000 presidential campaign as the Massachusetts state student coordinator, I knew a career in politics was not for me. First of all, at the turn of the twenty-first century, it was still uncouth for a female US senator to wear pants (an unwritten rule) or abstain from wearing pearls—and the last thing I ever wanted to do was wear a dress or pearls. (There were even Senate doorkeepers who could refuse people entry to the Senate floor if they were deemed to be dressed inappropriately. Need we mention that—in 2023—Missouri's

House of Representatives voted to restrict women's attire in the House chamber by requiring them to wear jackets to cover their arms and chests.) The only woman in national politics who felt relatable to me at the time was Hillary Clinton, because she refused traditional gender roles (with apologies to those chocolate chip cookies) and specifically refused to be subservient or to play dumb. She was unapologetic about her intelligence, which was stunningly refreshing. She bucked the traditional role of First Lady, especially when she ran for the US Senate. When I was an intern at the Democratic Senatorial Campaign Committee in 2000, what I distinctly remember was how much the Democratic Party hated her—it wasn't only the Republicans who painted her as a power-hungry Lady Macbeth. From my political experience, I thought that to be a credible political candidate in the future I would have to sell myself (fundraise); I would have to marry a man and have children; and, most important of all, I would have to become religious—more precisely, a Christian. But I could not fathom making any of these choices. I did not want that life. So I entered my senior year of college in crisis, with zero postgraduation plans and an uncertain future.

Fortunately, the first day of the fall semester, I decided on a whim to sit in on a Shakespeare lecture delivered by a very popular professor. I had never seen a woman like her before. She was magnificent—tall, strong, erudite, and passionate. She wore a perfectly tailored black pantsuit. She commanded the stage and delivered a masterpiece performance with blazing confidence. At the end of the lecture, the audience in the theater, full of students and locals, gave her a standing ovation—what I soon came to understand was just a regular occurrence for her. Prior to that semester, I had taken only one course taught by a female professor, and she was shy and deferential, and seemed to have disappeared from the government department after giving birth to her first child. She was my image of what a female professor looked like. That is, until that Shakespeare lecture. Completely enchanted by the end of the hour, I had a new vision for the type of woman I wanted to become.

Just as we fashion ourselves in relation to positive role models, we also create ourselves through, or in response to, negative relations. I think one reason I found lesbianism so attractive is that I didn't want to replicate the lives of the women I grew up around in the 1980s. I didn't want to be trapped at home as a caretaker to a husband or children. I saw that standard lifestyle as deeply stifling and deadening. Lesbianism felt like freedom to me, an openness to explore myself and my desires.

This pathway, of course, is specific to me. I fully understand that others find motherhood empowering and fulfilling. Toni Morrison spoke about how "motherhood is freedom" for Black women, given the history of chattel slavery, in which Black women were denied the experience of motherhood and of having a family, as their children were taken from them and sold into slavery. (The state still takes away their children, who are either brutally murdered by the police or, under state surveillance, taken by Child Protective Services.) But in my own life, one reason I find lesbianism desirable is because I can have sex free from the specter of accidental pregnancy, which was my greatest fear as a teenage athlete trying to land a scholarship to escape my provincial hometown. I have never had to worry about birth control or the morning-after pill, or the harassment I'd face if I needed an abortion. (To be clear, I'm referring to my chosen sex life and not situations of sexual assault or rape—these are acts of violence; they are not sex.) My lesbianism has ensured that my body is mine.

Yet throughout my twenties I refused to call myself a lesbian. The term felt old, dowdy, and depressing. I was in academia at the time, where it was much cooler and much more chic to be *queer*. Queer was radical. It was edgy. It was a (political) statement. Queer meant freedom from the strictures of heteronormative identities and from their expectations. It meant *Fuck you, I don't want to be a part of your society anyway!* Everyone, at least in the humanities, seemed to call themselves queer—even the people in monogamous, heterosexual marriages with multiple children. These folks were adamantly queer.

People, of course, can choose their own identities, which can change as people evolve. In a 2012 interview with *Rorotoko*, Lauren Berlant said honoring the process of life means we should rethink stagnant identity categories and instead understand sexuality as a "process rather than a foreclosing identity"—a narrative, not an ontological, event. Our self-creation, too, is not a one-time event or declaration (such as a coming out). It is a lifelong cultivation of who we are and are becoming as we accumulate knowledge and experience over time. As such, sexuality is accurately conceived not as a fixed identity but as Fawaz's "taking shape," or as Berlant's notion of a "history of patterning or style [of attachment] that develops over time, in relation to law, norms, and the accidents and incidents of ordinary life."

Because our lives are uniquely situated, how sexuality takes shape is different for everyone. But for me, two things happened that made me reconsider my sexual identity. First, *The L Word.* That powerful, smart, and funny femme women (yes, sorry to the butches) who identified as lesbian appeared on my TV screen for six seasons, beginning in the mid-aughts, offered the type of visibility that allowed me to reimagine who I was, who I could see myself becoming, and how I identified. Beyond one or two characters dealing with internalized homophobia, none of the characters were ashamed of their sexuality, their desires, or their pleasure. They were defiant and built their own Los Angeles Lesbian Bubble. This representation changed my perception of lesbians. *The L Word* showed me that lesbians did not necessarily wallow in the well of loneliness but were living proudly and authentically. And I found this attractive.

The second occurred just slightly later, in the early 2010s, when I was living-laughing-loving in Brooklyn, the land of queer-women abundance, in my early thirties. While dating, I began to notice the frequency of misogynistic behavior by queer women directed at femme and feminine women, who were criticized for conforming to gender stereotypes. At the same time, I kept meeting other queer people who described their identity in terms of the negative—they were queer because they were *not* women; they were queer because they were *against* marriage. This negative construction made *queer* feel reductive and reactionary to me, which I found disconcerting because my queerness had felt so pleasurable and joyful. *Queer* soon felt like an identity not existing in freedom but one situated in an antagonistic binary with heteronormativity, locking it into the same subjugated and inferior position as *woman* was in the gender binary.

I wanted the identities I chose to be positive, based in dignity, joy, pleasure, and love. Light and not oppressive. Audre Lorde defined *lesbian* as "love between women [that] is open and possible." And I wanted my life to feel that way, too—open and possible. So, I stopped identifying as *queer* and started identifying as *lesbian*. This identity, like all identities, is more than just sexual; it is also political: To love women meant to put women first and to situate myself first and foremost in relation to them. How I have lived my lesbianism, of course, is idiosyncratic to me. For example, if I watch porn, it will only and ever be gay male porn. And I have no problem admitting that men are attractive—just because I think some men are pretty doesn't mean I want to fuck them. Also, I think flannel is hideous, and I never, ever, want to go camping. Does this make me a bad lesbian? I just think it means I live my lesbianism on my own terms.

A significant factor in choosing to become a lesbian was also a matter of timing and time. My experiences with other women, of loving their bodies, taught me how to love my own body. A part of my identity work is to define what *lesbian* means to me, and that when I say I love women, I mean all women, cis and trans and beyond. At the same time, I periodically enjoy using the word *queer* in its more traditional sense of strangeness, of not quite fitting in—a feeling I have always had that is not distinctly related to my sexuality but rather to a deeper feeling of being untimely. My queerness, then, is rooted in an uncanny feeling of simultaneously existing in two different worlds. Admittedly, the friction produced from this feeling has more often than not made me feel frustration above all else. While I understand *queer* signifies liberation for some people, I've experienced my queerness most acutely as a punctuated strangeness. It is something I have at times happily assumed as part of my idiosyncratic perspective on things, while at other times it has imbued me with terrible frustration.

Just as there are reasons I stopped identifying—at least in terms of my sexuality—as queer, there are plenty of reasons why people have stopped identifying as lesbian. Increasingly in recent years, an extremely vocal cohort of transphobic lesbians have aligned themselves with the white supremacist patriarchy and taken to the media to attack trans women. These lesbians also have discriminated against trans women in queer community spaces. It is no wonder why, especially for younger generations, *lesbian* has felt exclusionary and antiquated, and it is perfectly understandable to me why someone would reject the label. I believe it is my responsibility, as someone who has chosen this identity, to be vocal about how I define *lesbian*, rather than sitting in silence and allowing the identity to be co-opted and maligned by transphobic bigots.

MY JOURNEY IN WOMANHOOD

I am part of a very long line of lesbians who were called tomboys as children. *Tomboy* is a slightly deviant yet largely socially acceptable form of girlhood because it's implied that tomboys, having appropriated their own version of boyhood, have no sexual desire for boys (and therefore have no sexual desire at all, especially not for other girls)—to the relief of parents everywhere. Around the age of nine, however, I became very upset that I could no longer play outside without a shirt on. I was angry I couldn't join boys' sports teams, even though I was as good as, if not better than, most of them. And I was furious I wasn't allowed to work in my grandfather's construction company—"Girls don't pour concrete," my father told me. (I realized after the fact that part of my father's reasoning was that he didn't want me, then just entering my teenage years, to be harassed by the male workers.)

When I was a child, I was terrified of puberty. As a competitive swimmer aspiring to become an Olympian, I remember watching in horror when my female teammates began growing breasts and hips. I did not want to be weighed down by tits in the water. I wanted a thin, sinewy torso like the guys on my team. And I did not want to become a woman. My changing body made me feel like I was sliding into a future life—of a husband, children, and domesticity—that was, to me, no life at all.

I can recall the internal struggle to fight this slide into womanhood throughout my childhood and teenage years. I didn't see myself as having a gender or a sexuality because I had fashioned myself to be an athlete. That was my identity. I trained and conditioned and ate and slept to become an athlete. A machine of muscles, a fortress against weakness, impregnable to distractive emotions. Perhaps this is another reason why I find the paranoia about trans and nonbinary people playing sports absurd. Competitive athletes inculcate a vision of themselves as champion athletes. They train for hundreds of hours, for years, to develop the endurance, power, and technique they need to perform at the top of their field. When a swimmer dives into the water, they aren't thinking, *How do I swim like a girl?* They're thinking about their breath or a technique they need to keep in mind to beat the clock for their personal best—when I swam butterfly, I kept my focus on my hips. Likewise, when I played tennis, I never once thought, *How do I serve this ball like a girl?* If anything, my thoughts amounted to *Hit the fucking shit out of this ball!* Despite being forced into a traditional gender identity, no one *competes* as a gender. Serena Williams didn't become the GOAT by thinking, *Well, I better be nice and hit this ball gently, like a good girl should.*

Consequently, when I realized that my career as an athlete was over, during my freshman year in college, I became incredibly depressed. I had always been an athlete, so without sports—without practices and competitions to structure my days—I had no idea who I was or, frankly, how to live. It was during this time that my identity crisis, connected to my gender dysphoria, bloomed into an eating disorder. This was a way I could control my body and prevent it from becoming a woman. I refused to eat and worked out religiously, and, after a few months, my hair started falling out and my monthly periods stopped.

Upon reflection, perhaps I was trying to become a woman—the ideal, thin woman that society told me I was supposed to be. I've never felt "at home" in my body, and, considering the sexist body ideals forced onto women, I doubt most women have felt at home in their bodies. In fact, I felt the most alienated from my body when it was arguably at its most feminine ideal.

When I lost a lot of weight and stopped menstruating, my track coach sent me to the doctor, and I was put on hormones (three continuous rounds of progesterone). This occurred around the time that my eating disorder morphed into bulimia. It was as if I tried the opposite strategy in order to obliterate myself, eating and eating until I could not feel myself. I wanted people to stop looking at me, and they did—for a little while, anyway.

My body expanded in new ways, which I hid in sweatpants and sweatshirts. Most uncomfortable of all was how my breasts swelled. Even when they were small, I had always hated them. But when I gained all that hormone-induced weight, compounded by my bingeing, I had to strap them down in tight sports bras and navigate my movement around them. In pain and depressed, I sought a breast reduction, and after months of pleading with my mother's health insurance company (as a twenty-one-year-old, I was thankfully still covered under her plan), I was able to get the surgery covered by insurance.

The morning of my surgery, I told my surgeon to "take them all off." I didn't want breasts. I never had. And I finally had the opportunity to be rid of them forever.

"I can't do that," the surgeon responded, as he drew the circles of my new breasts on my body with a thick blue marker. "You need breasts—you're a girl."

You're a girl.

This old shibboleth has been patronizingly inflicted on generations of children. Usually, upon hearing it, I'd rage and then try to find a way to circumnavigate the barrier, often by changing direction or finding an alternative or developing a new goal. (Or, when I was a child, outright defying my parents and other adults.) But this particular experience was devastating because I was so close to being free of the things I couldn't get rid of myself. Instead of helping me, patriarchal authority told me I had to have them. Because I was a girl.

Later in my twenties, I realized that I had spent my youth in constant combat with the box of acceptable girlhood (and, later, womanhood) I was supposed to fit into. Not only had I not wanted to be forced into the physical restraints of womanhood, but I did not want to marry a man or have children—which is what womanhood had meant. That is, becoming a woman felt impossible because I could not separate being a woman from men or from heterosexuality.

It wasn't until I worked as that Shakespearean's research assistant—saw her and her female partner, also brilliant and strong, living openly and having fulfilling lives and successful careers—that I witnessed what life outside of heterosexuality could look like. And it wasn't until a year after that, when I had kissed a woman for the first time, that I was able to see myself differently. I was finally starting to approach myself with openness and acceptance.

These experiences, among others, helped me see the connections between gender and sexuality. In *Females*, Andrea Long Chu wrote that gender and sexuality have a complementary relation: "If sexual orientation is basically the social expression of one's own sexuality, then gender is basically the social expression of someone *else*'s sexuality. In the former case, one takes an object; in the latter, one *is* an object." And, it turns out, I find immense pleasure in being the object of women's desire. The sexual dynamic at play in this complementary relation is one I think about in terms of what a friend (okay, an ex) of mine called "BuFu": the Be You / Fuck You paradigm. Do I want to be you? Do I want to fuck you? Maybe it's both? I don't think this dynamic is exclusive to homosexual tendencies—I mean, admit it, my straight lady friends: When you admire the six-pack abs you see on guys, it's not only because you want to lick them like you're playing a xylophone with your tongue, right? Some of you would kind of love a ripped torso, too.

My experience of gender throughout the more than four decades I have been alive has proven to me that identity is socially constructed. I have negotiated my various identities between my own desires and patriarchal impositions, and I have experienced my gender and sexuality as cocreations with other women and through being inspired by them.

I have never been one kind of woman. Admittedly, I have not always been or wanted to be a woman. When I was a girl, I did not want to become a woman. When I was anorexic, I was seen as the ideal woman, even though I despised myself. When I was fat, I was an invisible woman but a visible spectacle. And when, at the height of what I call my queer years, in my late twenties, I shed thirty pounds, got some tattoos, grew out my body hair, and shaved my head, I was called "it" by children in my neighborhood.

My identity as a woman has and will continue to be a journey (especially as I have hit perimenopause and my body is changing, seemingly daily, in unimagined ways). I have reached a point in my life where forty-plus years of experience has taught me that freedom is found in self-creation, particularly, in this patriarchal world, in how I create and express my womanhood. It is liberating to think about our lives not as static or stuck inside identity boxes but as narrative journeys of our becoming. What if we changed how we thought about ourselves? Unlocked ourselves from the identity boxes we were told to get into? What feelings of freedom and power might come from this reimagination?

ACCOUNTABILITY IN MUTUAL CREATION

The freedom practice of self-creation is anchored in accountability—not only for the choices we make but in respecting the self-creation of others. Our lives are interconnected, our freedoms interdependent, and therefore our self-creation is fundamentally mutual creation, in terms of both communication and expression. Mutual creation represents how our self-creation emerges from personal encounters and relationships, cultural influences and inspirations, and education and experiences, as well as from the societal forces of the white supremacist cis-heteropatriarchy.

Self-creation is collaboratively produced; individual choices and actions are influenced and situated by the collective. Our self-creation only becomes meaningful in society.

Self-creation, furthermore, is not just about cultivating a personal ethics. As mutual creation, it necessitates a political commitment to freedom, which demands accountability. We must understand and account for how identities work socially and how they operate within the white supremacist cis-heteropatriarchy. In our society, no two identities are created equal, exist equally, or are bestowed with the same amount of political or social power. Our identities, rather, are hierarchized according to the structure of the patriarchy. And within this hierarchy, our privilege and power relate to how we are *perceived*.

This was precisely philosopher Kwame Anthony Appiah's point in his response, in a 2020 Ethicist column in the *New York Times Magazine*, to a Jewish American man who asked if it was ethical if he chose not to identify as a white person. "Being white is not just a matter of identifying as white; it involves being treated as white, and that isn't up to you," Appiah wrote. "So, however you think of yourself, your whiteness is doing work in social life."

The social work of identities—the power and privilege they confer—is beyond our individual control because identities are *social* constructions that take shape within our specific white supremacist cis-heteropatriarchal society. Appiah elaborated:

> It is not up to us as individuals to determine the meaning of our racial terms. . . . What "white" means in America isn't up to each of us to decide on our own. To change those meanings, we'd have to work together to change practices. If you don't want to be white because you repudiate white supremacy or the racialization of public life, you first have to work alongside others to unmake an unjust social order.

The meaning of white identity, Appiah emphasized, is not up to this one man, or to any one person. Identity is language we use to describe ourselves, but its possession is beyond our individual grasp. Yet, because identities are socially constructed, Appiah noted, we do have the power to work together to change their meaning over time.

Because of the social work of identities, taking accountability for our self-creation means abstaining from choosing identities in bad faith—which is the opposite of authenticity. A choice made in bad faith is one in which a person deliberately refuses to acknowledge the social meanings and advantages of identities within a white supremacist cis-heteropatriarchy. Authenticity, for Beauvoir, is to practice freedom from one's own situatedness—not from the situatedness of others, as Appiah remarked.

Let me put this another way: You can choose any identity you want, but you cannot choose the power and privilege conferred by it. You can choose the identity but not the -*ism*.

So, sure, you can choose your race. But you in no way can choose your experience of racism. To be clear, we all experience racism; our society and its institutions are saturated by it. But we do not all experience racism equally. Those of us who are light skinned—white and white passing—are positively affected by racism. We benefit from how white supremacist institutions have accepted and supported light-skinned people based on skin color alone. The bad faith of light-skinned people—white people, no matter their ethnicity—who choose to be Black is that their choice ignores the privilege and power they have in our supremacist society. This bad-faith choice is a form of gaslighting—because we see them. Their whiteness is visible in the world.

White women produce further insult and harm when they appropriate racially marginalized identities for their professional advancement. We've seen several viral news stories about white women, specifically in academia, who built their careers on claims that they were Black or Latina or Native American—heritages later revealed to be false. For example, historian Jessica A. Krug outed herself (to preempt others from outing her) in a 2020 blog post on Medium, confessing: "I have eschewed my lived experience as a white Jewish child in suburban Kansas City under various assumed identities within a Blackness that I had no right to claim." Less than a week after publishing the post, she resigned from her tenured professorship at George Washington University.

This type of passing is what journalist Erin Aubry Kaplan has called "passe noir." Blackface has been documented for decades, Kaplan explained, but there is something specific going on when white women pretend to be women of color in the privileged space of academia. "No matter how woke or 'down' they are, white people who claim to be Black (or let us think they are) are not joining the cause so much as self-serving," she wrote in a 2020 *Los Angeles Times* article. "Their academic work would not be nearly as emotionally resonant if they presented it as white people. They would be seen as standing outside of it, and many white people desperately want in," she noted. This is an aspect of white supremacy, whereby "white interest in Black people can only be prurient or transactional."

It is unethical and inauthentic for white women—women who are perceived as white in society and who *because of this perception* benefit from whiteness—to deliberately appropriate Blackness for their economic gain, professional opportunity, and/or personal pleasure. Notoriously, Rachel Dolezal built an entire career not simply by identifying as Black but by laying claim to Black experiences she never had. Such inauthenticity is nothing less than white consumption of Black identity, whereby, as Ijeoma Oluo observed in *Mediocre*, white people "take what they want from other cultures in the name of love and respect, while distorting or discarding the remainder of that culture for their comfort."

Yes, the category of race is a construct, but it was constructed with the intention to systemize oppression. Nineteenth-century (pseudo)scientists used bodily attributes and phenotypes to classify people into races in order to justify racism. Several studies over the past two decades, including the Human Genome Project, have proven race is not biological or genetic. In fact, all humans are 99.9 percent genetically identical. Neither does race correlate with geographic ancestry (we see how phenotype, especially skin color, can vary even among our immediate biological relatives).

Race is not real, but racism is. A person's race is connected to not just their lived experience but also the lived experiences of generations past. According to writer Isabel Wilkerson, caste systems are "fixed assignments" based entirely on what people look like. Despite being a socially constructed system, she observed, caste "embeds into our bones an unconscious ranking of human characteristics and sets forth the rules, expectations, and stereotypes that have been used to justify brutalities against entire groups within our species. In the American caste system, the signal of rank is what we call race, the division of humans on the basis of their appearance. In America, race is the primary tool and the visible decoy, the front man, for caste."

At the same time, part of the power of whiteness, sociologist Tressie McMillan Cottom told us, is the very idea of its elasticity. This is also a product of how colorism works within our white supremacist society—a dark-skinned person cannot lay claim to whiteness as easily as a pale-skinned person can lay claim to Blackness. "Black people can rarely gatekeep the boundaries of blackness," Cottom observed. In her reading—and *read*—of Dolezal, she noted that this "is why the artist formerly known as a white woman Rachel Dolezal drove so many Black people mad. Dolezal had not only presented herself as a Black woman. She had not only adopted our hairstyles, our culture, and our struggles as her own. She had done so and there was nothing that Black people could do about it. Dolezal did not need to convince Black people that she was Black. She only had to convince white people."

Some people, including NBA legend Kareem Abdul-Jabbar in an opinion piece for *Time*, have expressed their appreciation for Dolezal for exemplifying the artificiality of race. Yet the reality of racism means that if a person is born into a family that for generations has benefited from whiteness, such that she herself is afforded all those privileges and opportunities granted to that race, then it is her responsibility to own that whiteness. Not cast it off or pretend like it doesn't exist. No. She must own it, which includes taking accountability for the injustices of whiteness that have been borne throughout history. Freedom is realized through a commitment to dismantling racism—it does not mean colonizing Blackness for profit or professional advantage or for social influence as a kind of performative allyship.

We are together responsible for creating the conditions to tear down society's oppressive hierarchies. A part of this responsibility, as Baldwin contended in "The White Problem," is acknowledging that identities are nothing but "invented realities." But this also means, because language is constructed by *us*, that there is a radical potential for their reinvention. "The price for this transformation is high," Baldwin observed, because "every white citizen in this country will have to accept the fact that he is not innocent, because those dogs and those hoses are being turned on American children, on American soil, with the tacit consent of the American Republic; those crimes are being committed in your name. Black people will have to do something very hard, too, which is to allow the white citizen his first awkward steps toward maturity."

Accountability in this capacity entails not only respecting the freedom of people to self-identify but willingly reckoning with our history. It means, if you're white, not being "colorblind" but seeing how colorism and racism operate in your life and surroundings. As Sara Ahmed observed in "A Phenomenology of Whiteness," "Whiteness is only invisible for those who inhabit it, or those who get so used to its inhabitance that they learn not to see it, even when they are not it." To make whiteness visible, then, requires white people to develop a critical consciousness. This work can begin with acts of self-reflection and questioning, and several recent books—including Layla Saad's *Me and White Supremacy*, Ibram X. Kendi's *How to Be an Antiracist*, and W. Kamau Bell and Kate Schatz's *Do the Work! An Antiracist Activity Book*—offer practices on learning how to become antiracist that are grounded in methods similar to the internal process of freedom work described here. Acknowledging and becoming aware of systemic racism in the United States is the first step. Learning how racism is rooted in our culture and institutions is the next step in the process of unlearning certain mindsets and behaviors complicit with white supremacy.

The accountability grounding our mutual creation can upend the power dynamics of our society and, I believe, work to dismantle the white supremacist cis-heteropatriarchy. The choice to take accountability for our identities and self-expression is essential to creating spaces of freedom that, in turn, encourage others to do the same. Collectively, then, we can create affirmative spaces of belonging that encourage authenticity and self-expression. Such spaces are crucial for historically marginalized and oppressed people to feel the safety and security necessary to share their own histories, ideas, and stories.

STORYTELLING AS FREEDOM

Through language we communicate ourselves to others and make meaning of our lives. But the language of identity is just one facet of this self-creation. I have included my stories not only to illustrate how I have chosen to live my identities of *woman* and *lesbian* but also to show how I relate to these identities as launchpads as I evolve over time, and in my desires and politics.

We each relate to our own set of intersecting identities in different ways throughout the course of our lives. If my identities are touchstones, my stories convey the meaning of who I have become over time—because our lives are far richer, much more complex, and more nuanced than any identity could ever represent.

Stories account for the parts of our lives that don't fit neatly into identity boxes. In form, stories resemble the process of life, as a narrative of continual becoming. The power of storytelling is that it allows us to express not only who we are but who we want to become. "I believe that telling our stories, first to ourselves and then to one another and to the world, is a revolutionary act," writer and activist Janet Mock wrote in her first memoir, *Redefining Realness*, about the need for trans women, and

Black trans women specifically, to tell their own stories. "We need stories of hope and possibility, stories that reflect the reality of our lived experiences. When such stories exist, as Barbara Smith remarked, 'then each of us will not only know better how to live, but how to dream.'"

It is for these reasons that women must write their own stories. Because if they do not, someone else will. Arguably, there is no greater expression of power than controlling the narrative, and, in particular, the story of one's life.

Writing our own stories, however, is more than simply assuming a position of authority over our own lives. Storytelling is a communal act that has a social function. It is self-creation but also collective creation, or cocreation. Whose language, whose stories, and whose ideas are the building blocks of our creation? Whom are we writing for? And for what purpose? The creative potential, here, is to eradicate and create anew both language and the conventions of storytelling. Like our self-creation, our stories do not need to conform to the patriarchal myth of the heroic individual who defies all odds to singularly save society. They do not even need to be linear, conforming to the morality of the form.

"A journey . . . is supposed to have a beginning, middle, and end, right? Well, the road is not like that at all," Gloria Steinem wrote in *My Life on the Road*. In her writing and activism, Steinem has reiterated that her own feminist journey has never been one she's made alone—despite being a solo traveler. Her encounters and the relationships she has made on her travels have made her the feminist icon she is today. While traveling throughout India in the 1950s, for example, she was able to participate in community talking circles, "groups that gather with all five senses, and allow consciousness to change." These groups, she explained, "taught me to talk as well as to listen. They also showed me that writing, which is solitary, is fine company for organizing, which is communal. It just took me a while to discover that both can happen wherever you are."

Historically, men have been the authoritative storytellers of humanity. Their stories have been taught as accurate and objective history, fed to us as schoolchildren in state-approved textbooks. These storytellers have had the power to decide which events are worth recording. Through this editing process, they have determined and judged the heroes and villains. They have imposed their morality and their values on the world.

The power of stories accrues over time and comes through their appropriation and repetition, both of which produce and reinforce what Omega Institute cofounder Elizabeth Lesser, in *Cassandra Speaks*, called an "uncontested value system"—in this case, a system built on sexist values intended to glorify and uphold men, largely through the objectification and vilification of women. The morality of these stories is based in gender stereotypes, with women conceived of as either obstacles or trophies. They also serve as warnings to women: Speak up or act out and your tongue will literally be cut out of your mouth, like Lavinia's.

The perennial challenge for women inheres in how impossible patriarchal society has made it for us to become storytellers. Especially in an increasingly connected world where the demands of capitalism mean we are expected to be available 24/7, how do we even find the time, the space, and the (financial) ability to create? Creativity requires imagination that can only come from rest, to recall Tricia Hersey's manifesto.

Beauvoir understood this challenge in historical terms. "As long as [woman] still has to fight to become a human being," she asserted in *The Second Sex*, "she cannot become a creator." Societal constraints have denied women the freedom to create, and creativity is essential to imagining a freer world. Yet, Beauvoir noted, there are "a thousand fine bonds" that stifle women's creativity by restricting her freedom. "I have already said," she wrote, "how hostile the street is: eyes everywhere, hands waiting: if she wanders absentmindedly, her thoughts elsewhere, if she lights a cigarette in a cafe, if she goes to the cinema alone, an unpleasant incident can quickly occur. . . . This concern rivets her to the ground and self. Her wings are clipped."

The world is hostile to women's creativity: whether it is the persistent, looming threat of violence; the feeling of being under continual surveillance; the compounding pressure of societal expectations; or the stress of financial limitations. (And, I want to note, when women do create—whether the medium is the written word or music or film or art—we often witness their creative genius dismissed as unserious autobiographical musings.) This hostility is unsurprising, given that for centuries the only valid form of women's creation was procreation.

Creating our own stories can reconfigure society's power dynamics. We can write women—write ourselves—as the protagonists of our stories. We can become the storytellers and wrest control of the word, of the narrative, from men who seek to pin us down and lock us inside their tales. "I write to record what others erase when I speak, to write the stories others have miswritten about me, about you," Gloria Anzaldúa wrote in a letter she addressed to third world women writers. "To discover myself, to preserve myself, to make myself, to achieve self-autonomy."

The freedom to create demands a foundation of safety—a safe space—from which to create. This is, again, why accountability is so crucial. If we do not feel safe, comfortable, at rest, and secure in ourselves and our surroundings, we are in no position to feel the vulnerability necessary to creation. "One reason that safe spaces are so threatening to those who feel excluded, and so routinely castigated by them, is that safe spaces are free of surveillance by more powerful groups," Collins explained about the necessity of safe spaces for Black women and other women of color. These spaces also allow for the possibility of taking control of the narrative and rewriting the story in our own words and on our own terms. She added that this safe space is both external, as in a physical location where women congregate and share their experiences, and internal, in terms of a mental space decluttered of racist and misogynist language and imagery.

These spaces of storytelling, therefore, can serve as lifesaving and life-preserving spaces for women, especially for marginalized communities. Mock has articulated how writing the story of her gender journey was a "gift," because doing so forced her to be honest with herself and, she wrote, "unapologetic about the layered identities I carry within my body, and reclaiming the often erased legacy of trans women's survival that enabled me to thrive as a young, poverty-raised trans woman of color." Her memoirs, among so many others, including Glennon Doyle's *Untamed* and Carmen Maria Machado's *In the Dream House*, have inspired the creation of spaces for shared dialogue, conversation, and community building. These are spaces of freedom.

THE RADICAL POTENTIAL OF CREATIVITY

Through storytelling, women are able to break through and break free of the identity categories that stifle us, hinder our expression, and erect barriers to seeing and building a community with other women. One of the simplest ways we can practice a freedom feminism is by writing our own stories *and* deeply listening to the stories of others.

In this way, storytelling is liberating. In an essay for NPR, V (the artist formerly known as Eve Ensler) wrote about the power of language "to transform our cells, rearrange our learning patterns of behavior, and redirect our thinking." She described how her depression lifted only after she and her mother discussed the sexual and physical violence she experienced at the hands of her father—which had become a suffocating silence between them. Giving language to what happened allowed V and her mother "to eventually face our deepest demons and deceptions and become free."

Storytelling allows us to work out, work through, and imagine our lives in new ways, with or without identities, in language that we deliberately choose. "Self-definition and self-determination [are] about the many varied decisions that we make to compose and journey toward ourselves, about the audacity and strength to proclaim, create, and evolve into who we know ourselves to be," Mock observed. "It's okay if your personal definition is in a constant state of flux as you navigate the world." Stories not only describe where we've come from, but where we want to go. There is a freedom in dreaming of ways to be, to exist, and to live in the world yet to be realized.

When I think about the fundamental importance of creativity to women's freedom, my mind immediately goes to Audre Lorde's "Poetry

Is Not a Luxury." In this 1977 essay, she argued for the necessity of poetry as a "revelatory distillation of experience," observing that "it forms the quality of the light within which we predicate our hopes and dreams toward survival and change, first made into language, then into idea, then into more tangible action."

The quality of light she referred to is not just the language or images we use but the textures of them, the perspective we place on them. The value system. "The quality of light by which we scrutinize our lives," she began, "has direct bearing upon the product which we live, and upon the changes which we hope to bring about through those lives. It is within this light that we form those ideas by which we pursue our magic and make it realized."

It is through creativity that we can change the very quality of light through which we understand, assess, create, and place value on ourselves and others.

Creativity is powerful because it gives form to formless forces, the energies and desires within us that we seek to know. And this power of the imagination is available to anyone. Lorde's light isn't cast as a spotlight. It shines on all of us.

Practicing freedom in the choices we make and the lives we create allows us to live with care and consideration, as well as find meaning and joy. We are responsible for the lives we create and the choices we make along the way. Self-creation is mutual creation—of each other, of the communities we want, of our values, and of our politics. The freedom practice of self-creation that can liberate *woman* from the gender binary, therefore, also can liberate the feminist movement from the cage of identity politics.

CHAPTER 6

FREE YOUR MOVEMENT

What does Britney Spears have to do with Black Lives Matter (BLM)? Arguably very little, at least on the surface. Yet what unites them is a profound sense of freedom—individual and collective, respectively—that has inspired broad-based movements worldwide.

Both movements have been subjected to backlash: #FreeBritney was brushed off as a joke, a baseless conspiracy fomented by obsessed fans of a "crazy" white female pop star; while BLM was derided as a terrorist threat, because Black people demanding the recognition of their human dignity is, apparently, very upsetting to white people.

While incomparable in many ways, the two movements represent the dual aspects of the third practice of freedom: the freedom to move—both personally and collectively.

The freedom to move is about more than just individual mobility and access; it's about the ability to create movements: deliberate, constructive actions that catalyze and generate new relationships, alliances, collaborations, and coalitions that can do the work of changing our institutions. The power of movements is based in the ideas that fuel them, that inspire people to come together and work toward the realization of a shared goal or values.

Even though freedom work begins with and within the self, we do not create the conditions for our freedom on our own. From collaborations to collectives, circles to communities, it is only by coming together and forming movements that our freedom work can achieve scale, transcending our individual efforts to effectively change our society and its institutions.

No one person can tear down the white supremacist cis-heteropatriarchy—because, if it were possible, a woman would've done it already. The fact is, we need each other. And we need to understand and learn from the past to break free from it. That means not only addressing the historic forms of oppression that have limited our accessibility and movement but also taking account of what has kept us—including ourselves, our own biases, and, within the feminist movement specifically, our racism, ableism, homophobia, and transphobia—from forming relationships and building a movement together.

#FREEBRITNEY

Like other movements, #FreeBritney did not emerge overnight.* The movement to free Britney Spears from her oppressive conservatorship began more than a decade ago. In 2009, a year after her conservatorship was established, the website FreeBritney.net launched to shed light on the unnecessary restrictions that—we have come to learn—stripped her of her autonomy, dignity, and civil rights. Since then, a coalition of fans, feminists, disability rights activists, and civil rights organizations have come together on several fronts—from podcasts to documentaries to courthouse protests—to liberate Britney from her conservatorship.

---

* In 2022, #FreeBritney evolved into #JusticeForBritney as the movement refocused its agenda, after securing Britney's freedom from her conservatorship, on winning legal and financial remediation for the singer. But the original moniker is still used in relation to questions about the authenticity of activity on Britney's Instagram account and the extent to which she is indeed free.

Their combined digital and grassroots activism worked to raise visibility about her situation, articulate the various forms of injustice and abuse she suffered under the conservatorship, and relentlessly pressure the courts to take up the case.

Documentaries by the *New York Times* and Netflix revealed that Britney repeatedly attempted to subvert and extricate herself from her conservatorship. But she was thwarted at every turn by her family, her management, and the security team hired by her conservators to surveil her every move (even illegally recording her through her devices and in her own bedroom). According to her own court statement in June 2021, the audio of which was leaked onto YouTube and published in full at NPR, she was forced to work, punished if she refused or if she was too sick to perform, threatened with losing custody of her children, denied friendships, forced into rehab, drugged with lithium and unknown quantities of other drugs, and subjected to medical procedures, including multiple blood tests a week and the forced use of an IUD to prevent pregnancy.

From the collective efforts of the movement, she gained her legal freedom. That it took thirteen years to liberate Britney despite all her privilege—her whiteness, her wealth, and her millions of fans who believed her and served as a built-in visibility campaign—indicates the extent of the monumental uphill battle faced by people trapped in abusive conservatorships.

"#FreeBritney movement," Britney wrote on Twitter shortly after a Los Angeles court suspended her father's control of her finances and set an official hearing date to end the conservatorship, "I have no words . . . because of you guys and your constant resilience in freeing me from my conservatorship . . . my life is now [going] in that direction!"

A few weeks later, after the court terminated the conservatorship on November 12, 2021, Britney posted an Instagram video to thank the movement for saving her life: "My voice was muted and threatened for so long, and I wasn't able to speak up or say anything. . . . I honestly think you guys saved my life." In the same video, she acknowledged her privilege, adding, "I'm here to be an advocate for people with real disabilities and illnesses. . . . Hopefully my story will make an impact and make some changes in the corrupt [conservatorship] system." That impact has already been made in terms of raising awareness about the dehumanization and exploitation of disabled people in conservatorships. According to the National Council on Disability's 2018 report, there are estimated to be more than 1.3 million Americans legally bound in conservatorships or guardianships, with more than $50 billion of their assets in the hands of guardians or conservators. In September 2022, California governor Gavin Newsom signed a law limiting the power of conservatorships. "This measure is an important step to empower Californians with disabilities to get needed support in caring for themselves and their finances, while maintaining control over their lives to the greatest extent possible," he said in a statement.

Britney's fight felt personal to me—and not just because for nearly twenty-five years her music has brought me immense joy and pleasure (and helped lift me out of my severe depression in college). As a feminist cultural critic, what I see in her experience of being trapped in a heinous conservatorship is the crystallization of what I have identified as the three primary forms of women's oppression: of mind, body, and movement. By the patriarchal state and the patriarchal father, she was denied the freedom to make choices about her life; denied the freedom to control her body; and denied the freedom to move, to leave her house, spend time with her friends, and go wherever she wanted whenever she wanted.

Britney often has contextualized her total lack of freedom in terms of driving and dancing—two expressions of bodily autonomy that bring her joy. The pattern of association between driving and freedom, in particular, is startling once you notice how abundant it is in interviews readily available online and in print.

Take the 2008 MTV documentary *Britney: For the Record*, which was filmed shortly after the instantiation of the conservatorship. The newness of the confining structure, still emergent in its full panoptic effects, is apparent in how unfiltered and unmediated some of the footage is, including scenes of an on-camera disagreement between Britney and her father, as well as Britney's emotional reference to her conservatorship's "restraints." At one point in the documentary, Britney is asked, "When did you last feel free?" Her response is immediate and unequivocal: "When I got to drive my car a lot." She added, "I love driving my car. There's something about being able to drive your car that allows freedom." Seconds later, she said, "I haven't been able to drive my car."

The freedom to move and control one's movement—this is what driving a car means to Britney. "In American consumer lore," New York University professors Andrew Ross and Julie Livingston wrote in a 2022 *New York Times* opinion piece, "the automobile has always been a 'freedom machine.'" Driving provides an escape (from, among others, the paparazzi, despite being chased by them); provides solace, solitude, and privacy; and, given the many occasions in which she—like many of us—sings and dances to music while driving, affords a kind of creative interlude from the daunting realities of life. For Britney, as well as countless teenagers and young adults, driving a car is the first real liberation from parental control.

This liberation, however, is more often than not foreclosed to Black and brown youth—a product of the racist social forces and systemic policing in the United States that originated in slave patrols, which were expressly created to prevent Black movement, escape, and liberation from enslavement. Historically, Black people's movement was always interpreted as a threat to white supremacist society (to recall Stordeur on the proliferation of the n-word as retaliation against Black liberation). And it is a history that has carried forward, from Black children being bullied and spat on while walking to school after *Brown*, to three white supremacist vigilantes chasing and gunning down Ahmaud Arbery, who was out for a run in a South Georgia neighborhood, in February 2020. Movement is freedom—which is why those in power intently focus on preventing and eliminating it.

The freedom to move depends in large part on one's societal privilege—specifically, one's race. "The rite of passage and the feeling of freedom that follows passing a driver's test is effectively dissolved when the license is placed in Black hands," author and journalist Brianna Holt wrote in an article at the *Guardian*. From sundown towns to racial profiling, "driving while Black" can prove and has proven deadly. Daunte Wright, Caron Nazario, Philando Castile, Sandra Bland, and Tyre Nichols are just a handful of the countless Black drivers who have been harassed and/or killed by police. For Black and brown people, the freedom experienced by driving is constrained by the perennial threat of violence at the hands of the police and racist vigilantes with guns.

The freedom to move is also tied to capital, to the labor economy, and specifically to earning a living in an increasingly prevalent gig economy. In June 2022, Jayland Walker, a DoorDash driver, was shot dozens of times—too many for the medical examiner to determine the exact count—by police in Akron, Ohio, who attempted to pull him over during a traffic stop. Last year, a number of Black and racially marginalized DoorDash drivers across the nation were murdered while on the job, from Oakland, California, to Detroit, Michigan, to Prince George's County, Maryland. The risks associated with driving for racially marginalized people fundamentally affect their safety, well-being, prosperity, and health.

The freedom to move is bodily autonomy activated through space and time. The connection between this freedom and the freedoms of choice and of self-creation is, in fact, bodily autonomy. It is no wonder, then, that driving her car is the first thing Britney mentions when describing the independence she felt after the termination of her conservatorship:

> I'm just grateful honestly for each day and being able to have the keys to my car and being able to be independent for a woman and owning an ATM card, seeing cash for the first time, being able to buy candles. . . . It's the little things for us women, but it makes a huge difference, and I'm grateful for that. It's nice. It's really nice.

Again, no one person has the power to create the conditions of their freedom. Not even Britney Jean Spears—an internationally famous, wealthy, American, white woman—who was deprived of these freedoms and her civil rights until a movement formed and fought to liberate her. Even as I write this, online conversation about her social media content has veered to skepticism about the extent to which Britney is indeed free and what, exactly, freedom looks and feels like for someone trapped and abused for more than a decade.

And while I was writing this book, another campaign fighting for the liberation of another Brittney took shape: Basketball star Brittney Griner was detained by the Russian government on February 17, 2022, on charges of carrying hashish oil in her luggage. She was convicted in August and, upon the rejection of her appeal in October, sentenced to nine years in a penal colony.

Capital operates at the core of the racism, misogyny, and homophobia of Griner's detainment. Griner is a Black, queer, masculine-of-center woman. She is a professional athlete, a two-time Olympic gold medalist, and one of several WNBA players who play overseas during the league's off-season, where they can easily double their salary. The gender pay disparity between WNBA and NBA players is startling. NBA players earn salaries in the millions. According to 2022 data posted at the Hoops Geek, the average 2021–2022 NBA salary was $8.5 million, with the median salary at $4,347,600 and bench players earning approximately $4.2 million. In contrast, according to the WNBA's 2020 Collective Bargaining Agreement, which runs through 2027, WNBA players average $130,000 annually. "That pay gap," Jennah Haque noted in an article at *Bloomberg*, "sends about half the [WNBA's] 144 players overseas for most of the year, where they can supplement their earnings—sometimes by $1 million dollars while being jetted around on private planes and indulging in a luxe life sponsored by Russian oligarchs."

Shortly after the news broke of Griner's detainment, multiple concerted efforts launched to fight for her release and return home. Primarily led by Black women, these included the We Are BG campaign—organized by Griner's agent, Lindsay Kagawa Colas; Black women advocacy groups; fellow WNBA players; and Griner's wife, Cherelle Griner; the political organization Black Feminist Future's #BringBrittneyHome campaign; and the relentless work of several groups like the Black Women's Leadership Collective and the Southern Black Girls and Women's Consortium.

These campaigns highlighted how the intersection of systemic oppressions operated both in Griner's detainment and in the media's coverage of her. Griner was a political pawn for Russian president Vladimir Putin—not just in the context of the Russian invasion of Ukraine but in the larger historical context of tensions between the United States and Russia. And while the geopolitics at play made Griner's situation vastly different from that of Britney Spears, the pervasive silence surrounding Griner's case nonetheless devastatingly illustrated how our society has historically cared less about Black women, especially queer Black women. Cherelle Griner, as well as WNBA legend and four-time Olympic gold medalist Lisa Leslie, spoke about how her supporters were instructed (by unnamed sources) to remain silent. The implication was that speaking out and bringing visibility to Griner's detainment would only impede her potential release.

Yet silence was the point. And while it is commonly understood as a tactic to facilitate the release of political prisoners like Griner, it is also a tactic of suppression. These Black-women-led groups strove to counter this tactic. Rallies, demonstrations, letter-writing campaigns, and online petitions combined to keep pressure on US officials to not ignore this Black queer woman. The collective power of their sustained efforts was essential to securing Griner's release on December 8, 2022.

"It took Black women sending a strong message to the world that we had to do everything that we could possibly do to get Brittney home," Jotaka Eaddy, founder of the Win with Black Women collective, told *The Hill* on the day of Griner's release. "It took the work and the voices of so many that have leveraged their platforms, their individual power, to help join the corps of so many Americans, especially Black women, to say that we must bring Brittney home and we will not stop saying her name, we will not stop standing in solidarity, we will not stop pushing until she's safely home."

BLACK LIVES MATTER

BLM illustrates the magnitude of a social movement's transformative power to completely reframe and elevate nationwide conversations about racism, health inequities, disenfranchisement, and police violence, and how these issues are connected. The roots of the global movement are diverse and diffuse. The organizational name and brand were established in 2013 as an online platform by three seasoned organizers and activists—Alicia Garza, Patrisse Cullors, and Opal Tometi.* The activism at the heart of BLM, to be clear, extends beyond the formal organization and includes a global network foundation, nonprofit and for-profit organizations, an action fund, and a political action committee. The Black Lives Matter Global Network Foundation is just one of dozens of groups within the coalition of the Movement for Black Lives (M4BL), which first convened at a conference in 2015 at Cleveland State University to strategize and establish a policy platform. The scope of these multi-issue, multidirectional movements is what gives BLM and M4BL such potency in its unyielding commitment to the abolition of anti-Black and racist institutions, laws, policies, and social norms. This abolition effort, as the 2016 M4BL platform stated, is "to move towards a world in which the full humanity and dignity of all people is recognized." The movement's platform outlined six demands—including reparations, divestment in carceral institutions, and community control of

---

* I understand the origin story of Black Lives Matter is complex. Here, I specifically refer to the beginning of the organizational part of the movement coined, with a hashtag, Black Lives Matter in a social media post by Alicia Garza in 2013, which the mainstream media has portrayed as representing the collective movement for Black lives, organizationally formed under the coalition of the Movement for Black Lives (M4BL). I recognize and acknowledge that BLM is one part of the capaciousness of activism, especially at the community level, focused on the liberation of and justice for Black people by abolishing the many systems of oppression. No single person or persons represent the totality of this or any movement.

laws and policies—for not just abolition but also the formation of Black political power and Black self-determination.

BLM ignited a profound and ongoing change in our society. It has changed the fabric of American culture and politics, changed the language we use to discuss police violence and systemic discrimination. It has transformed how we discuss American racism, and how we understand the foundations of this nation's history as rooted in Indigenous genocide and African enslavement. It has forced even some of the most unwilling among us—those who have clung to "colorblindness" as a testament that they *Are! Not! Racist!*—to *see* racism, to bear witness to the horrors and terrorism inflicted upon Black people by the state and by its white citizens. BLM has become a force in our political landscape, and, through myriad grassroots and organizational efforts, has paved the way toward the abolition of the systems and institutions that perpetuate racism.

"Movements are the story of how we come together when we've come apart," Garza wrote in *The Purpose of Power*. To be effective, she noted, movements require "sustained organizing" by "individuals, organizations, and institutions." Organizations are the spaces where movements acquire their literal structure—where people come together to set an agenda and build relationships and communities—that sustains those movements over time.

Garza emphasized that "hashtags do not start movements—people do," and, as a nod to the antiracist and feminist movements that have come before BLM, pointed out that "movements do not have official moments when they start and end, and there is never just one person who initiates them."

Contrary to portrayals in popular entertainment, social movements are not made of one or five white guys but rather consist of a broad coalition of people. Organizational work is distinct from activism in structure, intention, and temporality; while types of the latter—from online petitions to street protests—are incorporated into the former. Despite the hero narratives depicted in movies and television, the actual work of social movements is done by dozens upon dozens, if not hundreds and thousands, of people, not just because their lives depend on it but because there exists a collective consciousness about the values of accountability, dignity, and care. Writer and activist Sarah Schulman uncovered what the quality of this consciousness was in her historical analysis, in *Let the Record Show*, of what inspired people to join ACT UP:

> These were people who were unable to sit out a historic cataclysm. They were driven, by nature, by practice, or by some combination thereof, to defend people in trouble through standing with them. What ACT UPers had in common was that, regardless of demographic, they were a very specific type of person, necessary to historical paradigm shifts. In case of emergency, they were not bystanders.

To not be a bystander is to make a choice to act. Schulman's observation underscores an important commonality threaded through all effective social movements: They include people who may not have personally experienced, say, homophobia or racism, but who know that for society to change they must speak up and do something. They must *choose to intervene.*

To not be a bystander is, in a sense, the definition of what it means to be a *citizen*: to choose to take part in the collective society, to hold oneself accountable to the public.

Movements are not singular occurrences. They cannot be narrowed down to one protest or letter-writing campaign or sit-in. They also are not random, temporary reactions to violence but deliberate, intentional, organized, and sustained efforts. The most transformative social movements, furthermore, are not those that fight for equality within the white supremacist patriarchy but those that seek to abolish oppressive systems, institutions, and traditions. These movements change us, change how we move, and change how we engage with and relate to each other in the world. These movements and their respective organizations, such as M4BL, ACT UP, and the Black Panthers, have been revolutionary because they sought to provide the care to their respective communities that society's various systems—government, health care, and education—refused to provide them.

Movements vary in scope, shape, size, and mission. Yet, no matter the size or agenda, what singularly defines them is the fact that they begin with *people*, with collective mobilization. But they do not end there. Moms Demand Action, a nationwide grassroots movement of nearly ten million supporters whose mission is to change America's gun culture and fight for federal gun legislation, began with Shannon Watts sharing her anger and frustration with government inaction in a post with her seventy-five Facebook friends after the Sandy Hook shooting in 2012. "You should never underestimate a bunch of pissed-off moms," Watts told Katie Couric in a March 2021 interview. The movement's success has relied on its volunteers having conversations with their social networks online and offline, protesting gun violence in marches and public events, and even running for elected office—Lucy McBath and Marie Newman launched their political careers in the US Congress as Moms Demand members. In the 2022 US midterm elections, 140 Moms Demand volunteers supported by the movement's newly formed political training program, "Demand a Seat," were elected to office in states across America.

STRATEGIC CONTAINMENT

The freedom to move, without encumbrance or impediment, without surveillance or policing, without fear of violence or incrimination or imprisonment. This expression of freedom consists of the extension of our bodies into the world, into spaces that may or may not include us, that may or may not welcome us. This movement in public spaces—walking, running, dancing, marching, riding commercial or public transit—is dangerous for female- or feminine-presenting people and especially for women of color; genderqueer, nonconforming, and trans women; migrant and refugee women; and disabled women. Pregnant people's movement, too, is now at risk because *Dobbs* has ushered forth an assault by conservative state legislators and antiabortion advocates attempting to legally prevent the interstate travel of people seeking abortions.

Restricting women's movement has been a primary mode of their oppression for centuries. By controlling where, how, when, and with whom women move, men have not only claimed authority over women's bodies but over spaces, both public and private. While private spaces like the home have been established as sites of women's containment—morally enforced and racially coded through the language of domesticity and civility (and tied to the labor of racially marginalized women within those private spheres)—public spaces have been designed by men, exclusively for men. These spaces, traditionally prohibited to women, have been more often than not inhospitable to female- and feminine-presenting bodies moving through them. Until the early twentieth century, women's moral character was questioned if they were found walking out in the streets. The bicycle-riding New Woman, replete in her unlawful bloomers, was a radical sight.

And, I think, this is especially true if those spaces were vehicles of women's movement. Take the nineteenth-century argument in favor of banning women from traveling on locomotive trains. Critics claimed that "women's bodies were not designed to go at 50 miles an hour" because their "uteruses would fly out of [their] bodies." The misogynistic fear of the "wandering womb" was also cited as just cause for denying women the right to an education—the key to surpassing their situatedness through learning critical thinking, language, communication, and social skills and building relationships with their classmates and teachers. Again, moving bodies and moving minds give women too much independence from men for men's comfort. Thus, the threat of women's movement is often reframed and coded in language of protection—that women must be protected from such risky things. And, oh look, men will control them, I mean, *protect* them.

While laws, regulations, and social norms have eased over time concerning women's mobility and admission into traditionally male spaces—from colleges to the US Congress—what has been arguably more pernicious, and unchanging, is the pervasive threat of violence against our movement. And the historical threat of violence that has conditioned women to police and regulate their own movement. This self-policing is the very social conditioning Beauvoir spoke of in *The Second Sex* and what geographer Leslie Kern, in *Feminist City*, called "the social function of women's fear":

> Fear restricts women's lives. It limits our use of public spaces, shapes our choices about work and other economic opportunities, and keeps us . . . dependent on men as protectors. This all works to prop up the heteropatriarchal capitalist system in which women are tied to the private space of the home and responsible for domestic labor within the institution of the nuclear family. It's the system that benefits men as a group and upholds the status quo very effectively.

It's the misogynist version of the panopticon, of Big Brother, who is always watching, always ready to punish women if they step out of bounds or transgress the social limitations placed upon their movement. White female bodies are prized possessions that must remain fixed and pinned, like objects, to domestic spaces, while Black and brown female bodies are only permitted mobility in the service of white people. No matter what equal rights are given to women, this relentless terrorism is produced *socially*, as a social function that laws cannot remedy or prevent but can only redress through the carceral system and forms of punishment.

It is really no surprise that the top responses to a 2020 viral social media survey asking "What would you do if there were no men on Earth for 24 hours?" all concerned the ability to move without threat of violence from men. The most popular answer was "go on walks at night." Indeed, tens of thousands of women responded with versions of that same answer. "Ride bikes with my best friend at night"; "run around at night blasting music into my headphones without feeling like I need to take one out"; and "walk alone in the city and just breathe."

These informal survey results coincide with those of additional studies about societal constraints on women's movement. A landmark 2014 research survey by the nonprofit Right to Be (formerly Hollaback!) and Cornell University about street harassment in forty-two cities around the world concluded that "85 percent of US women report[ed] experiencing their first harassment before age 17," and "more than 81.5 percent of European women have been harassed before age 17." A 2019 study by NORC at the University of Chicago found that 81 percent of women reported some form of sexual harassment, 30 percent reported unwanted genital flashing, and 27 percent reported being physically followed.

These experiences change us—change how we behave and our patterns of movement.

Just to offer one experience of mine: I used to go running in Fort Tryon Park, in "upstate Manhattan," in the morning after sunrise. Often, I would encounter gay trysts—usually guys blowing other guys—in little nooks among the brush. Knowing they were out there because they were closeted at home, I would usually laugh and yell "get a room" as I ran by (sometimes leaping over legs and buttocks). These occasions surprised me in the sense that I was focused on my run; they were unexpected obstacles I would have to hurdle over or haphazardly move around in order to not fall into a dirt hole and twist my ankle—which happened, twice. But they did not offend or bother me, because they were there to fuck each other, not to violate passersby.

Then one morning, as I was running up a hill, I saw a man standing at the top wearing a tan trench coat. As soon as I had clear sight of him, he flashed me. My immediate response was disbelief—like, did I really just see a penis and hairy balls at 6:45 in the morning? Then I felt sick to my stomach. Shaking, I turned around and ran right back to my apartment. After that encounter, I stopped running in the park in the morning. I changed my schedule to run later in the day, and I avoided that hill. Like so many women, I made it *my* responsibility to ensure something like that didn't happen again.

My experience is far from unique. A 2017 *Runner's World* survey reported that 43 percent of female runners—compared to just 4 percent of male runners—were harassed on a run. We hear news stories of women murdered while out on a run, and who are then blamed for running too early in the morning or too late at night. The risk is so common as to have a name: running while female.

No space, public or private, ensures women's safety. Statistically, more women are murdered in the home by their intimate partners than they are by strangers outside of it. In a society intent on controlling women, women's movement—a physical declaration of their agency and autonomy—is a challenge to patriarchal authority. If the ideal woman is an object, then fixing a woman in place is a tactic to achieve this objectification. Violence is the enforcement, and the threat of it reinforces women's social conditioning to regulate themselves. The lifelong burden of self-circumscription is ignored because it is expected of women—because society has told us that we encourage or deserve violence if we are not careful or if we step out of bounds.

The "patriarchy has taught women to shrink themselves," Mona Eltahawy said. Women have been conditioned to contort themselves to take up the smallest physical space possible in order to not elicit any unwanted attention or harassment. This conditioning has materialized in the female body ideals that, from a young age, are ingrained into us as the right way to be a woman. It is not surprising that the ideal female body is tiny, lithe, soft yet thin, fit but not too muscular. Women must appear small and weak for men to feel big and strong—the visual effects of which reinforce the sexist beliefs that men can do things women can't.

Correlative to physical stature, women have been taught that they should take up the tiniest space possible, and that they should be exceedingly happy with the tiny amount of space they have been given by men in society. The tireless vigilance this conditioning has produced is what we often refer to as having a situational awareness. Sociologists Fiona Vera-Gray and Liz Kelly have studied, both individually and in collaboration, how this situational awareness takes effect, consciously and unconsciously, in women's habits of self-evaluation and self-restraint. Kelly coined this arduous yet invisible work of trying to minimize the chance of being harassed or assaulted as "safety work." In an article on the subject, Vera-Gray and Kelly described how safety work is mentally and physically labor intensive because it is intended to preempt harm. "Women learn to adapt their behaviour and movements," they wrote, "habitually limiting their own freedom in order to prevent, avoid, ignore, and ultimately dismiss what they experience as ordinary."

Despite this meticulously calibrated behavior, women end up in a catch-22 because our patriarchal society and its institutions find a way to blame and punish women for failing to prevent someone else from choosing to assault them—*the catch being that women know this*. "The pre-emptive nature of safety work is intended to prevent the very forms of escalation that would confirm whether such work was needed in the first place," Vera-Gray and Kelly elaborated on another facet of this catch-22. "With no way to know when they're getting it right, women are caught: blamed if they do not act to prevent sexual violence, yet unable to claim any success for the inevitable, numerous, times that they do."

What woman hasn't done safety work? *Multiple* kinds of safety work: holding your keys between your fingers as a makeshift weapon; carrying mace or pepper spray; parking your car close to a building's entrance or under parking lot lights; not standing too close to the subway tracks; making sure you're entering a subway car with multiple people already inside; running from the subway to your apartment after sundown; wearing your desired outfit under heavier, darker, and less revealing clothing (or transporting the outfit you want to wear in a bag and changing into it after you have arrived safely at your destination); or wearing sunglasses or headphones to signal to others that their glares or comments can't reach you. This work is even more arduous for people with mobility and accessibility concerns, as most public spaces and forms of transportation still fail to adequately account for people with disabilities.

Safety-work tactics are not universal. Different people experience different risks associated with their *perceived* identities. Choosing to travel together or in packs—the familiar refrain of "safety in numbers"—might work for cisgender, feminine-presenting white women yet can prove dangerous for Black, brown, and Indigenous women, as well as for gender-nonconforming, queer, and trans women. Recall, in 2015, the group of Black women kicked off a Napa Valley Wine Train because they were laughing—*on a wine train!* Members of the Sistahs on the Reading Edge book club—ten of eleven of whom were Black, and who ranged in age from their late 30s to 85—had gathered to discuss their latest book pick. "The train is set up to be with your friends, to drink wine and have a good time," Lisa Johnson, one of the members, told the *San Francisco Chronicle*. "We were thinking, 'Who are we offending?'"

Apparently, their joy—and specifically their Black joy—offended the people on board. To add insult (and potentially fatal injury), police were waiting for them when they were escorted off the train. "It was humiliating," Johnson added. "I felt like it was a racist attack on us. I feel like we were being singled out."

Women and feminine-presenting people are policed differently according to how they are racially profiled. In this case, it's not simply that Black women's movement was policed (trains were historically racially segregated spaces); it's that their humanity—evinced through their unapologetic expression of joy—was labeled unruly, uncivil, and indecorous, if not criminal.

Femme lesbians traveling alone may elicit unwanted male attention and harassment, but when traveling with a partner, they may provoke an entirely different form of harassment, depending on the partner's gender presentation. When I've been partnered with feminine women, men ogle and whistle and buy us drinks and beg for threesomes. When I've been partnered with trans or masculine-of-center people, we have been sneered at and verbally attacked in public.

Because public spaces have been historically segregated by the gender binary in addition to race, they have been particularly dangerous for trans, nonbinary, and gender-nonconforming people. The most notorious example concerns the use of public restrooms. Try to imagine, if you are or appear cisgender, the typical stress of having to pee so badly you are literally holding yourself together with your hands while praying there is an available stall free of—let's just say—*debris*. And now imagine this stress compounded with the very real potential threat of being harassed while trying to make it to the toilet before your bladder bursts. Trans and gender-nonconforming people just want to pee in peace, without harassment, harm, and arrest. The consequential safety work of trying to avoid this violence has resulted, according to the 2015 US Transgender Survey, in nearly 60 percent of trans people saying they avoid public restrooms—with 8 percent reporting urinary tract infections, kidney infections, and related health issues because of it. And yet somehow this basic need to empty one's bladder has captured the public's attention and has been a major point of debate in the media, statehouses, and the courts. It's stunningly ridiculous—stunning in how ridiculous it is—that people relieving themselves has become a flashpoint in the culture wars. What's next, adjudicating trans farts? Watch out, they can't be contained!

LGBTQ+ people are encumbered with additional safety work as preemptive measures when they travel, whether for business or pleasure. Homosexuality is still illegal in sixty-nine countries and punishable by death in eleven of them. In addition, trans and gender-nonconforming people must travel with personal documentation to prove their gender identity if they are interrogated at airports or at their destinations. The 2015 US Transgender Survey reported that a major barrier to getting this documentation is the financial cost. And for about a third of the survey's nearly twenty-eight thousand respondents, not having documentation with a name or gender that matched their gender expression resulted in harassment, abuse, and refusal of service. Since April 2022, US citizens have been able to choose the nonbinary gender designation "X" on passport applications. Yet, by the end of 2022, only three major airlines (United, American, and Delta, with other carriers promising to do so by 2024) offered the option—resulting in significant problems at check-in when passports and airline tickets show different gender identifications. Even in bars, nightclubs, and other social event spaces designated as feminist or queer, it is not unusual for trans and gender-nonconforming people to encounter harassment and discrimination.

MOVEMENT CONSTRUCTS SPACE

Liberation does not emerge from just any type of movement. It must be deliberate. As a freedom practice, movement must have intentionality. To live a considered life, our practice should endeavor to embody what Beauvoir referred to as "constructive movement": the thoughtful action or extension of oneself in the world.

Constructive movement, Beauvoir explained, is movement directed toward the realization of what she calls a "genuine freedom" that liberates us from our situatedness. We can only break free of the specific situations of our lives by making connections and building relationships. As Beauvoir said in *The Ethics of Ambiguity*, "It is other men who open the future to me, it is they who, setting up the world of tomorrow, define my future." Only other people can liberate us from our situatedness—a fact that marks the very beginning of our personhood, as we are pulled out and lifted up at birth to symbolize our joining humanity. (Not to mention that each of us are here because someone gestated us, hopefully by choice.)

Constructive movement realizes and enhances our individual and collective freedom. Critically, such interactions make us feel alive and imbue our lives with meaning. This is because freedom, Beauvoir contended, remains "abstract and empty," purely theoretical and hypothetical, if it remains unacted upon. We find meaning in deliberate movement that works to ensure the freedom of others. This is the significance of *constructive* in constructive movement: It builds, it nurtures and uplifts. As Beauvoir said: "The individual is defined only by his relationship to the world and to other individuals; he exists only by transcending himself, and his freedom can be achieved only through the freedom of others." We can only transcend the limits of our individually situated freedom with other people. Freedom in this capacity is a feeling experienced and expressed through movement and connection.

Movement is constructive when it is rooted in accountability, whereby we choose to take into account past experiences, learn from them, and act in the present with intention. It is action, in other words, grounded in a critical consciousness. This means that the future we want is in our hands, but what that future looks like is contingent upon how we redress historical wrongs. If we are truly committed to freedom, then we must collectively reckon with and repair the intergenerational impacts of slavery, genocide, and criminalization. "I am not free until everybody is free." Fannie Lou Hamer and innumerable civil rights activists and leaders have told us this.

The power of movement, therefore, is not simply that it is an expression of freedom but that it makes and unmakes space. Movement and space enfold each other, give each other definition and meaning that extend through time but are not necessarily permanent. Each space can be defined and redefined, claimed and reclaimed, by the qualities and intentions of the actions that make it. We make movements. We can build, and rebuild, worlds.

A freedom feminism is a world-building practice.

Inverting our understanding of the relation between movement and space, I know, may seem illogical, since we tend to think space establishes the physical parameters available for movement to happen. But the space I refer to here is not empty, geometric space. Rather, in the scope of this project about feminist ethics and remaking feminist values, I speak of ethical space—*social* and *political* space.

The force of our movements—feelings and intentions—establishes space through inscription. A space acquires meaning and significance because of the movements that make it. The intentions and qualities underlying rites, rituals, sermons, and prayers, for instance, carve a space that is holy and sacrosanct and therefore define that space as a site of worship or a house of religion. The space of a classroom, to take another example, is a site of learning. And, evident during the COVID-19 pandemic, a classroom can be made anywhere. During summer sessions, my classrooms often would materialize outside the college building, usually on the grassy and rocky knolls of Central Park. The learning practices—my lectures and lessons, our close readings of texts, student questions, conversation, and debate—combined to make our classroom.

Even the ancient Greeks knew you didn't need to be surrounded by four solid walls to *learn*.

Furthermore, the classrooms built by these movements—dialogue and intellectual exchange—simultaneously constituted our respective roles. My role as professor only acquired significance and purpose in my interactions with students. (I was not, for instance, a professor to the baristas at the coffee shop where I would pick up some much-needed caffeine en route to class.) Movement activates and realizes our social roles and scripts through our encounters with each other, and the repetition of these encounters—for example, meeting twice a week for fifteen weeks a semester—instantiates the parameters of the roles and dynamics in a relation between people. (This is why I will always call my fourth-grade teacher Mrs. Allegro.) It also creates the culture of a space.

If movement makes space, and the physicality of movement is finite, then there is radical potential in what our movement—our movements, collectively and over time—can do. Our movements, in effect, can reinscribe, reimagine, reclaim, or even dismantle a space's existing meaning, purpose, and functionality. It is significant to recognize the power of movement to create space in this regard, because understanding that movement creates space means world-building—and more precisely world rebuilding akin to Ruha Benjamin's idea of "reworlding"—is possible. Inverting our understanding of the relation between space and movement, therefore, allows us to comprehend our agency in a world where most of us, most of the time, feel completely powerless. No space is permanent, no meaning is fixed or unchangeable. That movement makes space means change is possible—no space is eternally set in stone, literally or figuratively. We can tear down monuments, remake spaces, and remake the world to reflect our values.

We have witnessed the power of movements to make and remake space in the removal of Confederate monuments across the nation. Monumentalizing racism and slavery is antithetical to our multiracial democracy because it glorifies and commemorates the systemic dehumanization of Black people. The removal of monuments, therefore, constitutes the remaking and reclaiming of space, which is why white supremacists are so quick to fight against Confederate monument removal, claiming these monuments should remain in place because they are representative of US history and their heritage. However, this argument fails to account for the difference between a monument and history—not all history needs to be monumentalized. This is one reason why we have *books*, because they are tools with which to learn and study history through a critical lens.

Some of these social change efforts have been ensnarled by the forces of capitalism, which render them as rebranding and commercial opportunities. Take, for instance, plantations, which have been rebranded as luxury wedding and event venues in a superficial attempt to whitewash slavery and its abuses. Or the Airbnb rental in Greenville, Mississippi, that advertised a "1830s slave cabin"—what became a 2022 viral story on TikTok resulted in the listing's removal and Airbnb's promise to remove all listings that were formerly housing for the enslaved in the United States from its site. Meanwhile Colonial Williamsburg, a popular tourist destination, is nothing less than a site of society-wide gaslighting of this nation's history of enslavement, genocide, and criminalization of Black and Indigenous peoples. (In collaboration with UNESCO's Slave Route Project and dozens of sites and museums, the Colonial Williamsburg Foundation established the Slavery and Remembrance website in 2014 as a token gesture toward history.)

The movement to create and recreate space is also achieved through language. For example, organizations and institutions have begun to include Indigenous and tribal land recognition acknowledgments at their events. These moments recognize that an event is taking place on Indigenous lands, with the implicit, and sometimes explicit, mention of Indigenous genocide, Indigenous erasure, and the colonization of their lands by white Europeans. While it could come across as an empty checking-the-box gesture, "the acknowledgment of the land is a way of transforming and undoing the intentional erasure of the Indigenous people of the land," Kimberly Morales Johnson, a tribal member of the

Gabrielino-Tongva, told *LAist*. "By stating our name, by talking about us, by making 'Gabrielino-Tongva' a word that people know, it makes them consciously think about the land that they're occupying and standing on, and that they're guests of the land." The acknowledgment, in other words, makes non-Indigenous people aware of their situatedness in the larger history of land occupation. And this public awareness can increase public knowledge of this long-overlooked American history.

As verbal recognition of the land's original inhabitants, this kind of acknowledgment is a first step in the effort to restore the lands to Indigenous peoples. And while change begins with language, it is, again, only a first step. Indigenous-led nonprofits throughout North America like the Native Governance Center, NDN Collective, and Native Land Digital offer online resources for how to take action beyond land acknowledgment, including defending the land from corporate extraction, donating to Indigenous-led organizations, and participating in the LandBack movement to return Indigenous lands to their original stewards.

MOVEMENT AS COLLECTIVE CREATION

Movement crystalizes the values that represent and are represented by the people who have made a space. The 2020 documentary *Crip Camp* illustrates the power of movements to make spaces of dignity and belonging crucial to a historically marginalized and oppressed group. *Crip Camp* recounts the stories of disabled youth who created their own community at Camp Jened in the 1970s—a critical decade for disability rights nationwide. From the mid-1800s onward, cities like San Francisco and Chicago passed "ugly laws" that outlawed disabled people and those deemed "diseased, maimed, mutilated or in any way deformed" from public spaces. Concurrent with the passage of such laws was the proliferation of medical institutions—hospitals, homes, and sanitariums—as the designated spaces to segregate physically and psychosocially disabled people from society.

Camp Jened provided the opportunity for people with disabilities to live and socialize outside of exclusively medicalized spaces. "Some can remember the precise moment when they were in a space inhabited entirely by people like them for the first time," writer s. e. smith noted in "The Beauty of Spaces Created for and by Disabled People." "For disabled people, those spaces are often hospitals, group therapy sessions, and other clinical settings. That is often by design; we are kept isolated from each other."

Whereas most institutions and infrastructure have been built in ways that ignore or hide disabled people, the space of Camp Jened was built by and for disabled youth, centering their humanity, needs, and desires. "Personal assistance was built into the fabric of the camp," Srinidhi Raghavan, colead of programs at India-based disability rights nonprofit Rising Flame, wrote in an article about the documentary. "Disabled people helped each other shower, get dressed, learn how to kiss, eat, get into the pool, and move around. For many of them it was the first time they were living independently and learning to take care of each other. It was a time of exploration of their identities, personalities and growing together as a group." Ragahvan continued, "It was a space for disabled youth in 70s America to sit together and talk about freedom, privacy, dating—things the world outside hadn't made room for them to speak."

The documentary features interviews with a handful of camp-goers, each of whom describes their experience as the first time they had ever felt seen, heard, and recognized as fully human—and, importantly, as sexual human beings. The relationships, both sexual and platonic, formed at Camp Jened were vitally important to camp-goers. The bonds built from this experience continued into adulthood and informed the camp-goers' disability rights activism, specifically for Section 504 of the Rehabilitation Act (which protects students with disabilities) and, later, the Americans with Disabilities Act.

By highlighting sexuality, *Crip Camp* flips the script about people with disabilities. The documentary makes it abundantly clear that disabled teens are horny like most teenagers. The camp, in fact, is saturated with so much teenage sexual energy and sexual freedom that a crabs outbreak sends almost everyone into quarantine.

We can see a correlation between the practice of self-creation and the practice of movement: We make ourselves and make spaces simultaneously. Bodies are defined by what they do and do with each other, and their movements—encounters, interactions, and assemblages—make space. These practices mutually inform each other over time. And it is through encounters with others that our self-expression finds the expanse and limitations of its freedom.

The boundaries, borders, and norms of a space are enacted and codified through people's actions, their intended roles, and how they move. Melissa Febos wrote about this beautifully in her essay collection *Girlhood*, in her reflections on how her work as a pro-domme shaped her early experiences at cuddle parties. These parties, intended to explore touch and different kinds of intimacy, were framed by a set of rules that establish the space—from "pajamas stay on the whole time" to "you don't have to cuddle anyone at a Cuddle Party, ever," to "you are encouraged to change your mind."

For Febos, this exploration sparked an introspection about what felt comfortable for her own body. After the first cuddle party, she observed feeling unnerved by "how powerful"—even though "enthusiastic consent" was a rule of the party—"my instinct was to give them what they wanted, as if I didn't have a choice." That is, this radically open space of exploration and experimentation afforded her the emotional space to realize how deeply she's been conditioned to serve men and fulfill their needs, despite the established parameter of enthusiastic consent.

This realization came in part through a discussion with her wife, the poet Donika Kelly, who also attended the party and whose experience was strikingly different from her own.

Empathy and accommodation are not synonymous. In fact, I suspect that the instinct to subsume one's own desires or comfort for the desires or comfort of another may ultimately inhibit empathy. Donika's impression of the cuddle party was not marked particularly by the desperation of others because she did not feel threatened by their need. She said no easily. Also, she was interested in cuddling. Which is all to say that it wasn't the cuddle party; it was me.

Febos then connects her feelings to her previous work as a pro-domme, which had "conditioned [her] to override [her] own comfort." At the same time, she acknowledged that sex work "gave her a vocabulary with which to name [her] boundaries."

Febos's second time at the cuddle party was conditioned both by her first experience and the insights she gained from it, which effectively changed her interactions with other partygoers. While she still begrudgingly accommodated a man who threw his arms around her for a hug without her consent, her awareness deepened and clarified her understanding about herself, her boundaries, and her desires. "The work that these parties are doing and making space for is revolutionary," she reflected. "It has the power to transform the most devastating aspects of our society. . . . I don't know what else would have prompted me to collect this detailed information about my own comfort, about what kinds of touch felt acceptable and what kinds did not. . . . I needed a space where I could say no with explicit support."

Constructive movements can create spaces of radical openness, where we are free to express ourselves and to speak openly, without restraint or fear of harm. These are spaces, Eltahawy asserted, "where we can express the revolutionary identities we can fashion free of patriarchy and its attendant chokeholds . . . spaces of risk and vulnerability to explore transgression."

Eltahawy borrowed her definition of radical openness from bell hooks, who believed we each have the freedom to choose how we move and position ourselves in the world. We can choose to stand alongside the white supremacist patriarchy and act like attendant foot soldiers, or we can, hooks asserted, "stand in political resistance with the oppressed, ready to offer our ways of seeing and theorizing, of making culture towards the revolutionary effort which seeks to create space where there is unlimited access to the pleasure and power of knowing, where transformation is possible. The choice is crucial," she continued. "It shapes and determines our response to existing cultural practice and our capacity to envision new, alternative, oppositional aesthetic acts. It informs the way we speak about these issues, the language we choose."

Spaces of radical openness are those of creativity and invention. In many ways, they differ from safe spaces that foreclose challenging conversations to maintain control and comfort. With freedom as their architecture, spaces of radical openness are dream spaces where we can imagine new ways of living and relating to one another. They are spaces, to return to Hersey, where time feels generous and not constricted by the exhausting demands of capitalism. They can be spaces unscarred by gender oppression and the patriarchal strictures and scripts of the gender binary.

Fundamentally, constructive movements and the spaces they make and unmake remind us of our interdependence, of how all life on this planet exists in a delicate ecosystem. These are movements that emphasize our human points of connection, including "a desire to be seen and valued, to make each day count, to be loved and to love in return," Garza said. "A movement where we resist replicating the same dynamics that we fight against."

A FREEDOM FEMINIST MOVEMENT

We must relinquish the equality mindset and fight to eradicate all binaries that work to enforce the white supremacist cis-heteropatriarchy. The equality feminism that has relied upon the gender binary has forced us to claim our secondary sex status as an ethical and political position in order to justify feminism. And yet the consequence is that our efforts have either intentionally or inadvertently strengthened the patriarchy by utilizing the very operating principle that upholds the patriarchal house.

The gender binary has socially conditioned women to accept our subjugation. Equality feminism leverages this binary as a political standpoint (of powerlessness) from which to petition the patriarchy for the same rights as men. Cleaving to the binary has resulted in a feminism built on relationships in which "the basis for bonding was shared victimization, hence the emphasis on common oppression," hooks observed in *Feminist Theory*. "This concept of bonding directly reflects male supremacist thinking. Sexist ideology teaches women that to be female is to be a victim."

White women's tears perform this ideology, as Ruby Hamad deftly explained in *White Tears/Brown Scars*. They are integral to the success of equality feminism, particularly its carceral elements, by assisting in the vilification and incarceration of Black and brown men. These tears, furthermore, perform victimization intended to obfuscate and exempt white women from accountability and specifically from reckoning with their own racism. White women's tears symbolize the political position and strategy of equality feminism.

Consequently, this very bond—the basis of the movement in a shared victimization—prevents our liberation and justice. The feminist movement is severely limited by a politics composed of strategies and actions focused on and in reaction to men. To change the structure of the movement, women must break free of the shared bond of victimization—break free of the gender binary that instantiates this dynamic and women's subjugated position.

Instead, bonds should be based in our shared strengths and resources. "We can bond on the basis of our political commitment to a feminist movement that aims to end sexist oppression," hooks said. "Given such a commitment, *our energies would not be concentrated on the issue of equality with men or solely on the struggle to resist male domination. . . .* Before we can resist male domination we must break our attachment to sexism; we must work to transform the female consciousness" (emphasis mine).

It's not only that the work begins within us—what I have referred to as the internal process of freedom—but it also must materialize in practices not framed by, centered on, or opposed to men. This is because, as hooks showed us, everyone—not only women—is negatively affected by misogyny.

What a feminist movement based in freedom demands of each of us is a shift in mindset, a change in consciousness that comprehends how the personal is political—how individual choice is collective choice, individual action is collective action, and individual movement is collective movement. Everything we do has impact, even if that impact is imperceptible to us. Our task, as feminists, is to make that which is imperceptible perceptible.

Letting go of the equality mindset means we must let go of the man in the mirror. We must, as Barbara Johnson argued in the conclusion to *The Feminist Difference,* decenter men as the frame of reference for our politics:

> *As long as feminist analysis polarizes the world by gender, women are still standing facing men. Standing against men, or against patriarchy, might not be structurally so different from existing for it.* A feminist logic that pits women against men operates along the lines of heterosexual thinking. But conflicts among feminists require women to pay attention to each other, to take each other's reality seriously, to face each other. This requirement that women face each other may not have anything erotic or sexual about it, but it may have everything to do with the eradication of the misogyny that remains within feminists, and with the attempt to escape the logic of heterosexuality. It places difference among women rather than exclusively between the sexes. Of course, patriarchy has always played women off against each other and manipulated differences among women for its own

purposes. Nevertheless, *feminists have to take the risk of confronting and negotiating differences among women if we are ever to transform such differences into positive rather than negative forces in women's lives* (emphasis mine).

I quote the passage above in full because it completely revolutionized my understanding of feminism when I first read it, more than twenty years ago. I hope it does the same for you.

Feminism isn't—and shouldn't be—a war between men and women. Feminism shouldn't be about men at all. Yet feminism will continue to center men if its politics remains wedded to the gender binary.

We must break free from the gender binary and all other dualisms that limit the scope of our liberation efforts. Feminism, if it is to proceed as a freedom movement, requires women to face each other, to engage with and understand our differences as the source of our creative vitality and of new futures. Only through constructive movements can we more thoughtfully address the differences and disagreements among us. Only then will we create a feminist movement for all of us.

Reorienting feminism toward freedom begins on the individual level, within oneself, and then extending interpersonally. The fundamental linkage between the personal and the social, the *encounter*, is the building block of a social movement. When tens and hundreds of thousands of people decide to change how they encounter each other, as Benjamin outlined in her method of reworlding, those intimate relations scale to recreate the fabric of society.

Focusing on the interpersonal level of the encounter allows us to rethink, as hooks asked of us, the type of bond underlying the feminist movement. hooks's enjoinder is for feminists to never lose sight of the affective power of the emotions that bind and drive our greater cause. But her intention, to me, is to divorce two often blurred or overlapping standpoints: that of the oppressed and that of the victim. Like Elizabeth Grosz, who asserted that feminists must not be afraid of power, hooks encouraged us to take stock of the power we do have through our freedom to make choices and take action, no matter how small or inconsequential they may seem to us. The point of claiming our freedom and power is that doing so situates both as the "shared strengths and resources" upon which feminists can build bonds.

Essential to this work of building bonds in freedom is homosociality, a term most commonly applied to the social glue that has sustained and strengthened the patriarchy for centuries. From ancient Greek male-only academies to men's clubs, football teams, and college fraternities, these single-sex spaces have excluded women (or anyone not considered man enough) for the purpose of deepening male relationships and establishing fidelity to other men. These relations may or may not be sexual but fundamentally serve to establish power dynamics between men and strengthen their bonds. (Just think about fraternity initiations that involve some kind of sodomitical or sex act as a ritual of belonging. Or even physical exchanges—the butt and crotch pats and chest bumps of sports events, between not only players but also fans—and language of affection like *bro*. All are cultural symptoms of male homosociality.)

A deliberate strategy of the patriarchy has been to not only keep women separated from each other—by limiting their movement and accessibility—but ideologically divided and opposed to each other. Because when women are busy fighting each other, the logic goes, they cannot build a movement together. Patriarchal laws and norms have foreclosed female homosociality, instead dictating that women's primary relationships should be with men. The political economy of sex, Gayle Rubin explained decades ago, has been the trafficking of women between men to form contractual bonds and alliances. This is widely evident in traditional marriage ceremonies, which begin with one man handing over the possession of the woman to another man, with the marriage itself establishing a contractual bond between families. Heterosexuality, to recall Adrienne Rich, is first and foremost a political institution that strengthens the patriarchy by keeping women apart. And separating women, feminist scholar and organizer Charlotte Bunch observed, serves several purposes: "It makes women define themselves through men; it forces women to compete against each other for men and the privilege which comes through men and their social standing. . . . The very essence, definition, and nature of heterosexuality is men first."

Just as equality feminism has relied on the gender binary, it has also relied on the logic of heterosexuality to advance its political agenda. From the very origins of the US feminist movement for equality, white women seeking safety, security, education, money, and civic power did not form alliances with women of color and other marginalized and dispossessed people but with the people in power—white men.

A feminist freedom movement, therefore, demands that we break through the barrier that has historically separated us, a barrier that has worked hand in hand with the gender binary:

Heterosexuality.

WE MUST BECOME LESBIANS

I truly wish I were referring to scissoring, but alas, I am not referring to the grand sapphic act but to the removal of men—and, more precisely, the patriarchy—from our mindset and our politics. We must scissor them out and place women at the center of our mindset and our politics. This demands we abolish the very structure of heterosexuality that has framed the movement on and in reaction to men. "No feminist per se has advanced a solution outside of accommodation to the man," Jill Johnston argued in *Lesbian Nation.* "Until all women are lesbians there will be no true political revolution."

To deprogram our equality mindset, to scissor out the patriarchy, and to encourage women to regard themselves without the man in the mirror and face each other without male mediation—this is what it means to become a lesbian. Less of a fixed box and more like a launchpad. An ethics of lesbianing. A politics of "lesbianing together," to quote Pennsatucky in *Orange Is the New Black.* This is possible only by liberating *woman* from the gender binary and committing to destroying all dualisms associated with that binary. The ethics and the politics are not in the identification but in the *doing*. As Bunch said,

> Being a Lesbian means ending your identification with, allegiance to, dependence on, and support of heterosexuality. It means ending your personal stake in the male world so that you join women, individually and collectively, in the struggle to end your oppression. Lesbianism is the key to liberation and only women who cut their ties to male privilege can be trusted to remain serious in the struggle against male dominance.

Scissoring out the patriarchy is not misandry. Decentering men from our mindset and politics is in no way the equivalent of hating them. Rather, in Rich's words, men simply become "irrelevant" to our self-worth and to our political vision. "When we are totally, passionately engaged in working and acting and communicating with and for women," Rich said, "the notion of 'withdrawing energy from men' becomes irrelevant: we are already recycling our energy among ourselves."

Becoming a lesbian requires internal work, a recalibration, an awakening of the mind to cultivate a lesbian consciousness—what the Radicalesbians, in their 1970 manifesto, called "a new consciousness of and with each other." This consciousness comprises the internal work of freedom that, in turn, informs our external practices, especially our relationships. For Lorde, "the true feminist deals out of a lesbian consciousness whether or not she ever sleeps with women." And while reluctant to reduce the word to "sexual terms alone," she cheekily added, in her 1980 interview with the poet Karla Hammond, "Our sexuality is so energizing why not enjoy it too?"

Developing a lesbian consciousness is a liberatory tool that works to decenter the patriarchy and deprogram our equality mindsets. We can decondition ourselves of the patriarchal strictures, gender norms, and expectations that have hemmed us in. The space that this work creates allows for a genuine freedom to flourish, in part because it liberates the erotic within us and between us—the vital force of our self-creation, our encounters, and our movement.

Lorde made it a point to reclaim the erotic as women's "most profoundly creative force" from the patriarchy, which conscripted it as harmful and immoral. In "The Uses of the Erotic," she explained that the erotic is "creative energy empowered" because it connects us to ourselves and to other people, serving as a "bridge" between women who have been conditioned to distrust and not form relationships with each other—again, aspects of compulsory heterosexuality. The erotic, she elaborated, is a wellspring of joy because of the connections and emotions it produces. It can be, but is not purely, sexual. And, importantly, the erotic informs our consciousness, Lorde wrote, by becoming "a lens through which we scrutinize all aspects of our existence, forcing us to evaluate those aspects honestly in terms of their relative meaning within our lives." From this consciousness we can choose to live otherwise, create our lives and build relationships and communities with intention.

As a creative energy activated in encounters, the erotic fuels "love as a practice of freedom," what hooks said can transform our consciousness, by dismantling our supremacist mindset, and "liberate ourselves and others." As such, it is a practice that begins within the self and is rooted in accountability and care. "Awareness is central to the process of love as the practice of freedom," she observed. "If we discover in ourselves self-hatred, low self-esteem, or internalized white supremacist thinking and we face it, we can begin to heal."

Constructive movements fail if they lack a culture of accountability and care. The accountability demanded of a feminist *movement* critically includes the care of repair work. It means, to recall Johnson once more, women must "face each other" and "take the risk of confronting and negotiating differences among women if we are ever to transform such differences into positive rather than negative forces in women's lives." And we face each other not through violent confrontation or unilateral communication but through sustained engagement—the deep listening and radical honesty necessary to build trust and, hopefully, the bonds hooks spoke of.

To overcome the barriers—and false binaries—that have separated us, we must commit to a vision of feminism that centers freedom. We must develop a politics of freedom that values dignity, accountability, care, and justice.

So much of this work begins with ideas—the catalysts of change that inform our mindsets, guide our actions, and inspire movements. The ideas in this book may make you deeply uncomfortable, since encountering new or unfamiliar ideas can prove disquieting. Frankly, they are intended as jolts to our system, to how we think and how we envision feminism and our feminist politics. The choice in how you move forward after reading this book is, of course, yours. But for new ideas to take root and flourish, and for new relationships and political formations to take shape, we must embrace discomfort.

Our freedom, and our feminism, depend on it.

CONCLUSION

Freedom and Beyond

If I perceive my ignorance as a gap in knowledge instead of an impera-
tive that changes the very nature of what I think I know, then I do not
truly experience my ignorance. The surprise of otherness is that moment
when a new form of ignorance is suddenly activated as an imperative.
—Barbara Johnson, "Nothing Fails Like Success"

Generation after generation, feminists have carried the mantle of
equality as the noble cause of our liberation and in service of the
greater purpose of democracy. Yet this fidelity has not ushered forth
our total liberation. Even worse, equality has chained us to the white
supremacist cis-heteropatriarchy while being interpreted as a type of
freedom—freedom within the system. As long as we play by the rules.

A feminism dedicated to equality cannot offer us the ideas, language,
or framework to create fulfilling lives. Women's agency and bodily autonomy will always be criticized, constrained, and denied by an ideology
that seeks equivalence and sameness with white men. Filtered through
and rendered within the white supremacist cis-heteropatriarchy, we
have seen time and again how the ideal of equality has turned out to be

anything but equality in practice. And if we don't *feel* equal, if we aren't *treated* equally, what good is it?

Structural forms of equality—laws that guarantee equal rights and protections—have failed to account for centuries of misogyny, racism, and discrimination baked into the very systems in which we live. Once you open your eyes to it, it is impossible not to see the lie of equality. That the United Nations recently determined that gender equality is "300 years away" proves that equality is an absurdity.

So what if, realizing the failures of equality, we decide to ask, What else?

This book carries with it several intentions. As a book of ideas, I hope it helps disrupt the equality mindset, helps us understand how equality has failed us and how it has limited our self-creation and bodily autonomy and therefore offers us no pathway to the recognition of the full dignity of our humanity. The equality mindset cannot lead us to collective justice because equality only operates within the existing systems, institutions, and societal structures. And, as we've witnessed with alarming frequency in recent years, the logic of equality has been utilized in service of the status quo and against justice efforts.

I would love for women to read this book and realize that equality simply isn't good enough. It is a mediocre white male ideal. Any feelings of shame or guilt they have about their power, pleasure, and joy are products of patriarchal social conditioning. "The surprise of otherness," as Barbara Johnson called it, should crack us open and catalyze within us a reconsideration of what we know and how we know it. What "truths" have we been taught that may fundamentally serve to oppress us? I think of someone within my devoutly Christian family who has punished herself—starved herself to the point of suffering permanent illness—for decades because she chose to have an abortion. The misogyny of her religious morality has produced the belief that what she did was wrong, and she has reinforced this belief as truth by harming herself.

I also hope that when people, especially those who believe that society only listens to them when they speak from a place of powerlessness, read this book, they feel their power—the power they have over their actions and choices, despite their situatedness—in order to understand what they *can* control within their own lives. Freedom comes through claiming ownership and responsibility for one's choices. The power of freedom helps us realize that the systems and institutions we live in are not agentic, autonomous entities but things *people* have built and *people* control. More importantly, I want readers to understand that the limitations of our lives are not fixed or finite. Rather, the boundaries of our lives are porous and can be transcended through practices of freedom and specifically through our relationships with each other.

I want us to expand how we think and who we think we are and can become. Fundamental to our liberation is realizing that the gender binary is not just a social construct but the most significant structural support of the white supremacist cis-heteropatriarchy. Equality feminism has wedded us to this binary. And it is only when we free ourselves of the gender binary that women can define ourselves on our own terms.

There is an egregious belief that if we get rid of the gender binary, women will be erased from society. This could not be further from the truth. Eliminating the gender binary categorically unchains women from men. This does not mean denying women relationships with men. Rather, getting rid of the gender binary means *man* no longer dictates the parameters of the *woman* you can become. Gender is not an either-or choice. *Woman* does not have to be the opposite of *man*. Instead of thinking about gender in an oppositional pair of boxes, what if we thought of *woman* as one constellation within a universe of genders? What if we understood our gender as a lifelong becoming, as a self-expression that changes over time, as our bodies age and as our desires evolve? In fact, destroying the gender binary might be the best way to remove the antagonistic barriers between men and women. Because if we stop conceiving of men and women as opposites—from opposite planets, as Social Darwinism notoriously espoused—then maybe we'd find much more common ground. And maybe we'd have more fulfilling relationships with each other. I mean, if heterosexuality is your thing.

In writing this book, I came to realize that it was by really letting go of the gender binary that I could further let go of the woman I was *supposed* to be. The writing process helped me work through the vestiges of patriarchal conditioning about my body and my gender. I feel freer, less restricted, and less preoccupied with how I look, especially since I have entered perimenopause and have seen and felt my body change, quite dramatically, in just a couple of years. Only by letting go of the gender binary could I really become a woman on my own terms. For me, from a freedom mindset, *woman* is nonbinary.

This book has two broader intentions. The first is to reclaim freedom from its dominant American usage of unadulterated, unfettered, unthoughtful individualism. Freedom does not mean doing whatever you want whenever you want. That isn't freedom. It's solipsism. It's willful ignorance of the undeniable fact that we live in the world among billions of other people and life-forms, including Earth itself, and that we are interdependent on each other for our well-being and the future of all life on this planet.

White freedom has proven more threatening—and deadly—than liberating. Because how free do we feel when mass shootings are a daily occurrence in our communities? At our Fourth of July parades, at our cultural festivals, and in our schools? Our schools are sites of learning, of opening our minds. They are inherently vulnerable spaces that expose us to new ideas and new ways of thinking. It infuriates me when I hear, after yet another school mass shooting, criticism that a school was not prepared for it. Of course it wasn't prepared for it! A school is not a war zone; it is not intended to be a fortress—or a prison. It is intended as a place of learning, which requires generosity and openness. The horrific scene of cops in Uvalde, Texas, standing in the hallway outside two Robb Elementary classrooms with an arsenal of guns and ballistic shields and yet refusing to save the students and teachers in those classrooms should be all the proof we need that guns, and so-called good guys with guns, do not stop gun violence. More cops and more guns in schools do not make schools safer—and they certainly don't make students, especially racially marginalized students, feel safer.

Because our freedoms are linked, and because the current conditions of our lives can only be surpassed through encounters and relationships, a feminist freedom is the antithesis of the rabid selfishness that defines the white freedom of the ideological right. Freedom is a *personal* feeling, but it is *socially* realized and experienced. The capacity of our freedom—of our collective freedom—is determined by our awareness of our intersubjectivity and dictated by our commitment to accountability and care.

Freedom, furthermore, is not an object or commodity. It is a continuous practice that can be ignited in every new moment, in each new encounter or opportunity, of our lives. Part of the failure of equality feminism has been the assumption that once an "equal" right has been won, the fight is done. Now more than ever we know this to be false, as recently seen with how voting rights and abortion rights have been under attack and withdrawn. Rights are neither permanent nor guaranteed, even constitutionally. The fight takes place in each moment of each day. "You have to act as if it were possible to radically transform the world," Angela Davis said. "And you have to do it all the time." Freedom is not like checking a box; rather, it is constitutive of the journey of our lives. None of us are finished products and neither is freedom work. And so, if feminists took up the call of freedom, we could change the teleology—and the vision—of the movement.

Reclaiming freedom isn't just about America's endless—and, for many, endlessly tiring—culture wars. It also helps us reconsider our own debates and disagreements within feminism by moving away from the equality mindset and the gender binary and, ultimately, identity politics. Centering a feminist politics on freedom also allows us to reimagine the relationship between the individual and the collective as not antagonistic but intertwined. The equality mindset has been responsible for this antagonism, I think, particularly as it espouses the patriarchal values of capitalism and individualism that have come to be known as quintessentially American. As such, equality feminism construes *individual* success as *feminist* success. Did so-and-so female multimillionaire celebrity or CEO get paid the same as the male multimillionaire celebrity or CEO? Yes? Success!

Among a number of feminists, Susan Faludi has rightly criticized what she has called this "individualist style of feminism," epitomized by *Lean In* and celebrity feminisms. This style not only reduces a mass movement to personal choice but has proven to be a "double-edged sword," Faludi wrote in the *New York Times*, "because if an individual embodies the principle [of feminism], the principle can be disproved by dethroning the individual." If feminism pivots toward freedom, it can break free of this antagonistic binary of the individual and the collective.

This pivot liberates feminism by expanding its philosophical capacity beyond the single issue of gender and beyond the individual to consider, more broadly, how our intersubjectivity, our interconnectedness, conditions our freedom. Here, my mind jumps to the virtual, and how our lives are increasingly lived online. Social media companies have trained us to value personalization at the expense of—literally for their profit off of—our privacy. This is not the self-creation of freedom but capitalist commodification. Only a feminism that centers freedom—dignity, accountability, and justice—can help us strategize and develop policies to protect our privacy and our personhood. And since *Dobbs*, we have already witnessed how these companies are selling our personal data to the highest bidder, including the state. In August 2022, Motherboard obtained court documents revealing that Facebook gave private messages sent between Nebraskan seventeen-year-old Celeste Burgess and her mother about the teen's at-home medication abortion to the police; both were then arrested and charged both with multiple crimes. Social media companies are only able to offer "free" services by selling our private data. Feminists will be grappling with many more indignities and rights violations online in the coming years—and freedom, not equality, can help us generate the strategies and talking points to fight back.

Furthermore, feminists contending with the shortcomings of the sex positivity movement vis-à-vis the #MeToo movement could think through the tension and reframe the debate utilizing the definition of freedom I put forth here, based in accountability and care. Because sexual freedom is not carelessness. It is care-*fullness*. It is understanding that you are responsible for the choices you make, that you are accountable to the people you choose to be intimate with. From a feminist-freedom lens, accountability inheres in and is constitutive of sex positivity and sexual freedom, more generally. The ethic of care that inheres in freedom, too, means that we must extend our care work to sex workers, rather than demonize them. Carceral strategies that result in their criminalization and incarceration are not forms of care that improve their well-being or respect their human dignity.

We—not just feminists but especially feminists—need to reclaim freedom and situate it as the North Star of the feminist movement. This is tied to the second, larger intention of this book: to stop playing by the patriarchy's rules. To no longer agree to the terms and conditions of the debate over our lives. Because if we keep playing by their rules, if we continue to seek the same rights and privileges as men, if we continue to use the same language and definitions prescribed by the logic of equality and the principle of the gender binary, then we will continue to lose—our rights, our bodily autonomy, our dignity, and our lives.

We should not predicate our fight for bodily autonomy on equality unless we want men to continue to control and define our bodies. Bodily autonomy will remain a foregone conclusion, for example, if we continue to participate in the misogynistic pro-choice/pro-life framework—a framework even deployed in the *Dobbs* decision, in which Justice Alito and his concurring judges repeatedly opined about protecting the life of a fetus without remotely considering the life of the real, legal, pregnant person. A world in which justice is understood as care and accountability rather than as incarceration and punishment will remain out of reach if we continue to remedy violence with more violence under the guise of justice.

Breaking Free encourages us to let go of old ways of thinking, behaving, and engaging with other people in the world. In this book, I have offered ideas, logics, and ways of thinking about ourselves and our actions in the hope that we reevaluate our values, redefine concepts and language, refuse supremacist frameworks, and reclaim the narrative. That is power. Controlling the narrative—in terms of establishing the set definitions of the language and frameworks—is the key to our collective freedom.

Capitalism is our bugbear and is certainly the bugbear of this book. It is the fuel of the white supremacist cis-heteropatriarchy, and it is integral to equality feminism and its subsidiaries, commodity feminism and carceral feminism. In calling for a reevaluation of values, my hope is that if we change our values, we can, in turn, trigger a butterfly effect that changes where the money goes—who gets it and how it is distributed. Capitalism may be inescapable, but we still have the power to decide what we do with our capital. Where we invest and spend our money, for better or worse, represents the *materialization of our values*. Changing our priorities means changing where we put our money—from a freedom mindset, this amounts to allocating less money for policing and militarization and more for housing, health care, and education. What if, for example, a *fraction* of the more than $800 billion allocated to the Department of Defense in 2023, or a fraction of the $30 billion given to so-called crime prevention and, more broadly, law enforcement, were invested elsewhere? What if the people we elected to office decided to reroute money directed to the nuclear weapons program and to hiring more police officers and prosecutors to, say, a universal basic income? Or public education? Or, dare I say it, universal health care?

Community groups and nonprofit collectives are already doing this revaluing and revisioning work under the guiding vision that government budgets are moral documents that should reflect the values of that constituency. In New Jersey, the city of Newark has undergone a seismic change in policing and public safety since 2016. A coalition led by a group of residents known as the Newark Community Street Team worked with local government and police to craft several community-led and systems-led strategies focused on crime prevention and trauma healing rather than punishment. And after fifty years of being considered among the country's most violent cities, as of 2020, Newark was no longer on that list.

While the equal right to vote is not guaranteed, and voting itself—as the organization Indigenous Action has observed—is not an act of harm reduction, those of us who can vote do have the power to elect representatives who value people over profits. Cultivating what some call a "conscientious capitalism" is not the final goal in our journey to creating a freer and more caring world, but it is a start. Being conscientious about where we spend our money and thinking about who gets it are the first steps to changing the flow of capital. We need to develop a critical consciousness about any and all power—here, financial power—we have in our hands.

But again, because our lives are differently situated, not all of us can make the same choices or take the same risks. This reality—the reality that many of us grew up with little to no money or few resources—is why I am reluctant to take a purist perspective on capitalism. Many of us have needed to take the jobs we could get in order to pay our rent, cover our medical expenses, and put food in our bellies. Compromise, ethical compromise, inheres in self-preservation. Not all of us have a trust fund and an apartment fully paid for by Mommy and Daddy that allow us to live radically queer anarchist lives and criticize people for "working for the man."

I have spent years figuring out where the line is for me—where I can still stand in my integrity while keeping a roof over my head and taking care of my cats (and, yes, myself). There will always be capital, or systems of exchange. But if we change our thinking, if we change our values and are ethically committed to living those values, I am hopeful we can transform capitalism as we know it.

I began this conclusion with an epigraph—the only one in the book—that for decades has been a quote that has catalyzed my own curiosity and made me unafraid to ask questions. As I would always tell my students, there are no bad or wrong questions. Barbara Johnson has taught me

Breaking Free

to always ask, "What else?" And this "What else?" is born from the imperative of perceiving one's ignorance and a commitment to curiosity.

What if we continued to ask, What else?

What else besides equality?

What else besides the gender binary?

I think the answer can be found in another of Johnson's texts, specifically in the passage I quoted earlier, which arguably inspired this entire book, and which I quote again because its message needs repeating:

> As long as a feminist analysis polarizes the world by gender, women are still standing *facing* men. Standing against men, or against patriarchy, might not be structurally so different from existing *for* it. A feminist logic that pits women against men operates along the lines of heterosexual thinking. But conflicts among feminists require women to pay attention to each other, to take each other's reality seriously, to face each other. The requirement that women face each other may not have anything erotic or sexual about it, but it may have everything to do with the eradication of the misogyny that remains within feminists, and with the attempt to escape the logic of heterosexuality. It places difference *among* women rather than exclusively *between* the sexes. Of course, patriarchy has always played women off against each other and manipulated differences among women for its own purposes. Nevertheless, feminists have to take the risk of confronting and negotiating differences among women if we are ever to transform such differences into positive rather than negative forces in women's lives.

If equality feminism relies on the patriarchy's organizational principle of the gender binary, then the *polarization* this engenders means feminism will continue to relinquish its cause to the concerns of men and in the service of men.

Freedom is not the opposite of equality. Rather, the ideas and practices of freedom put forth in this book reveal to us that the answer to the "What else?" question about equality is *mutuality*.

266

Mutuality finds dignity in difference—it does not conceive of human dignity in terms of sameness, or the hateful belief of only respecting the dignity and humanity of people who look like you. Rather, it is a shared understanding of and respect for our self-creation as mutual creation. Our freedom work falters if we fail to understand our mutual coexistence and interdependence, both for our survival and for us to thrive. An ethics of mutuality means that we value accountability and care as levers of freedom and justice.

Mutuality can also transform our politics outside the constricting and exclusionary identity politics that has dominated the feminist movement. The equality mindset has bound the feminist movement to the gender binary, which has resulted in a lot of infighting about the identity of *woman*. Instead, freedom feminism emphasizes the politics of mutuality because it acknowledges that our lives—and our oppressions—are linked. Through this lens, we can create a broad-based, diverse political movement that, rather than fighting for rights on an identity-by-identity basis, reimagines a politics focused on sites of collective struggle that strive for justice and to realize our human dignity and freedom.

"Imagine living in a world where there is no domination, where females and males are not alike or even always equal, but where a vision of mutuality is the ethos shaping our interaction," bell hooks wrote in *Feminism Is for Everybody*. "If equality is evoked as the only standard by which it is deemed acceptable for people to meet across boundaries and create community, then there is little hope," she said. "Fortunately, mutuality is a more constructive and positive foundation for the building of ties that allow for differences in status, position, power, and privilege whether determined by race, class, sexuality, religion, or nationality."

Mutuality does not render our humanity—our rights or our worth—in terms of a supremacist hierarchy or binaries. Instead of the discrimination of difference, which has constituted our nation's systems and institutions, we find dignity in difference. Mutuality, in terms of honoring our mutual dignity and providing mutual aid, allows us to recognize and account for the specific needs of individuals and communities.

Guided by a vision of freedom, feminists can create a world that values the dignity, belonging, and joy of all people, a world in which justice is exacted through care and accountability. Where love is a power, not a weakness. A world in which we are encouraged to create authentic lives. A world in which we are truly free.

ACKNOWLEDGMENTS

Generations of women made this book possible, two of whom are recorded in the dedication. My grandmother Angela Bianco and my mentor Barbara Johnson taught me, in different ways, the meaning of life and that every person can decide *how* they will live each day, even in the face of death. Illness took them too soon—both died at the age of 61—yet their lessons have made me the person I am today and the person I aspire to become.

Inspiration for this book came from women like my grandmother and BJ whose ideas and activism have informed me, including Simone de Beauvoir, Audre Lorde, bell hooks, Barbara Smith, Angela Davis, and Elizabeth Grosz, among several others. I have attempted to incorporate as many of these women as possible into this book to show that no idea is the creation of one person in one moment but rather is an immanence of a collective of people over time.

My agent, Laura Mazer, at Wendy Sherman Associates, believed in me and in this project when no one else did. Thank you, Laura, for being my champion.

To my editor, Colleen Lawrie; my production editor, Kelly Anne Lenkevich; and the entire team at PublicAffairs—especially Pete Garceau, whose incredible cover design captured the fiery essence of this project, and Brittany Smail for her meticulous copyedits—thank you for investing in this project and making this book a reality. And thank you, Colleen, for ushering this book through the editorial process with such grace and aplomb.

Thank you to Sara Krolewski for her thoughtful fact-checking, and Peter Majerle is owed a lifelong debt for fact-checking nearly the entire manuscript at the eleventh hour and providing me much-needed peace of mind.

Kristin Cofer took amazing photos of me for this book and for the book's publicity. Thank you for making me look good and for also taking photos of me with my cats.

So many friends and fellow feminists fought and cared for this book, from the proposal stage to the chapter-reading process to the proofing stage. Mona Eltahawy, Darnell Moore, Charlotte Clymer, Soraya Chemaly, Caroline Simard, Michelle Garcia (and her mama!), Carrie Kholi-Murchison, Renée Jacobs, and Lisa Dorfman supported this project through their words, insights, and invaluable feedback.

Thank you to Sarah Schulman for reading the entire manuscript and proffering extremely idiosyncratic Sarah Schulman feedback that pushed me to do essential revisions.

The absolute, incisive brilliance and expert minds of Jill Filipovic and Claire Potter sharpened my ideas and my writing in unimaginable yet crucial ways. They leveled this book up!

My BB, Meredith Bennett-Smith, read and edited multiple versions of this manuscript. For years, she has been my second set of eyes and has been integral to this project. Thank you, BB, for making me a better writer, for giving my ideas a home (at Mic, Quartz, and now, NBC), and for being my friend.

Friends have been my lifeline throughout this—particularly isolating—experience. They have checked in on me and encouraged me at moments when I thought I had nothing left to give.

I love you, Vicky Bond, for being My Ultimate Virgo and always telling it like it is, knowing not to sugarcoat a damn thing with me.

Acknowledgments

I love you, Noor Noman, for your generosity of spirit and your fearlessness in living, and for your daily affirmations that reassured me despite all my anxiety and doubt. Also, thank you for swooping in and doing essential proofing at the end of this process. I am sorry-not-sorry to say that I will be saving all your voice notes, for all of posterity, and for my pleasure.

Along with Noor and BB, my *SATC*—Sapphics and the Caira—group would be incomplete without Caira Conner, whose wisdom and compassion have filled my heart.

I am deeply grateful for the friendship of "KRay" Karen Costa, Tracy Gilchrist, and Grace Moon, all of whom have been in my life for years—KRay, since the beginning of my life—and each of whom have, in their own way, helped me keep my feet on the ground. I extend this gratitude to my broader circle of friends and family—especially Amedeo Tumolillo, Grace Chu, Nicole Hoschuetzky, Miriam Weiskind, Juanita Erb, Karman Kregloe, Bridget McManus, Jill LaLonde, Derrick Clifton, Sarah Fonseca, Rebecca Ward, Melissa Abad, Marie Rutkoski, Kate Gormley, Caroline Modarressy-Tehrani, Kera Bolonik, Gerard McGeary, Steven Syrek, Chris Roney, Saga Mellbin, Adele Gilani, Gabrielle Korn, Lynn Ballen, Trish Bendix, Kathryn Lounsbery, Hannah Skelton, Francesca Bianco, Maria Bianco-Falcone, AdriAnn Bianco, TJ Bianco, and Charene Scheeper.

I am extremely fortunate to count Aida Mariam Davis as a coconspirator and friend. Aida, you have given me so much life these past couple of years. Thank you for *seeing* me and for *getting* me and for your vision of a future filled with belonging, dignity, justice, and joy.

Bridget Sweetin-Lilla has taught me the meaning of friendship. Bridget, from airmailing donuts to reading my manuscript, from sending cat memes, daily, to our hours-long phone conversations, you have been my rock, and you have kept me from burning it all down.

Holding down a full-time job while writing a book is no joke. Thank you to my bosses—David Johnson and Eric Nee—for allowing me to carve out a work schedule that opened the time I needed to write this book, and thanks to my entire *Stanford Social Innovation Review* team for their encouragement. Brian Karo, thank you for *community*—two gay peas in a walnut shell. And a special shout-out is owed to Barbara Wheeler-Bride for always stepping up and stepping in when I would hit panic mode or when I would proverbially throw up my hands and yell, "Technology!"

Thank you, Andrea Rees Davies, for being my first reader and for being a stable presence in my life as I worked my way through the book-writing and publication process.

Last, but certainly not least, I must acknowledge the four furballs that have been my constant companions: Simone de Beauvoir, Freddie Nietzsche, (Amanda) Gorman, and Audre THEE Lorde. While not quite as profound as the philosophers and poets they are named for, these creatures have certainly transformed me and given me comfort and joy at the most challenging of times.

And if you've made it this far: Thank you, dear reader, for engaging with me in this book.

BIBLIOGRAPHY

The materials on the following list served as both inspiration and sources for the writing of this book:

Abdulrahim, Raja, and Patrick Kingsley. "Al Jazeera Reporter Is Killed in West Bank." *New York Times*, May 11, 2022. www.nytimes.com/2022/05/11/world/middleeast /al-jazeera-journalist-killed-west-bank.html.

Adams, Abigail. Letter from Abigail Adams to John Adams, March 31, 1776. Adams Family Papers. www.masshist.org/digitaladams/archive/doc?id=L17760331aa.

Adams, Char. "Black Women Played a Critical Role in Helping to Free Brittney Griner." NBCBLK, NBC News, December 13, 2022. www.nbcnews.com/news/nbcblk/black -women-played-critical-role-helping-free-brittney-griner-rcna61020.

Adams, John. Letter from John Adams to Abigail Adams, April 14, 1776. Adams Family Papers. www.masshist.org/digitaladams/archive/doc?id=L17760414ja.

Aday, Tara. "The Effectiveness of the Violence Against Women Act (VAWA) in Creating System-Level Change." *SPHNA Review* 11, no. 1 (2015). https://scholarworks.gvsu .edu/cgi/viewcontent.cgi?article=1042&context=spnhareview.

Ade, Yewande. "Disability Was Treated Like a Crime for Many Years." *History of Yesterday* (Medium), April 19, 2022. https://medium.com/history-of-yesterday.com/it-was -once-illegal-to-be-ugly-in-america-fd07df79d3e6.

Advancing New Standards of Reproductive Health. *The Turnaway Study*. 2020. www .ansirh.org/research/ongoing/turnaway-study.

Ahmed, Sara. *Complaint!*. Durham, NC: Duke University Press, 2021.

Ahmed, Sara. *Living a Feminist Life*. Durham, NC: Duke University Press, 2017.

Ahmed, Sara. "A Phenomenology of Whiteness." *Feminist Theory* 8, no. 2 (August 2007). https://journals.sagepub.com/doi/abs/10.1177/1464700107078139.

Alexander, Michelle. *The New Jim Crow: Mass Incarceration in the Age of Colorblindness*. New York: The New Press, 2011.

All People Created Equal Act, HB 194, 2015 Session. New Hampshire. www.gencourt .state.nh.us/legislation/2015/HB0194.pdf.

American Muslim Bar Association. "The Islamic Principle of Rahma: A Call for Reproductive Justice." April 15, 2022. www.ambalegal.org/ambainthenews/the-islamic -principle-of-rahma-a-call-for-reproductive-justice.

Anderson, Elizabeth S. "What Is the Point of Equality?" *Ethics* 109, no. 2 (January 1999): 287–337.

Anderson, Piper. "Building a Culture of Accountability." *Stanford Social Innovation Review*, June 28, 2021. https://ssir.org/articles/entry/building_a_culture_of_account ability.

Antonio Vitolo; Jake's Bar and Grill, LLC v. Isabella Casillas Guzman, Administrator of the Small Business Administration, Nos. 21-5517/5528 (6th Cir, May 27, 2021). https:// int.nyt.com/data/documenttools/sixth-circuit-rrf-decision/32353ea5090fabb/full .pdf.

Anzaldúa, Gloria. *Borderlands/La Frontera: The New Mestiza*. San Francisco: Aunt Lute Books, 2018.

Anzaldúa, Gloria. "Speaking in Tongues: A Letter to Third World Women Writers." In *Women Writing Resistance: Essays on Latin America and the Caribbean*, edited by Jennifer Browdy de Hernandez. Boston: South End Press, 2003.

AP Stylebook (@APStylebook). "Avoid the vague 'officer-involved' for shootings and other cases involving police." Twitter, August 25, 2020. https://twitter.com/apstylebook /status/1298283084631150592?lang=en.

Appiah, Kwame Anthony. "I'm Jewish and I Don't Identify as White. Why Must I Check That Box?" *New York Times Magazine*, October 13, 2020 (updated May 19, 2021). www.nytimes.com/2020/10/13/magazine/im-jewish-and-dont-identify-as-white -why-must-i-check-that-box.html.

Arcidiacono, Peter, Josh Kinsler, and Tyler Ransom. "Legacy and Athlete Preferences at Harvard." National Bureau of Economic Research, working paper 26316, September 2019. www.nber.org/papers/w26316.

Arendt, Hannah. "Freedom and Politics, a Lecture." In *Thinking Without a Banister*, edited by Jerome Kohn. New York: Schocken Books, 2018.

Arendt, Hannah. "What Is Freedom?" In *Between Past and Future*. New York: Penguin Books, 2006.

The Armed Conflict Location & Event Data Project. "Anti-LGBT+ Mobilization on the Rise in the United States," June 16, 2022. https://acleddata.com/2022/06/16 /fact-sheet-anti-lgbt-mobilization-is-on-the-rise-in-the-united-states/.

Arp, Kristana. *The Bonds of Freedom: Simone de Beauvoir's Existentialist Ethics*. Chicago: Open Court, 2001.

Ascher, Carol. *Simone de Beauvoir: A Life of Freedom*. Boston: Beacon Press, 1981.

Assar, Vijith. "An Interactive Guide to Ambiguous Grammar." *McSweeney's*, September 3, 2015. www.mcsweeneys.net/articles/an-interactive-guide-to-ambiguous-grammar.

Bibliography

Associated Press. "House of Representatives Passes Equal Pay Bill for US Women Athletes." *ESPN*, December 22, 2022. www.espn.com/soccer/united-states-usaw /story/4837135/house-of-representatives-passes-equal-pay-bill-for-us-women-ath-letes.

Associated Press. "Medical Examiner Says Jayland Walker Was Shot Dozens of Times." *NPR*, July 15, 2022. www.npr.org/2022/07/15/1111760958/jayland-walker-autopsy -shot-akron.

Associated Press. "An Ohio Police Officer Was Cleared in the Shooting of Teenager Ma'Khia Bryant." *NPR*, March 12, 2022. www.npr.org/2022/03/12/1086283433 /police-officer-cleared-makhia-bryant-shooting.

Aswad, Jem. "Read Britney Spears' Full Statement Against Conservatorship: 'I Am Trau-matized.'" *Variety*, June 23, 2021. https://variety.com/2021/music/news/britney -spears-full-statement-conservatorship-1235003940/.

Austin, Sophie. "After #FreeBritney, California to Limit Conservatorships." *The Hill*, Sep-tember 30, 2022. https://thehill.com/homenews/ap/ap-u-s-news/ap-after-freebritney -california-to-limit-conservatorships/.

Bachman, Rachel. "U.S. Women's Soccer Games Outearned Men's Games." *Wall Street Journal*, June 17, 2019. www.wsj.com/articles/u-s-womens-soccer-games-out -earned-mens-games-11560765600.

Baker, Carrie N. "'An Inclusive Constitution': Professor Julie Suk on the Equal Rights Amendment." *Ms.* April 2, 2021. https://msmagazine.com/2021/04/02/equal-rights-amendment-era-constitution-julie-suk/.

Baldwin, James. *The Cross of Redemption: Uncollected Writings*. Edited by Randall Kenan. New York: Vintage International, 2010.

Baldwin, James. *James Baldwin: Collected Essays*. Edited by Toni Morrison. New York: The Library of America, 1998.

Baldwin, James. *The Price of the Ticket: Collected Nonfiction 1948–1985*. Boston: Beacon Press, 1992.

Bambara, Toni Cade, ed. *The Black Woman: An Anthology*. New York: Simon & Schuster, 1970.

Basile, Kathleen C., Sharon G. Smith, Marcie-jo Kresnow, Srijana Khatiwada, and Ruth W. Leemis. "The National Intimate Partner and Sexual Violence Survey: 2016/2017 Report on Sexual Violence." Centers for Disease Control and Prevention, June 2022. www.cdc.gov/violenceprevention/pdf/nisvs/nisvsReportonSexualViolence.pdf.

Baumgardner, Jennifer, and Amy Richards, eds. *Manifesta: Young Women, Feminism, and the Future*. New York: Farrar, Straus and Giroux, 2000.

Beal, Frances M. "Double Jeopardy: To Be Black and Female." In *Words of Fire: An An-thology of African-American Feminist Thought*, edited by Beverly Guy-Sheftall, 146–156. New York: The New Press, 1995.

Beauvoir, Simone de. *The Ethics of Ambiguity*. Translated by Bernard Frechtman. New York: Carol Publishing Group, 1996.

Beauvoir, Simone de. *Pyrrhus and Cineas*. In *Simone de Beauvoir: Philosophical Writings*, edited by Margaret A. Simons, with Marybeth Timmermann and Mary Beth Mader. Chicago: University of Illinois Press, 2004.

Beauvoir, Simone de. *The Second Sex*. Translated by Constance Borde and Sheila Malovany-Chevallier. New York: Alfred A. Knopf, 2010.

Beauvoir, Simone de. *Simone de Beauvoir: Philosophical Writings*. Edited by Margaret A. Simons, with Marybeth Timmermann and Mary Beth Mader. Chicago: University of Illinois Press, 2004.

Beck, Koa. *White Feminism: From the Suffragettes to Influencers and Who They Leave Behind*. New York: Atria Books, 2021.

Beety, Valena. *Manifesting Justice: Wrongly Convicted Women Reclaim Their Rights*. New York: Citadel Press, 2022.

Bell, W. Kamau, and Kate Schatz. *Do the Work! An Antiracist Activity Book*. New York: Workman Publishing, 2022.

Benjamin, Ruha. *Viral Justice: How We Grow the World We Want*. Princeton, NJ: Princeton University Press, 2022.

Bergson, Henri. *Creative Evolution*. Translated by Arthur Mitchell. Mineola, NY: Dover Publications, 1998.

Bergson, Henri. *Matter and Memory*. Translated by N. M. Paul and W. S. Palmer. New York: Zone Books, 1991.

Berlant, Lauren. *Cruel Optimism*. Durham, NC: Duke University Press, 2011.

Berlant, Lauren. "On Her Book *Cruel Optimism*." *ROROTOKO*, June 4, 2012. http://rorotoko.com/interview/20120605_berlant_lauren_on_cruel_optimism/?page=2.

Berlant, Lauren. *The Queen of America Goes to Washington City: Essays on Sex and Citizenship*. Durham, NC: Duke University Press, 1997.

Berman, Russell. "Ruth Bader Ginsburg Versus the Equal Rights Amendment." *Atlantic*, February 15, 2020. www.theatlantic.com/politics/archive/2020/02/ruth-bader-ginsburg-equal-rights-amendment/606556/.

Best, Amy L. *Fast Cars, Cool Rides: The Accelerating World of Youth and Their Cars*. New York: NYU Press, 2006.

Bianco, Marcie. "Britney Fans Angry at Justin Timberlake Have a Point." CNN Opinion, February 10, 2021. www.cnn.com/2021/02/10/opinions/britney-spears-documentary-justin-timberlake-accountability-bianco/index.html.

Bianco, Marcie. "Britney Spears' Conservatorship Fight Reflects One of Society's Most Sacred Desires." NBC Think, February 14, 2021. www.nbcnews.com/think/opinion/framing-britney-spears-freebritney-our-universal-desire-freedom-ncna1257812.

Bianco, Marcie. "*Grace and Frankie*'s New Season Pushes New Boundaries." Women's Media Center, June 6, 2016. https://womensmediacenter.com/news-features/grace-and-frankies-new-season-pushes-new-boundaries.

Bianco, Marcie. "HBO Max's New Abortion Doc 'The Janes' Is Timely, Haunting—and Ultimately Hopeful." NBC Think, June 8, 2022. www.nbcnews.com/think/opinion/hbo-maxs-new-abortion-doc-janes-timely-hopeful-rcna32472.

Bianco, Marcie. "International Women's Day Is Symbolic. The ERA Is Dead (Again). What Does Women's Equality Really Mean?" NBC Think, March 8, 2019. www .nbcnews.com/think/opinion/international-women-s-day-symbolic-era-dead -again-what-does-ncna980796.

Bianco, Marcie. "Miley Cyrus' Split with Liam Hemsworth Isn't Just Celebrity Gossip—It's a Blow to the Patriarchy." NBC Think, August 16, 2019. www.nbcnews .com/think/opinion/miley-cyrus-split-liam-hemsworth-isn-t-just-celebrity-fodder -ncna1042931.

Bianco, Marcie. "Nothing Says Misogyny Like Defining Feminism as Equality for All." Quartz, March 29, 2017. https://qz.com/943068/the-future-of-feminism-the-gender -revolution-has-stalled-because-feminists-think-empowement-is-more-important -than-power/.

Bianco, Marcie. "Queer Women Have a Lot to Worry About When They Travel for Work." Vice, January 7, 2020. www.vice.com/en/article/n7jbjw/queer-women-have-a-lot -to-worry-about-when-they-travel-for-work.

Bianco, Marcie. "'Respect for Marriage Act' Is a Pitiful Band-Aid." NBC Think, November 29, 2022. www.nbcnews.com/think/opinion/senate-vote-tonight-passes-gay -marriage-bill-band-aid-rcna59264.

Bianco, Marcie. "Women Running for Our Lives." Women's Media Center, August 23, 2016. https://womensmediacenter.com/news-features/women-running-for-our-lives.

Biden, Joseph R. "Statement from President Biden on the Equal Rights Amendment." White House, January 27, 2022. www.whitehouse.gov/briefing-room/statements -releases/2022/01/27/statement-from-president-biden-on-the-equal-rights -amendment/.

Black Feminist Future. "#BringBrittneyHome." https://blackfeministfuture.org/bring brittneyhome/.

Black, Meg. "Violence Against Women Is an Issue That Concerns Us All." UNICEF USA, December 10, 2018. www.unicefusa.org/stories/violence-against-women-issue -concerns-us-all/35247.

Blain, Keisha N. Until I Am Free: Fannie Lou Hamer's Enduring Message to America. Boston: Beacon Press, 2021.

Blistein, Jon. "Norma McCorvey, Jane Roe of 'Roe v. Wade,' Said She Was Paid to Take Anti-Abortion Stance." Rolling Stone, May 19, 2020. www.rollingstone.com /culture/culture-news/norma-mccorvey-jane-roe-roe-v-wade-pro-life-abortion -paid-1002550/.

Block, Melissa. "Olympic Runner Caster Semenya Wants to Compete, Not Defend Her Womanhood." NPR, July 28, 2021. www.npr.org/sections/tokyo-olympics-live -updates/2021/07/28/1021503989/women-runners-testosterone-olympics.

Bloom, Amy. In Love: A Memoir of Love and Loss. New York: Random House, 2022.

Bonn, Kyle. "Has USA Won the World Cup for Men? List of USMNT Results and Complete History at FIFA Soccer Tournament." Sporting News, March 30, 2022. www

.sportingnews.com/us/soccer/news/has-usa-won-world-cup-soccer-usmnt-history
-results-list/nghObzvajkdd7qfrwojd8tij.

Booker, Brakkton. "Driving While Black Is Still a Death Sentence." *Politico*, April 13, 2021.
www.politico.com/newsletters/the-recast/2021/04/13/driving-while-black-daunte
-wright-caron-nazario-492458.

Branigin, Anne. "A Battle Over Title IX: Can It Be Used to Exclude Trans Athletes?" *Washington Post*, September 29, 2022. www.washingtonpost.com/nation/2022/09/29
/connecticut-trans-athlete-lawsuit/.

Brenan, Megan. "Americans' Strong Support for Euthanasia Persists." Gallup, May 31,
2018. https://news.gallup.com/poll/235145/americans-strong-support-euthanasia
-persists.aspx.

Brooker, Jena. "Congress Promised Debt Relief to Farmers of Color. They Might Not
Get It." Grist, October 4, 2021. https://grist.org/agriculture/congress-promised-debt
-relief-to-farmers-of-color-they-might-not-get-it/.

brown, adrienne maree. *Emergent Strategies: Shaping Change, Changing Worlds*. Chico,
CA: AK Press, 2017.

Brown v. Board of Education at 65: A Promise Unfulfilled. Hearing Before the Committee on Education and Labor, US House of Representatives. 116th Cong. (2019). www
.govinfo.gov/content/pkg/CHRG-116hhrg36594/pdf/CHRG-116hhrg36594.pdf.

Brown, Wendy. *States of Injury: Power and Freedom in Late Modernity*. Princeton, NJ:
Princeton University Press, 1995.

Bruney, Gabrielle. "Abortion Is a Fundamentally American Act." *Jezebel*, July 4, 2022.
https://jezebel.com/abortion-american-history-1849079359.

Buckley, Cara, and Kate Hammer. "Man Is Stabbed in Attack After Admiring a Stranger."
New York Times, August 19, 2006. www.nytimes.com/2006/08/19/nyregion/19stab
.html.

Bunch, Charlotte. "Lesbians in Revolt." In *Women's Liberation! Feminist Writings That
Inspired a Revolution & Still Can*, edited by Alix Kates Shulman and Honor Moore,
210–215. New York: Library of America, 2021.

Bureau of Labor Statistics, US Department of Labor. "College Tuition and Fees Increase 63
Percent Since January 2006." *The Economics Daily*, August 30, 2016. www.bls.gov/opub
/ted/2016/college-tuition-and-fees-increase-63-percent-since-january-2006.htm.

Butler, Judith. *The Force of Nonviolence: An Ethico-Political Bind*. New York: Verso, 2020.

Butler, Judith. "Gender Performance: *The TransAdvocate* Interviews Judith Butler." By
Cristan Williams. *TransAdvocate*. www.transadvocate.com/gender-performance
-the-transadvocate-interviews-judith-butler_n_13652.htm.

Butler, Judith. *Giving an Account of Oneself*. New York: Fordham University Press, 2005.

Carlisle, Madeline. "Inside the Right-Wing Movement to Ban Trans Youth from Sports." *Time*,
May 16, 2022. https://time.com/6176799/trans-sports-bans-conservative-movement/.

Carmon, Irin. "I, Too, Have a Human Form." *New York Magazine*, May 19, 2022. https://
nymag.com/intelligencer/2022/05/roe-v-wade-draft-opinion-pregnant-body
-erased.html.

Carruthers, Charlene A. *Unapologetic: A Black, Queer, and Feminist Mandate for Radical Movements*. Boston: Beacon Press, 2018.

Castro, Mayra A. Rodríguez, ed. *Audre Lorde: Dream of Europe. Selected Seminars and Interviews: 1984–1992*. Berkeley: Kenning Editions, 2020.

Catalano, Shannon. *Intimate Partner Violence, 1993–2010*. US Department of Justice Bureau of Labor Statistics, September 29, 2015. https://bjs.ojp.gov/content/pub/pdf /ipv9310.pdf.

Centers for Disease Control and Prevention. "Working Together to Reduce Black Maternal Mortality." April 6, 2022. https://www.cdc.gov/healthequity/features/maternal -mortality/index.html.

Chisholm, Shirley. "For the Equal Rights Amendment—August 10, 1970," congressional floor speech at US House of Representatives. Iowa State University Archives of Women's Political Communication. https://awpc.cattcenter.iastate.edu/2017/03/21 /for-the-equal-rights-amendment-aug-10-1970/.

Chu, Andrea Long. *Females*. New York: Verso, 2019.

Chua, Charmaine. "Abolition Is a Constant Struggle: Five Lessons from Minneapolis." *Theory & Event* 23, no. 4 Supplement (October 2020): S-127–S-147.

Clarke, Cheryl. "Lesbianism: An Act of Resistance." In *Words of Fire: An Anthology of African-American Feminist Thought*, edited by Beverly Guy-Sheftall, 242–252. New York: The New Press, 1995.

Clarke, Cheryl. "New Notes on Lesbianism." In *The Days of Good Looks: The Prose and Poetry of Cheryl Clarke, 1980 to 2005*. Boston: Da Capo, 2006.

Cleary, Skye C. *How to Be Authentic: Simone de Beauvoir and the Quest for Fulfillment*. New York: St. Martin's Press, 2022.

CNN Newsource. "Physician-Assisted Suicide Fast Facts." KESQ News Channel 3, May 26, 2022. https://kesq.com/news/2022/05/26/physician-assisted-suicide-fast -facts-2/.

Coates, Ta-Nehisi. "I'm Not Black, I'm Kanye." *Atlantic*, May 7, 2018. www.theatlantic .com/entertainment/archive/2018/05/im-not-black-im-kanye/559763/.

Cogan, Marin. "Not All Religions Oppose Abortion." *Vox*, July 3, 2022. www.vox .com/2022/7/3/23190408/judaism-rabbi-abortion-religion-reproductive-rights.

Cohen, Susan A. "Abortion and Women of Color: The Bigger Picture." *Guttmacher Policy Review* 11, no. 3 (August 6, 2008). www.guttmacher.org/gpr/2008/08/abortion -and-women-color-bigger-picture.

Colbert, Soyica Diggs. *Radical Vision: A Biography of Lorraine Hansberry*. New Haven, CT: Yale University Press, 2021.

Collins, Patricia Hill. *Black Feminist Thought: Knowledge, Consciousness, and the Politics of Empowerment*. Rev. 10th anniversary 2nd ed. New York: Routledge, 2000.

Combahee River Collective. "A Black Feminist Statement." In *Words of Fire: An Anthology of African-American Feminist Thought*, edited by Beverly Guy-Sheftall, 232–240. New York: The New Press, 1995.

Committee for Abortion Rights and Against Sterilization Abuse (CARASA). 1979 pamphlet. In *Women Under Attack: Victories, Backlash, and the Fight for Reproductive Freedom*, edited by Susan E. Davis. Boston: South End Press, 1988.

Conrad, Ryan, ed. *Against Equality: Queer Revolution Not Mere Inclusion*. Chico, CA: AK Press, 2014.

Coontz, Stephanie. "Do Millennial Men Want Stay-at-Home Wives?" *New York Times*, March 31, 2017. www.nytimes.com/2017/03/31/opinion/sunday/do-millennial-men -want-stay-at-home-wives.html.

Cooper, Anna Julia. "The Status of Women in America." In *Words of Fire: An Anthology of African-American Feminist Thought*, edited by Beverly Guy-Sheftall, 44–49. New York: The New Press, 1995.

Cooper, Brittney C. *Beyond Respectability: The Intellectual Thought of Race Women*. Urbana, IL: University of Illinois Press, 2017.

Cooper, Marianne. *Cut Adrift: Families in Insecure Times*. Berkeley: University of California Press, 2014.

Coote, Anna, and Beatrix Campbell. *Sweet Freedom: The Struggle for Women's Liberation*. Oxford: Blackwell Publishers, 1987.

Cordano, Karen. "Running While Female." *HuffPost*, July 28, 2014. www.huffpost.com /entry/running-while-female_b_5562343.

Costas, Eliza. "Activist Shannon Watts on Mass Shooting in Boulder, Fighting Gun Violence." Katie Couric Media, March 12, 2021. https://katiecouric.com/news/shannon -watts-fighting-gun-violence/.

Cott, Nancy F. *The Grounding of Modern Feminism*. New Haven, CT: Yale University Press, 1987.

Cottom, Tressie McMillan. *Thick: And Other Essays*. New York: The New Press, 2019.

Covert, Bryce. "The Trump Administration Gutted the EEOC." *The Nation*, February 8, 2021. www.thenation.com/article/society/janet-dhillon-eeoc/.

Cowley, Stacy. "Judges Halt Race and Gender Priority for Restaurant Relief Grants." *New York Times*, June 14, 2021. www.nytimes.com/2021/06/14/business/restaurant -relief-fund-covid-sba.html.

Creative Interventions. *Creative Interventions Toolkit: A Practical Guide to Stop Interpersonal Violence*. 2012. www.creative-interventions.org/toolkit/.

CrimethInc. Ex-Workers Collective. *From Democracy to Freedom: The Difference Between Government and Self-Determination*, Ill. Ed. CrimethInc., 2017.

Crispin, Jessa. *Why I Am Not a Feminist: A Feminist Manifesto*. Brooklyn: Melville House, 2017.

Cruz, Caitlin. "Ohio Lawmaker Says Pregnancy from Rape Is an 'Opportunity.'" *Jezebel*, April 27, 2022. https://jezebel.com/ohio-lawmaker-says-pregnancy-from-rape-is -an-opportunit-1848849829.

Cusk, Rachel. *Aftermath: On Marriage and Separation*. London: Faber and Faber, 2012.

Bibliography

Daily Show with Jon Stewart. Season 20, "The Unborn Ultimatum." Aired January 15, 2015, on Comedy Central. www.cc.com/video/ouq3mw/the-daily-show-with-jon-stewart-the-unborn-ultimatum.

Dangelantonio, Matt. "What to Know About Land Acknowledgment, and Why It's Deeper Than Just a Statement." *LAist*, October 6, 2021. https://laist.com/news/what-to-know-about-land-acknowledgment.

Daniels, Cheyanne. "How Black Women Served a Critical Role in Securing Brittney Griner's Release." *The Hill*, December 8, 2022. https://thehill.com/policy/international/3767430-how-black-women-served-a-critical-role-in-securing-britney-griners-release/.

Daniels, Jessie. *Nice White Ladies: The Truth About White Supremacy, Our Role in It, and How We Can Help Dismantle It*. New York: Seal Press, 2021.

Darby, Seyward. *Sisters in Hate: American Women on the Front Lines of White Nationalism*. New York: Little, Brown, 2020.

Davis, Aida Mariam. "Dignity Is the Bedrock for Workplace Belonging." *Stanford Social Innovation Review*, April 26, 2021. https://ssir.org/articles/entry/dignity_is_the_bedrock_for_workplace_belonging.

Davis, Aida Mariam. "Diversity, Equality and Inclusion Have Failed. How About Belonging, Dignity and Justice Instead?" World Economic Forum, February 23, 2021. www.weforum.org/agenda/2021/02/diversity-equity-inclusion-have-failed-belonging-dignity-justice/.

Davis, Angela Y. "Angela Davis talk at SIUC on Feb. 13, 2014." James Anderson. YouTube video. www.youtube.com/watch?v=6s8QCucFADc.

Davis, Angela Y. *Freedom Is a Constant Struggle: Ferguson, Palestine, and the Foundations of a Movement*. Chicago: Haymarket Books, 2016.

Davis, Angela Y. *The Meaning of Freedom and Other Difficult Dialogues*. San Francisco: City Lights Books, 2012.

Davis, Angela Y. *Women, Race & Class*. New York: Vintage Books, 1983.

Davis, Angela Y., Gina Dent, Erica R. Meiners, and Beth E. Richie. *Abolition. Feminism. Now*. Chicago: Haymarket Books, 2022.

De Dijn, Annelien. *Freedom: An Unruly History*. Cambridge, MA: Harvard University Press, 2020.

Death with Dignity. https://deathwithdignity.org/.

Deleuze, Gilles. *Desert Islands and Other Texts: 1953–1974*. Edited by David Lapoujade. Translated by Michael Taormina. New York: Semiotext(e) Foreign Agents Series, 2004.

Deleuze, Gilles. *Negotiations, 1972–1990*. Translated by Martin Joughin. New York: Columbia University Press, 1995.

Delmont, Matthew. "There's a Generational Shift in the Debate over Busing." *Atlantic*, July 1, 2019. www.theatlantic.com/ideas/archive/2019/07/kamala-harris-and-busing-debate/593047/.

Dias, Elizabeth, and Ruth Graham. "Abortion Foes Ponder a World After Roe Falls." *New York Times*, May 8, 2022.

Dicker, Rory. *A History of U.S. Feminisms*. Berkeley: Seal Press, 2016.

Didion, Joan. "On Self-Respect: Joan Didion's 1961 Essay from the Pages of *Vogue*." *Vogue*, December 23, 2021. www.vogue.com/article/joan-didion-self-respect-essay-1961.

District of Columbia v. Heller, 554 US 570 (2008). https://scholar.google.com/scholar _case?case=6484080926445491577&q=district+of+columbia+v+heller&hl=en&as _sdt=6,33.

Dnika, J. Travis, Jennifer Thorpe-Moscon, and Courtney McCluney. *Emotional Tax: How Black Women and Men Pay More at Work and How Leaders Can Take Action*. Catalyst, October 11, 2016. www.catalyst.org/research/emotional-tax-how-black-women -and-men-pay-more-at-work-and-how-leaders-can-take-action/.

Dobbs v. Jackson Women's Health Organization, 597 US __ (2022). www.supremecourt .gov/opinions/21pdf/19-1392_6j37.pdf.

Döring, Nicola, M. Rohangis Mohseni, and Roberto Walter. "Design, Use, and Effects of Sex Dolls and Sex Robots: Scoping Review." *Journal of Medical Research* 22, no. 7 (July 30, 2020). www.ncbi.nlm.nih.gov/pmc/articles/PMC7426804/.

Douglas, Mary. *Purity and Danger: An Analysis of the Concepts of Pollution and Taboo*. New York: Taylor & Francis, 1966.

Dowd, Trone. "Why Are WNBA Players Being Told Not to Talk About Brittney Griner?" *Vice*, March 30, 2022. www.vice.com/en/article/bvnaez/brittney-griner-russia -political-prisoner.

Doyle, Jude Ellison S. "The Unavoidable Violence of Banning Abortion." Medium, May 9, 2022. https://judedoyle.medium.com/the-unavoidable-violence-of-banning -abortion-36c68da8f674.

Duster, Chandelis. "Stephen Miller-Led Group Emerges as Top Legal Foe of Biden Initiatives." CNN Politics, December 15, 2022. www.cnn.com/2022/12/14/politics /stephen-miller-america-first-legal-biden-initiatives/index.html.

Duster, Chandelis, and Janie Boschma. "Many Black Farmers Nationwide Struggling to Keep Their Farms Afloat as They Face Disparities Across the Board." CNN Politics, December 15, 2021. www.cnn.com/2021/12/15/politics/black-farmers-debt -relief-disparities/index.html.

DuVernay, Ava, dir. *13th*. Netflix, 2016.

Ebbert, Stephanie. "In Many States, Marriage Is Still a Defense Against Rape." *Boston Globe*, December 4, 2019. www.bostonglobe.com/metro/2019/12/04/many-states -marriage-still-defense-against-rape/VRPtncPSekrLSAyUX68O7O/story.html.

Eberhardt, Jennifer L. *Biased: Uncovering the Hidden Prejudice That Shapes What We See, Think, and Do*. New York: Penguin Books, 2020.

Echols, Alice. *Daring to Be Bad: Radical Feminism in America 1967–1975*. Minneapolis: University of Minnesota Press, 1989.

Eckert, Maddi. "Civil Rights Leader Angela Davis Speaks at Bovard." *Daily Trojan*, February 23, 2015. https://dailytrojan.com/2015/02/23/civil-rights-leader-angela-davis -speaks-at-bovard/.

Bibliography

Ehrenreich, Barbara. Barnard College commencement speech. 2004. www.mail-archive .com/culture@list.purple.com/msg00332.html.

Eisenberg, Jeff. "Counting Men as Women? Inside the Fuzzy Math of Title IX Compliance." *Yahoo Sports*, June 22, 2022. https://sports.yahoo.com/counting-men-as-women -inside-the-fuzzy-math-of-title-ix-compliance-132707743.html.

Elkin, Lauren. *Flâneuse: Women Walk the City in Paris, New York, Tokyo, and London.* New York: Farrar, Straus and Giroux, 2018.

Ellin, Abby. "'Death Doulas' Provide Aid at the End of Life." *New York Times*, June 25, 2021. www.nytimes.com/2021/06/24/well/doulas-death-end-of-life.html.

Elliott, Jane. "The Blue Eyes & Brown Eyes Exercise." https://janeelliott.com/.

Eltahawy, Mona. *The Seven Necessary Sins for Women and Girls.* Boston: Beacon Press, 2019.

Emergency Relief for Farmers of Color Act of 2021, S.278, 117th Cong. (2021). www .congress.gov/bill/117th-congress/senate-bill/278.

Ensler, Eve. "The Power and Mystery of Naming Things." NPR, March 20, 2006. www .npr.org/2006/03/20/5285531/the-power-and-mystery-of-naming-things.

Equal Justice USA and Newark Community Street Team. *The Future of Public Safety: Exploring the Power & Possibility of Newark's Reimagined Public Safety Ecosystem.* https://newarksafety.org/download/TheFutureOfPublicSafety.pdf.

Equal Pay for Team USA Act of 2022, S.2333, 117th Cong. (2023). www.congress.gov /bill/117th-congress/senate-bill/2333/text.

The Equal Rights Amendment: Achieving Constitutional Equality for All, Hearing Before the Committee on Oversight and Reform, 117th Cong. (2021).

ERA Coalition. "The Amendment." www.eracoalition.org/the-amendment.

Escobar, Sam. "Alok Vaid-Menon Wants to Degender Beauty. Will You Help Them?" *Allure*, May 21, 2022. www.allure.com/story/alok-vaid-menon-talking-beauty.

Fahs, Breanne, ed. *Burn It Down! Feminist Manifestos for the Revolution.* New York: Verso, 2020.

Fahs, Breanne. *Firebrand Feminism: The Radical Lives of Ti-Grace Atkinson, Kathie Sarachild, Roxanne Dunbar-Ortiz, and Dana Densmore.* Seattle: University of Washington Press, 2018.

Faludi, Susan. *Backlash: The Undeclared War Against American Women.* New York: Anchor Books, 1991.

Faludi, Susan. "Feminism Made a Faustian Bargain with Celebrity Culture. Now It's Paying the Price." *New York Times*, June 20, 2022. www.nytimes.com/2022/06/20/opinion /roe-heard-feminism-backlash.html.

Farrell, Molly. "Ben Franklin Put an Abortion Recipe in His Math Textbook." *Slate*, May 5, 2022. https://slate.com/news-and-politics/2022/05/ben-franklin-american -instructor-textbook-abortion-recipe.html.

Fawaz, Ramzi. *Queer Forms.* New York: New York University Press, 2022.

Febos, Melissa. *Girlhood: Essays.* New York: Bloomsbury Publishing, 2021.

Felice, Selene San. "Some Florida Schools Ask Student Athletes to Report Period Data." *Axios*, October 6, 2022. www.axios.com/local/tampa-bay/2022/10/06/florida-student -athletes-period-data.

Filipovic, Jill. "Brett Kavanaugh's Right to Privacy." *Jill Filipovic* (Substack), June 8, 2022. https://jill.substack.com/p/brett-kavanaughs-right-to-privacy.

Filipovic, Jill. *The H-Spot: The Feminist Pursuit of Happiness*. New York: Nation Books, 2017.

Fischel, Joseph J. *Screw Consent: A Better Politics of Sexual Justice*. Oakland: University of California Press, 2019.

Foucault, Michel. "The Ethics of the Concern for Self as a Practice of Freedom." In *Ethics: Subjectivity and Truth*, edited by Paul Rabinow, 281–302. New York: The New Press, 1997.

Fowler, Sarah. "She Founded Moms Demand Action for Gun Reform. 140 of Its Volunteers Won Office." *Washington Post*, December 8, 2022. www.washingtonpost.com /parenting/2022/12/08/shannon-watts-moms-demand-action/.

Fox Sports. "U.S. Victory Delivers 14,271,000 FOX Sport Viewers in FIFA Women's World Cup France 2019 Final." Press Pass, July 8, 2019. www.foxsports.com/press pass/blog/2019/07/08/u-s-victory-delivers-14271000-fox-sports-viewers-fifa-wom ens-world-cup-france-2019-final.

"Fran Lebowitz on Technology, Loneliness, and New York City." In *Still Spinning*, podcast. Joyce Theater, June 11, 2021. www.joyce.org/still-spinning-fran-lebowitz -technology-loneliness-and-new-york-city.

Francis, Marquise. "Newark Was One of the Deadliest Cities in the U.S. Now It Wants to Set an Example on Public Safety Reform." Yahoo News, June 25, 2022. news.yahoo .com/newark-was-one-of-the-deadliest-cities-in-america-now-it-wants-to-be -a-blueprint-for-public-safety-reform-163320757.html.

Frazier, Mya. "Stop Using 'Officer-Involved Shooting.'" *Columbia Journalism Review*, August 7, 2020. www.cjr.org/analysis/officer-involved-shooting.php.

Free, Laura E. *Suffrage Reconstructed: Gender, Race, and Voting Rights in the Civil Rights Era*. Ithaca, NY: Cornell University Press, 2015.

Freedman, Estelle B., ed. *The Essential Feminist Reader*. New York: The Modern Library, 2007.

Freedom for Immigrants. "Sexual Abuse, Assault, and Harassment in U.S. Immigration Detention Facilities." Complaint filed with the Office for Civil Rights & Civil Liberties, Department of Homeland Security. April 11, 2017. https://static1.square space.com/static/5a33042eb078691c386e7bce/t/5a9da297419202ab8be09c92 /1520280217559/SexualAssault_Complaint.pdf.

Freedom for Immigrants. "Widespread Sexual Assault." https://freedomforimmigrants .org/sexual-assault.

Fuller, Laurie, and Ann Russo. "Feminist Pedagogy: Building Community Accountability." *Feminist Teacher* 26, no. 2–3 (2016): 179–197.

Garbes, Angela. *Essential Labor: Mothering as Social Change*. New York: Harper Wave, 2022.

Bibliography

Garcia, Manon. *We Are Not Born Submissive: How Patriarchy Shapes Women's Lives.* Princeton, NJ: Princeton University Press, 2021.

Garza, Alicia. *The Purpose of Power: How We Come Together When We Fall Apart.* New York: One World, 2020.

Gay, Roxane. *Bad Feminist: Essays.* New York: Harper Perennial, 2014.

Gay, Roxane. "Why I've Decided to Take My Podcast Off Spotify." *New York Times,* February 3, 2022. www.nytimes.com/2022/02/03/opinion/culture/joe-rogan-spotify-roxane-gay.html.

Gearon, Jihan. "Indigenous Feminism Is Our Culture." *Stanford Social Innovation Review,* February 11, 2021. https://ssir.org/articles/entry/indigenous_feminism_is_our_culture.

Gerber, Marisa. "One Last Trip: Gabriella Walsh's Decision to Die—and Celebrate Life—on Her Own Terms." *Los Angeles Times,* August 1, 2022. www.latimes.com/california/story/2022-08-01/death-with-dignity-gabriella.

Gerhard, Ute. *Debating Women's Equality: Toward a Feminist Theory of Law from a European Perspective.* Translated by Allison Brown and Belinda Cooper. New Brunswick, NJ: Rutgers University Press, 2001.

Germain, Jacqui. "Student Debt Must Be Canceled, Not Just Paused, Elizabeth Warren Says." *Teen Vogue,* January 24, 2022. www.teenvogue.com/story/student-debt-cancellation-elizabeth-warren.

Gersen, Jeannie Suk. "If *Roe v. Wade* Is Overturned, What's Next?" *New Yorker,* April 27, 2022. www.newyorker.com/magazine/2022/04/25/if-roe-v-wade-is-overturned-whats-next.

Gillen, Nancy. "Caster Semenya Calls Out World Athletics in Scathing Tweet." GiveMeSport, March 22, 2022. www.givemesport.com/87989068-caster-semenya-calls-out-world-athletics-in-scathing-tweet.

Ginsburg, Ruth Bader. "Some Thoughts on Autonomy and Equality in Relation to Roe v. Wade." *North Carolina Law Review* 63, no. 2 (1985): 375–386. www.semanticscholar.org/paper/Some-thoughts-on-autonomy-and-equality-in-relation-Ginsburg/3a6311adf1b54ddf6d2adbdc56da95ddc84fadeb?p2df.

Goldin, Claudia. *Career & Family: Women's Century-Long Journey Toward Equity.* Princeton, NJ: Princeton University Press, 2021.

Goodman, Wendy. "Fran Lebowitz vs. the World." *New York Magazine,* December 29, 2020. www.curbed.com/article/fran-lebowitz-pretend-its-a-city.html.

Goodwin, Michelle. "No, Justice Alito, Reproductive Justice Is in the Constitution." *New York Times,* June 26, 2022. www.nytimes.com/2022/06/26/opinion/justice-alito-reproductive-justice-constitution-abortion.html.

Goyal, Nidhi. "As a Blind Woman, I Belong to a Community of Friendship, Love and Care." *Point of View* (Medium), October 15, 2018. https://medium.com/skin-stories/as-a-blind-woman-i-belong-to-a-community-of-friendship-love-and-care-5aa82bd28570.

Greenhouse, Linda. "A Surprising Argument Against Affirmative Action." *New York Times,* October 30, 2022.

Greer's Ranch Café et al. v. Isabella Casillas Guzman, in her official capacity as administrator of the Small Business Administration and United States Small Business Administration, 540 F. Supp 3d 638 (N.D. Tex. 2021). https://s3.documentcloud.org/documents/20773795/order-granting-tro-against-biden-administration.pdf.

Griffin, Phil, dir. *Britney: For the Record*. MTV, 2008.

Grimké, Sarah. *Letters on the Equality of the Sexes*. 1837. www.worldculture.org/articles/12-Grimke%20Letters,%201-3.pdf.

Grosz, Elizabeth. *Becoming Undone: Darwinian Reflections on Life, Politics, and Art*. Durham, NC: Duke University Press, 2011.

Grosz, Elizabeth. "Histories of the Present and Future: Feminism, Power, Bodies." In *Thinking the Limits of the Body*, edited by Jeffrey Jerome Cohen and Gail Weiss, 13–24. Albany, NY: SUNY Press, 2003.

Grosz, Elizabeth. *The Incorporeal: Ontology, Ethics, and the Limits of Materialism*. New York: Columbia University Press, 2017.

Grosz, Elizabeth. *The Nick of Time: Politics, Evolution, and the Untimely*. Durham, NC: Duke University Press, 2004.

Grosz, Elizabeth. *Space, Time, and Perversion: Essays on the Politics of Bodies*. New York: Routledge, 1995.

Grosz, Elizabeth. *Time Travels: Feminism, Nature, Power*. Durham, NC: Duke University Press, 2005.

Guy-Sheftall, Beverly, ed. *Words of Fire: An Anthology of African-American Feminist Thought*. New York: New Press, 1995.

Hais, Michael D., and Morley Winograd. "Biden Has Women to Thank for His Primary Victories." Brookings Institution, March 17, 2020. www.brookings.edu/blog/fixgov/2020/03/17/biden-has-women-to-thank-for-his-primary-victories/.

Hale, Matthew. *The History of the Pleas of the Crown*. Vol. 1. United Kingdom: Payne, 1800. www.google.com/books/edition/The_History_of_the_Pleas_of_the_Crown/u1FDAAAAcAAJ?hl=en&gbpv=0.

Halperin, Anna Danziger. "RBG's Long History of Expanding and Protecting Reproductive Rights." *Women at the Center* (blog), New York Historical Society, January 11, 2022. www.nyhistory.org/blogs/rbgs-long-history-of-expanding-and-protecting-reproductive.

Hamad, Ruby. *White Tears/Brown Scars*. Carlton, Victoria, Australia: Melbourne University Press, 2019.

Hamer, Fannie Lou. *The Speeches of Fannie Lou Hamer: To Tell It Like It Is*. Edited by Maegan Parker Brooks and Davis W. Houck. Jackson: University Press of Mississippi, 2011.

Hamilton, Michelle. "Running While Female." *Runner's World*, August 7, 2017. www.runnersworld.com/training/a18848270/running-while-female/.

Hampton, Deon J. "It's Not Uncommon for WNBA Players Like Brittney Griner to Compete in Russia. Here's Why They Do It." NBC News, March 7, 2022. www.nbcnews.com/news/us-news/not-uncommon-wnba-players-brittney-griner-compete-russia-rcna19068.

Bibliography

Hamraie, Aimi. "Designing Collective Access: A Feminist Disability Theory of Universal Design." *Disability Studies Quarterly* 33, no. 4 (2013). https://dsq-sds.org/article/view/3871/3411.

Hannah-Jones, Nikole. "School Segregation After Brown." ProPublica, May 1, 2014. https://projects.propublica.org/segregation-now/.

Hansberry, Lorraine. "Simone de Beauvoir and *The Second Sex*: An American Commentary." In *Words of Fire: An Anthology of African-American Feminist Thought*, edited by Beverly Guy-Sheftall, 128–142. New York: The New Press, 1995.

Haque, Jennah. "WNBA Players' $1 Million Paydays Vanish as Off-Season Opportunities Dry Up." *Bloomberg*, September 28, 2022. www.bloomberg.com/news/articles/2022-09-28/wnba-players-offseason-salaries-drop-due-to-russia-china-tensions.

Hark, Sabine, and Paula-Irene Villa. *The Future of Difference: Beyond the Toxic Entanglement of Racism, Sexism and Feminism*. Brooklyn: Verso, 2020.

Hayes, Chris, and Nikole Hannah-Jones. "Investigating School Segregation in 2018 with Nikole Hannah-Jones." Podcast and transcript. NBC Think, July 31, 2018. www.nbcnews.com/think/opinion/investigating-school-segregation-2018-nikole-hannah-jones-podcast-transcript-ncna896116.

Hekman, David R., Stefanie K. Johnson, Maw-Der Foo, and Wei Yang. "Does Diversity-Valuing Behavior Result in Diminished Performance Ratings for Non-White and Female Leaders?" *Academy of Management Journal* 60, no. 2 (March 3, 2016). https://journals.aom.org/doi/abs/10.5465/amj.2014.0538.

Heller, Nathan. "The Philosopher Redefining Equality." *New Yorker*, January 7, 2019. www.newyorker.com/magazine/2019/01/07/the-philosopher-redefining-equality.

Henig, Iszac. "I Chose to Compete as My True, Trans Self. I Win Less, but I Live More." *New York Times*, January 5, 2023. www.nytimes.com/2023/01/05/opinion/trans-athlete-swimming.html.

Hersey, Tricia. *Rest Is Resistance: A Manifesto*. New York: Little, Brown Spark, 2022.

Hicks, Donna. *Dignity: Its Essential Role in Resolving Conflict*. 2nd ed. New Haven, CT: Yale University Press, 2021.

Hill, Glynn A. "Transgender Girls Allowed to Play Girls' Sports in Utah, Judge Rules." *Washington Post*, August 21, 2022. www.washingtonpost.com/sports/2022/08/21/transgender-girls-utah-sports/.

Hirschmann, Nancy J. "Disability and Positive Liberty." In *Positive Freedom: Past, Present, and Future*. Cambridge: Cambridge University Press, 2021. www.cambridge.org/core/books/abs/positive-freedom/disability-and-positive-liberty/C2AC49F9421B2CB149F3AC75FF8D94AD.

Hirschmann, Nancy J. "Feminism and Freedom," In *What Is Freedom? Conversations with Historians, Philosophers, and Activists*, edited by Toby Buckle. New York: Oxford University Press, 2021. https://oxford.universitypressscholarship.com/view/10.1093/oso/9780197572214.001.0001/oso-9780197572214-chapter-5.

Hirschmann, Nancy J. *Gender, Class, and Freedom in Modern Political Theory*. Princeton, NJ: Princeton University Press, 2008.

Hirschmann, Nancy J. *The Subject of Liberty: Toward a Feminist Theory of Freedom*. Princeton, NJ: Princeton University Press, 2003.

History, Art & Archives, US House of Representatives. "The Southern Manifesto of 1956." March 12, 1956. https://history.house.gov/Historical-Highlights/1951-2000/The-Southern-Manifesto-of-1956/.

Hochschild, Arlie. *The Managed Heart: Commercialization of Human Feeling*. Berkeley: University of California Press, 1983.

Hocker, Cornelius. "Indiana Is One Step Closer to Banning Transgender Girls from Playing High School Sports." WRTV Indianapolis, January 25, 2022. www.wrtv.com/decodedc/politics/indiana-is-one-step-closer-to-banning-transgender-girls-from-playing-girls-sports.

Hoffman, Kelly M., Sophie Trawalter, Jordan R. Axt, and M. Norman Oliver. "Racial Bias in Pain Assessment and Treatment Recommendations, and False Beliefs About Biological Differences Between Blacks and Whites." *Proceedings of the National Academy of Sciences of the United States of America* 113, no. 16 (April 4, 2016): 4296–4301. https://doi.org/10.1073/pnas.1516047113.

Hogue, Ilyse, and Ellie Langford. *The Lie That Binds*. Sacramento, CA: Strong Arm Press, 2020.

Holladay, Hilary. *The Power of Adrienne Rich: A Biography*. New York: Nan A. Talese/Doubleday, 2020.

Holt, Brianna. "'We Don't Have the Benefit of the Doubt': The Fear of Driving While Black." *Guardian US*, April 22, 2021.

hooks, bell. *Ain't I a Woman: Black Women and Feminism*. Boston: South End Press, 1981.

hooks, bell. *All About Love: New Visions*. New York: Harper Perennial, 2000.

hooks, bell. "Choosing the Margin as a Space of Radical Openness." *Framework: The Journal of Cinema and Media*, no. 36 (1989): 15–23.

hooks, bell. *Feminism Is for Everybody: Passionate Politics*. New York: Routledge, 2015.

hooks, bell. *Feminist Theory from Margin to Center*. Boston: South End Press, 1984.

hooks, bell. *Outlaw Culture: Resisting Representations*. New York: Routledge, 1994.

hooks, bell. *Talking Back: Thinking Feminist, Thinking Black*. New York: Routledge, 2015.

Hoops Geek. "How Much Do NBA Players Make? Average Salary from 1990–2022." July 2, 2022. www.thehoopsgeek.com/average-nba-salary/.

Horowitz, Juliana Menasce, and Ruth Igielnik. "A Century After Women Gained the Right to Vote, Majority of Americans See Work to Do on Gender Equality." Pew Research Center, July 7, 2020. www.pewresearch.org/social-trends/2020/07/07/a-century-after-women-gained-the-right-to-vote-majority-of-americans-see-work-to-do-on-gender-equality/.

Hoyert, Donna L. "Maternal Mortality Rates in the United States, 2021." National Center for Health Statistics, March 2023. https://www.cdc.gov/nchs/data/hestat/maternal-mortality/2021/maternal-mortality-rates-2021.pdf.

Hull, Akasha (Gloria T.), Patricia Bell Scott, and Barbara Smith. *All the Women Are White, All the Blacks Are Men, but Some of Us Are Brave: Black Women's Studies.* 2nd ed. New York: The Feminist Press, 2015.

Human Rights Campaign. "United Against Hate—Fighting Back on State Legislative Attacks on LGBTQ+ People." www.hrc.org/campaigns/the-state-legislative-attack-on -lgbtq-people.

IEA. "Global Energy Review: CO2 Emissions in 2021." www.iea.org/reports/global-energy -review-co2-emissions-in-2021-2.

Igielnik, Ruth. "Most Americans Who Are Familiar with Title IX Say It's Had a Positive Impact on Gender Equality." Pew Research Center, April 21, 2022. www.pewre search.org/fact-tank/2022/04/21/most-americans-who-are-familiar-with-title-ix -say-its-had-a-positive-impact-on-gender-equality/.

ILR Worker Institute. "ILR and Hollaback! Release Largest Analysis of Street Harassment to Date." Worker Institute Blog, June 1, 2015. www.ilr.cornell.edu/worker -institute/blog/research-and-publications/ilr-and-hollaback-release-largest-analy sis-street-harassment-date.

INCITE! Women of Color Against Violence. "Community Accountability Factsheet." TransformHarm. https://transformharm.org/ca_resource/community-accountabil ity-factsheet/.

INCITE! Women of Color Against Violence. *Community Accountability Within the People of Color Progressive Movement.* July 2005. https://web.archive.org/web /20180219031741/http://incite-national.org/sites/default/files/incite_files /resource_docs/2406_cmty-acc-poc.pdf.

Indigenous Action. "Voting Is Not Harm Reduction—An Indigenous Perspective." February 5, 2020. www.indigenousaction.org/voting-is-not-harm-reduction-an-indig enous-perspective/.

Irigaray, Luce. *This Sex Which Is Not One.* Translated by Catherine Porter with Carolyn Burke. Ithaca, NY: Cornell University Press, 1985.

Jameel, Maryam. "More and More Workplace Discrimination Cases Are Being Closed Before They Are Even Investigated." *Vox*, June 14, 2019. https://www.vox.com/identities /2019/6/14/18663296/congress-eeoc-workplace-discrimination.

Janz, Heidi L. "Ableism: The Undiagnosed Malady Afflicting Medicine." *Canadian Medical Association Journal* 191, no. 17 (April 29, 2019): E478–E479. https://doi.org /10.1503/cmaj.180903.

Jewish Women's Archive. "A Quote from Epistle to the Hebrews." https://jwa.org/media /quote-from-epistle-to-hebrews.

Johnson, Akilah, and Dan Keating. "Whites Now More Likely to Die from Covid Than Blacks: Why the Pandemic Shifted." *Washington Post*, October 19, 2022. www.wash ingtonpost.com/health/2022/10/19/covid-deaths-us-race/.

Johnson, Barbara. *The Barbara Johnson Reader: The Surprise of Otherness.* Edited by Melissa Feuerstein, Bill Johnson González, Lili Porten, and Keja Valens. Durham, NC: Duke University Press, 2014.

Bibliography

Johnson, Barbara. *The Feminist Difference: Literature, Psychoanalysis, Race, and Gender.* Cambridge, MA: Harvard University Press, 1998.

Johnson, Barbara. *Mother Tongues: Sexuality, Trials, Motherhood, Translation.* Cambridge, MA: Harvard University Press, 2003.

Johnson, Barbara. *Persons and Things.* Cambridge, MA: Harvard University Press, 2008.

Johnson, Barbara. *A World of Difference.* Baltimore, MD: Johns Hopkins University Press, 1987.

Johnson, Carrie. "Senate Probe Found Some Federal Prison Staff Abused Female Inmates Without Discipline." NPR, December 14, 2022. www.npr.org /2022/12/14/1142520821/senate-probe-found-some-federal-prison-staff-abused -female-inmates-without-disci.

Johnson, Stephanie K., and David R. Hekman. "Women and Minorities Are Penalized for Promoting Diversity." *Harvard Business Review*, March 23, 2016. https://hbr .org/2016/03/women-and-minorities-are-penalized-for-promoting-diversity.

Johnston, Jill. *Lesbian Nation: The Feminist Solution.* New York: Simon & Schuster, 1974.

Jones, Alethia, Virginia Eubanks, and Barbara Smith, eds. *Ain't Gonna Let Nobody Turn Me Around: Forty Years of Movement Building with Barbara Smith.* Albany: State University of New York, 2014.

Jones, Kimberly Latrice. "#BLM How Can We Win? Kimberly Jones Powerful Speech." CARJAM TV. June 9, 2020. YouTube video. www.youtube.com/watch?v=llci8MVh8J4.

Jordan-Young, Rebecca M., and Katrina Karkazis. *Testosterone: An Unauthorized Biography.* Cambridge, MA: Harvard University Press, 2019.

Joshi, Shamani. "Man Who Married His Sex Doll Opens Up About His Marriage." *Vice*, February 18, 2021. www.vice.com/en/article/wx8ywm/man-married-sex-doll-viral -relationship.

Kaba, Mariame. "So You're Thinking About Becoming an Abolitionist." *LEVEL* (Medium), October 29, 2000. https://level.medium.com/so-youre-thinking-about -becoming-an-abolitionist-a436f8e31894.

Kaba, Mariame. *We Do This 'Til We Free Us: Abolitionist Organizing and Transforming Justice.* Chicago: Haymarket Books, 2021.

Kaba, Mariame, and Andrea J. Ritchie. *No More Police: A Case for Abolition.* New York: The New Press, 2022.

Kaiser Family Foundation. "Reported Legal Abortions by Race of Women Who Obtained Abortion by the State of Occurrence." 2019. www.kff.org/womens-health -policy/state-indicator/abortions-by-race/?currentTimeframe=0&sortModel=%7B %22colId%22:%22Location%22,%22sort%22:%22asc%22%7D.

Kaplan, Erin Aubry. "What's Going On with All the White Scholars Who Try to Pass as Black?" *Los Angeles Times*, October 8, 2020. www.latimes.com/entertainment-arts /books/story/2020-10-08/when-scholars-and-activists-pretend-to-be-black-an -essay.

Kaplan, Laura. *The Story of Jane: The Legendary Underground Feminist Abortion Service.* Chicago: University of Chicago Press, 2019.

Bibliography

Karakola, Eskalera. "Manifesto for a New Feminist Presence." In *Burn It Down! Feminist Manifestos for the Revolution*, edited by Breanne Fahs, 111–114. New York: Verso, 2020.

Katz, Jonathan Ned. *Routledge International Handbook of Sexuality Studies*. New York: Routledge, 2020.

Kelley, Robin D. G. *Freedom Dreams: The Black Radical Imagination*. Boston: Beacon Press, 2002.

Kendi, Ibram X. *How to Be an Antiracist*. New York: One World, 2019.

Kern, Leslie. *Feminist City: Claiming Space in a Man-Made World*. Brooklyn: Verso, 2020.

Kessler-Harris, Alice. *In Pursuit of Equity: Women, Men, and the Quest for Economic Citizenship in 20th-Century America*. New York: Oxford University Press, 2001.

Kim, Paul. "What Are the Environmental Impacts of Cryptocurrencies?" *Business Insider*, March 17, 2022. www.businessinsider.com/personal-finance/cryptocurrency -environmental-impact.

Kirchgaessner, Stephanie. "Revealed: Leaked Video Shows Amy Coney Barrett's Secretive Faith Group Drove Women to Tears." *Guardian*, August 26, 2022. www.theguardian .com/us-news/2022/aug/26/amy-coney-barrett-faith-group-people-of-praise?.

Kirkpatrick, Kate. *Becoming Beauvoir: A Life*. New York: Bloomsbury Academic, 2019.

Kleeman, Alexandra. "The Secret Toll of Racial Ambiguity." *New York Times Magazine*, October 20, 2021, updated November 22, 2021. www.nytimes.com/2021/10/20 /magazine/rebecca-hall-passing.html?searchResultPosition=1.

Koebler, Jason, and Anna Merlan. "This Is the Data Facebook Gave Police to Prosecute a Teenager for Abortion." *Motherboard*, August 9, 2022. www.vice.com/en/article /n7zevd/this-is-the-data-facebook-gave-police-to-prosecute-a-teenager-for-abortion.

Kravitz, Marshall. "The Gender Binary Is a Tool of White Supremacy." *An Injustice!* (Medium), July 14, 2020. https://aninjusticemag.com/the-gender-binary-is-a-tool -of-white-supremacy-db89d0bc9044.

Kriel, Lomi. "ICE Guards 'Systematically' Sexually Assault Detainees in an El Paso Detention Center, Lawyers Say." ProPublica, August 14, 2020. www.propublica.org /article/ice-guards-systematically-sexually-assault-detainees-in-an-el-paso-deten tion-center-lawyers-say.

Krug, Jessica A. "The Truth, and the Anti-Black Violence of My Lies." Medium, September 3, 2020. https://medium.com/@jessakrug/the-truth-and-the-anti-black-violence -of-my-lies-9a9621401f85.

Kruzel, John. "Federal Judge Says Biden Restaurant Fund Discriminated Against White Male." *The Hill*, May 19, 2021. https://thehill.com/regulation/554361-federal -judge-says-biden-restaurant-fund-discriminated-against-white-male/.

Lang, Nico. "South Carolina Just Enacted an Anti-Trans Sports Ban—and Louisiana Could Be Next." *Xtra*, May 18, 2022. https://xtramagazine.com/power/politics /south-carolina-anti-trans-sports-ban-223206.

Langford, Terri. "'If There's Kids in There, We Need to Go In': Officers in Uvalde Were Ready with Guns, Shields and Tools—But Not Clear on Orders." *Texas Tribune*,

June 20, 2022. www.texastribune.org/2022/06/20/uvalde-police-shooting-response -records/.

Langmaid, Virginia. "Study of Wealthy Nations Finds American Women Most Likely to Die of Preventable Causes, Pregnancy Complications." CNN, April 5, 2022. www .cnn.com/2022/04/05/health/us-women-health-care/index.html.

LeanIn.org and McKinsey & Company. *Women in the Workplace.* 2022. https://wiw -report.s3.amazonaws.com/Women_in_the_Workplace_2022.pdf.

Lebowitz, Fran. "Fran Lebowitz on Race and Racism." *Vanity Fair*, October 1, 1997. www .vanityfair.com/culture/2016/01/fran-lebowitz-on-race-and-racism.

Lebrecht, James, and Nicole Newnham, dir. *Crip Camp.* Netflix, 2020.

Lenthang, Marlene. "Jayland Walker Was Shot 46 Times by Ohio Police, Medical Examiner Says." NBC News, July 15, 2022. www.nbcnews.com/news/us-news/jayland -walker-was-shot-46-police-ohio-medical-examiner-says-rcna38392.

Lepore, Jill. "The Invention of the Police." *New Yorker*, July 13, 2020. www.newyorker .com/magazine/2020/07/20/the-invention-of-the-police.

Lesser, Elizabeth. *Cassandra Speaks: When Women Are the Storytellers, the Human Story Changes.* New York: Harper Wave, 2020.

Looker, Rachel. "'It's Time to Clear the Path to Equality': Senate Revisits Equal Rights Amendment After 40 Years." *USA Today*, March 5, 2023. https://www.usatoday .com/story/news/politics/2023/03/05/senate-ratify-equal-rights-amendment-era /11389985002/.

Lorde, Audre. *A Burst of Light and Other Essays.* Mineola, NY: Ixia Press. 2017.

Lorde, Audre. *The Cancer Journals.* San Francisco: Aunt Lute Books, 1980.

Lorde, Audre. "An Interview with Audre Lorde." By Karla Hammond. *American Poetry Review* 9, no. 2 (March/April 1980): 18–21.

Lorde, Audre. *The Selected Works of Audre Lorde.* Edited by Roxane Gay. New York: W. W. Norton, 2020.

Lorde, Audre. *Sister Outsider.* New York: Penguin Books, 2020.

Lovett, Laura L. "Rest in Power: Dorothy Pitman Hughes, Icon and Activist." *Ms.*, December 14, 2022. https://msmagazine.com/2022/12/14/dorothy-pitman-hughes/.

Macur, Juliet. "Simone Biles Dials Up the Difficulty, 'Because I Can.'" *New York Times*, August 3, 2021. www.nytimes.com/2021/05/24/sports/olympics/simone-biles -yurchenko-double-pike.html.

Mangino, Kate. *Equal Partners: Improving Gender Equality at Home.* New York: St. Martin's Press, 2022.

Mangino, Kate. "What to Actually Do About an Unequal Partnership: An Interview with Kate Mangino." By Anne Helen Petersen. *Culture Study* (Substack), August 17, 2022. https://annehelen.substack.com/p/what-to-actually-do-about-an-unequal.

Manne, Kate. *Down Girl: The Logic of Misogyny.* New York: Oxford University Press, 2017.

Manne, Kate. *Entitled: How Male Privilege Hurts Women.* New York: Crown, 2020.

Bibliography

Mapping Police Violence. https://mappingpoliceviolence.us/.

Marso, Lori Jo. *Politics with Beauvoir: Freedom in the Encounter*. Durham, NC: Duke University Press, 2017.

Martin, Nina, and Renee Montagne. "The Last Person You'd Expect to Die in Childbirth." In *Lost Mothers: Maternal Mortality in the U.S.*, NPR and ProPublica special series. NPR, May 12, 2017. www.npr.org/2017/05/12/527806002/focus-on-infants-during -childbirth-leaves-u-s-moms-in-danger.

Masters, Jeffrey. "Shatzi Weisberger: Meet the 91-Year-Old Death Educator." *Advocate*, April 28, 2022. www.advocate.com/lesbian/2022/4/28/shatzi-weisberger-meet -91-year-old-death-educator.

Maynard, Brittany. "Brittany Maynard Legislative Testimony." CompassionChoices, March 31, 2015. YouTube video. www.youtube.com/watch?v=Mi8AP_EhM94.

Maynard, Brittany. "My Right to Death with Dignity at 29." CNN Opinion, November 2, 2014. www.cnn.com/2014/10/07/opinion/maynard-assisted-suicide-cancer-dignity/.

McFadden, Syreeta. "Rachel Dolezal's Claim That She Is Black Is the Whitest Possible Way to Deal with Her Issues." NBC Think, May 6, 2018. www.nbcnews.com/think /opinion/rachel-dolezal-s-claim-she-black-whitest-possible-way-deal-ncna871656.

McGraw, Meredith. "Stephen Miller Group's Radio Ads Accuse Biden of 'Racism' Towards White Americans." *Politico*, October 31, 2022. www.politico.com/news/2022/10/30 /stephen-miller-ads-biden-racism-white-americans-00064148.

McIntosh, Peggy. "White Privilege Checklist." ALSO. http://also-chicago.org/also_site /wp-content/uploads/2017/03/white-privilege.pdf.

McLaughlin, Eliott C. "Police Officers in the US Were Charged with More than 400 Rapes over a 9-Year Period." CNN, October 19, 2018. www.cnn.com/2018/10/19/us /police-sexual-assaults-maryland-scope/index.html.

Merelli, Annalisa. "America's Legal Experts Believe We've Got the Abortion Debate All Wrong." *Quartz*, June 11, 2019. https://qz.com/1637066/legal-experts-say-the -abortion-debate-is-about-equality-not-privacy.

Mertens, Maggie. "The Title IX Loophole That Hurts NCAA Women's Teams." *Atlantic*, April 1, 2021. www.theatlantic.com/culture/archive/2021/04/march-madness -could-spark-title-ix-reckoning/618483/.

Mikelionis, Lukas. "White Population Aging Rapidly in U.S., Dying Faster Than Babies Are Born, Data Show." Fox News, June 21, 2018. www.foxnews.com/us/white -population-aging-rapidly-in-us-dying-faster-than-babies-are-born-data-show.

Milan Women's Book Collective. *Sexual Difference: A Theory of Social-Symbolic Practice*. Translated by Patricia Cicogna and Teresa de Lauretis. Bloomington: Indiana University Press, 1990.

Miller, Claire Cain. "Americans Value Equality at Work More Than Equality at Home." *New York Times*, December 3, 2018. www.nytimes.com/2018/12/03/upshot/americans -value-equality-at-work-more-than-equality-at-home.html.

Mock, Janet. *Redefining Realness: My Path to Womanhood, Identity, Love & So Much More*. New York: Atria Books, 2014.

Mock, Janet. *Surpassing Certainty: What My Twenties Taught Me.* New York: Atria Books, 2017.

Montañez, Amanda. "Visualizing Sex as a Spectrum." *Scientific American*, August 29, 2017. https://blogs.scientificamerican.com/sa-visual/visualizing-sex-as-a-spectrum/.

Moraga, Cherrie, and Gloria Anzaldúa, eds. *This Bridge Called My Back: Writings by Radical Women of Color.* 4th ed. Albany: State University of New York Press, 2015.

Morgan, Rachel E., and Barbara A. Oudekerk. *Criminal Victimization*, 2018. US Department of Justice Bureau of Justice Statistics, September 2019. www.nsvrc.org/sites/default/files/2021-04/cv18.pdf.

Morris, Andrea. "Meet the Man Who Test Drives Sex Robots." *Forbes*, September 27, 2018. www.forbes.com/sites/andreamorris/2018/09/27/meet-the-man-who-test-drives-sex-robots/?sh=2aa825f7452d.

Movement Advancement Project. "Gay/Trans Panic Defense Bans." Accessed October 20, 2022. www.lgbtmap.org/equality-maps/panic_defense_bans.

Movement for Black Lives. "About Us." https://web.archive.org/web/20190502120213/https://policy.m4bl.org/about/.

Mueller, Eleanor, and Alice Miranda Ollstein. "How the Debate over the ERA Became a Fight over Abortion." *Politico*, February 11, 2020. www.politico.com/news/2020/02/11/abortion-equal-rights-amendment-113505.

Muller v. Oregon, 208 USA 412 (1908). https://supreme.justia.com/cases/federal/us/208/412/.

Murray, Melissa. "The Equal Rights Amendment: A Century in the Making Symposium Forward." *Harbinger* 43, *N.Y.U. Review of Law & Social Change* (2019).

National Center for Transgender Equality. *The Report of the 2015 U.S. Transgender Survey.* 2016. https://transequality.org/sites/default/files/docs/usts/USTS-Executive-Summary-Dec17.pdf.

National Center for Women and Policing data. Reported in Conor Friedersdorf. "Police Have a Much Bigger Domestic-Abuse Problem Than the NFL Does." *Atlantic*, September 19, 2014. www.theatlantic.com/national/archive/2014/09/police-officers-who-hit-their-wives-or-girlfriends/380329/.

National Human Genome Research Institute. "Genetics vs. Genomics Fact Sheet." Last updated September 7, 2018. www.genome.gov/about-genomics/fact-sheets/Genetics-vs-Genomics.

National Organization for Women. "Chronology of the Equal Rights Amendment, 1923–1996." https://now.org/resource/chronology-of-the-equal-rights-amendment-1923-1996/.

National Sexual Violence Resource Center. "New Data—Sexual Assault Rates Doubled." October 10, 2019. www.nsvrc.org/blogs/new-data-sexual-assault-rates-doubled.

Nelson, Jennifer. *Women of Color and the Reproductive Rights Movement.* New York: New York University Press, 2003.

Nelson, Maggie. *On Freedom: Four Songs of Care and Constraint.* Minneapolis: Graywolf Press, 2021.

Neuwirth, Jessica. *Equal Means Equal: Why the Time for an Equal Rights Amendment Is Now*. New York: The New Press, 2015.

Ng, Brian. "Nonbinary Airline Passengers Ask: What's Gender Got to Do with It?" *New York Times*, June 22, 2022. www.nytimes.com/2022/06/22/travel/nonbinary -airline-passengers-tickets.html.

Nietzsche, Friedrich. *Basic Writings of Nietzsche*. Translated by Walter Kaufmann. New York: The Modern Library, 2000.

Nietzsche, Friedrich. *Daybreak: Thoughts on the Prejudices of Morality*. Translated by R. J. Hollingdale. Cambridge, UK: Cambridge University Press, 1986.

NPR Staff. "Read Britney Spears' Statement to the Court in Her Conservatorship Hearing." NPR, June 24, 2021. www.npr.org/2021/06/24/1009858617/britney-spears-transcript -court-hearing-conservatorship.

Obama, Michelle. *Becoming*. New York: Crown, 2018.

Oluo, Ijeoma. *Mediocre: The Dangerous Legacy of White Male America*. New York: Seal Press, 2020.

Onibada, Ade. "Sundown Towns Are Still a Problem for Black Drivers." *BuzzFeed News*, July 22, 2021. www.buzzfeednews.com/article/adeonibada/sundown-towns -racism-black-drivers-tiktok.

Order of the Good Death. "Death Positive Movement." www.orderofthegooddeath.com /death-positive-movement/.

Oxner, Reese. "Texas Agriculture Commissioner Sid Miller Alleges Aid to Farmers of Color Discriminates Against White Farmers in Suit Against Biden Administration." *Texas Tribune*, April 27, 2021. www.texastribune.org/2021/04/27/sid-miller-farmers -lawsuit/.

Pasulka, Nicole. "How 4 Gay Black Women Fought Back Against Sexual Harass- ment—And Landed in Jail." NPR, June 30, 2018. www.npr.org/sections/codes witch/2015/06/30/418634390/how-4-gay-black-women-fought-back-against -a-sexual-harasser-and-landed-in-jail.

Pauly, Madison. "It's 2019, and States Are Still Making Exceptions for Spousal Rape." *Mother Jones*, November 21, 2019. www.motherjones.com/crime-justice/2019/11 /deval-patrick-spousal-rape-laws/.

Petersen, Anne Helen. "The Work-from-Home Revolution Is Also a Trap for Women." *Bloomberg*, August 10, 2022. www.bloomberg.com/news/features/2022-08-10/work -from-home-jobs-haven-t-made-things-easier-for-women.

Pickert, Kate. "What's Wrong with the Violence Against Women Act?" *Time*, February 27, 2013. https://nation.time.com/2013/02/27/whats-wrong-with-the-violence-against -women-act/.

Piepzna-Samarasinha, Leah Lakshmi. *Care Work: Dreaming Disability Justice*. Vancouver: Arsenal Pulp Press, 2018.

Population Reference Bureau. "Black Women over Three Times More Likely to Die in Pregnancy, Postpartum than White Women, New Research Finds." December 2,

2021. www.prb.org/resources/black-women-over-three-times-more-likely-to-die -in-pregnancy-postpartum-than-white-women-new-research-finds/.

Powell, Michael. "What Lia Thomas Could Mean for Women's Elite Sports." *New York Times*, May 29, 2022. www.nytimes.com/2022/05/29/us/lia-thomas-women-sports.html.

Powers, Tom. "Evert's Farewell Sad Time." *St. Paul Pioneer*, September 3, 1989. Quoted in Mary Jo Kane, "Media Coverage of the Post Title IX Female Athlete: A Feminist Analysis of Sport, Gender, and Power." *Duke Journal of Gender & Law Policy* 3, no. 95 (1996): 95–127.

Pryor, Elizabeth Stordeur. *Colored Travelers: Mobility and the Fight for Citizenship Before the Civil War*, 203–245. Chapel Hill: University of North Carolina Press, 2016.

Pryor, Elizabeth Stordeur. "The Etymology of [N-word]: Resistance, Language, and the Politics of Freedom in the Antebellum North." *Journal of the Early Republic* 36, no. 2 (Summer 2016): 203–245.

Purnell, Dericka. *Becoming Abolitionists: Police, Protests, and the Pursuit of Freedom*. New York: Astra House, 2021.

Purnell, Dericka. "Why Do White Supremacists Want to Kill Black People?" *Guardian*, May 18, 2022. www.theguardian.com/commentisfree/2022/may/18/why-do-white -supremacists-want-to-kill-black-people.

Radicalesbians. "The Woman Identified Woman." *Women's Liberation! Feminist Writings That Inspired a Revolution & Still Can*. Edited by Alix Kates Shulman and Honor Moore, 145–150. New York: Library of America, 2021.

Raghavan, Srinidhi. "In Discussing Accessibility Solely Through the Disability Lens, We Limit Who Benefits from Access." *Firstpost*, December 13, 2020. www.firstpost .com/living/in-discussing-accessibility-solely-through-the-disability-lens-we-limit -who-benefits-from-access-9091341.html.

Raghavan, Srinidhi. "Thoughts on Crip Camp, and How Spaces with Disabled Leader- ship Can Make One Feel Seen and Heard." *Firstpost*, January 15, 2021. www.first post.com/living/thoughts-on-crip-camp-and-how-spaces-with-disabled-leadership -can-make-one-feel-seen-and-heard-9197001.html.

RAINN. "The Criminal Justice System: Statistics." www.rainn.org/statistics/criminal-justice -system.

Rankin, Lauren. *Bodies on the Line: At the Front Lines to Protect Abortion in America*. New York: Counterpoint, 2022.

RAPID. *Forced Out of Work: The Pandemic's Persistent Effects on Women and Work*. June 2022. https://static1.squarespace.com/static/5e7cf2f62c45da32f3c6065e/t/62bde72fc 48ebe6be04ea2da/1656612655531/rapid-women-and-work-factsheet-june2022.pdf.

Ravindran, Jeevan. "'You Guys Saved My Life,' Britney Spears Tells #FreeBritney Move- ment." CNN, November 17, 2021. www.cnn.com/2021/11/17/entertainment/brit ney-spears-conservatorship-freebritney-instagram-scli-intl/index.html.

Raymond, Elizabeth G., and David A. Grimes. "The Comparative Safety of Legal Induced Abortion and Childbirth in the United States." *Obstetrics & Gynecology* 119, no. 2 (part 1, February 2012): 215–219. https://pubmed.ncbi.nlm.nih.gov/22270271/.

Redstockings. "Redstockings Manifesto." In *Burn It Down! Feminist Manifestos for the Revolution*, edited by Breanne Fahs, 207–209. New York: Verso, 2020.

Reeves, Richard V., and Ember Smith. "The Male College Crisis Is Not Just in Enrollment, but Completion." Brookings Institution, October 8, 2021. www.brookings.edu/blog/up-front/2021/10/08/the-male-college-crisis-is-not-just-in-enrollment-but-completion/.

Reinhard, Beth, and Josh Dawsey. "How a Trump-Allied Group Fighting 'Anti-White Bigotry' Beats Biden in Court." *Washington Post*, December 12, 2022. www.washingtonpost.com/politics/2022/12/12/stephen-miller-america-first-legal-biden-race-policies/.

Reuters. "Britney Spears Thanks Free Britney Movement for Its 'Constant Resilience.'" October 6, 2021. www.reuters.com/world/us/britney-spears-thanks-freebritney-movement-its-constant-resilience-2021-10-04/.

Reuters. "Caster Semenya Offered to Show Officials Her Vagina to Prove She Is Female." *Guardian*, May 24, 2022. www.theguardian.com/sport/2022/may/24/caster-semenya-800m-world-athletics-hbo-interview.

Rich, Adrienne. *Blood, Bread, and Poetry: Selected Prose 1979–1985*. New York: W. W. Norton, 1994.

Rich, Adrienne. "Compulsory Heterosexuality and Lesbian Existence," *Signs* 5, no. 4 (Summer 1980): 631–660.

Rich, Adrienne. *On Lies, Secrets, and Silence: Selected Prose 1966–1978*. New York: W. W. Norton, 1979.

Richards, Zoë. "Oklahoma Governor Signs Country's Most Restrictive Abortion Ban into Law." NBC News, May 25, 2022. www.nbcnews.com/politics/politics-news/oklahoma-governor-signs-law-nations-restrictive-abortion-ban-rcna30584.

Right to Be. "The 5Ds of Bystander Intervention." https://righttobe.org/bystander-intervention-training/.

Risen, Clay. "Dorothy Pitman Hughes Dies at 84; Brought Black Issues to Feminism." *New York Times*, December 16, 2022. www.nytimes.com/2022/12/14/us/dorothy-pitman-hughes-dead.html.

Ritchie, Andrea J. *Invisible No More: Police Violence Against Black Women and Women of Color*. Boston: Beacon Press, 2017.

Roberts, Dorothy E. *Killing the Black Body: Race, Reproduction, and the Meaning of Liberty*. New York: Vintage, 1999.

Rocca, Corinne H., Goleen Samari, Diana G. Foster, Heather Gould, and Katrina Kimport. "Emotions and Decision Rightness Over Five Years Following an Abortion: An Examination of Decision Difficulty and Abortion Stigma." *Social Science & Medicine* 248 (March 2020). www.sciencedirect.com/science/article/pii/S0277953619306999?via%3Dihub.

Rodriguez, Barbara. "Why Bills to End Spousal Rape Loopholes Hit Snags." *The 19th*, May 28, 2021. https://19thnews.org/2021/05/why-bills-to-end-spousal-rape-loopholes-hit-snags/.

Rooney, Ben. "Women and Children First: Technology and Moral Panic." *Wall Street Journal*, July 11, 2011. www.wsj.com/articles/BL-TEB-2814.

Ross, Andrew, and Julie Livingston. "Once You See the Truth About Cars, You Can't Unsee It." *New York Times*, December 15, 2022. www.nytimes.com/2022/12/15/opinion/car-ownership-inequality.html.

Roth, Benita. *Separate Roads to Feminism: Black, Chicana, and White Feminist Movements in America's Second Wave*. New York: Cambridge University Press, 2004.

Rubin, Gayle S. *Deviations: A Gayle Rubin Reader*. Durham, NC: Duke University Press, 2011.

Russo, Ann. *Feminist Accountability: Disrupting Violence and Transforming Power*. New York: NYU Press, 2018.

Saad, Layla F. "'I Don't See Color' Is an Act of Racial Gaslighting." *Forge* (Medium), August 31, 2020. https://forge.medium.com/i-dont-see-color-is-an-act-of-racial-gaslighting-da5dca7063bb.

Saad, Layla F. *Me and White Supremacy: Combat Racism, Change the World, and Become a Good Ancestor*. Naperville, IL: Sourcebooks, 2020.

Sanchez, Chelsey. "Cynthia Nixon Defends Miranda's Storyline in the *Sex and the City* Reboot." *Harper's Bazaar*, January 28, 2022. www.harpersbazaar.com/celebrity/latest/a38923968/cynthia-nixon-defends-miranda-sex-and-the-city-reboot/.

Sarachild, Kathie. "Consciousness-Raising: A Radical Weapon." In *Women's Liberation! Feminist Writings That Inspired a Revolution & Still Can*, edited by Alix Kates Shulman and Honor Moore, 238–241. New York: Library of America, 2021.

Scarborough, William J., Ray Sin, and Barbara Risman. "Attitudes and the Stalled Gender Revolution: Egalitarianism, Traditionalism, and Ambivalence from 1977 through 2016." *Gender & Society* 33, no. 2 (2019). https://journals.sagepub.com/doi/10.1177/0891243218809604.

Schneir, Miriam, ed. *Feminism: The Essential Historical Writings*. New York: Vintage Books, 1972.

Schuller, Kyla. *The Biopolitics of Feeling: Race, Sex, and Science in the Nineteenth Century*. Durham, NC: Duke University Press, 2018.

Schuller, Kyla. *The Trouble with White Women: A Counterhistory of Feminism*. New York: Bold Type Books, 2021.

Schulman, Sarah. *Conflict Is Not Abuse: Overstating Harm, Community Responsibility, and the Duty of Repair*. Vancouver: Arsenal Pulp Press, 2016.

Schulman, Sarah. *The Gentrification of the Mind: Witness to a Lost Generation*. Oakland: University of California Press, 2013.

Schulman, Sarah. *Let the Record Show: A Political History of ACT UP New York, 1987–1993*. New York: Farrar, Straus and Giroux, 2021.

Scorsese, Martin, dir. *Public Speaking*. HBO Documentary Films, 2012.

Scott, Joan. "The Conundrum of Equality." In *Gender and the Politics of History*. 30th ann. ed. New York: Columbia University Press, 2018.

Scott, Joan. "Deconstructing Equality-Versus-Difference: Or the Use of Poststructuralist Theory for Feminism." *Feminist Studies* 14, no. 1 (1998): 32–50.

Sears, Jocelyn. "Why Women Couldn't Wear Pants on the Senate Floor Until 1993." *Mental Floss*, March 27, 2017. www.mentalfloss.com/article/93384/why-women-couldnt-wear-pants-senate-floor-until-1993.

Sernoffsky, Evan. "Black Women 'Humiliated' After Getting Kicked Off Napa Valley Wine Train." *San Francisco Chronicle*, August 24, 2015. www.sfchronicle.com/news/article/Black-women-humiliated-after-getting-kicked-6460912.php?t=1ff8fb808200af33be&cmpid=fb-premium.

Shakur, Assata. *Assata: An Autobiography*. Chicago: Lawrence Hill Books, 2001.

Shane, Charlotte. "The Right to Not Be Pregnant." *Harper's Magazine*, October 2022. https://harpers.org/archive/2022/10/the-right-to-not-be-pregnant-asserting-an-essential-right/.

Shelby County v. Holder, 570 US 529 (2013). https://supreme.justia.com/cases/federal/us/570/529/.

Shepardson, David. "Major U.S. Airlines to Allow Gender-Neutral Option on Ticket Reservations." Reuters, July 1, 2022. www.reuters.com/world/us/major-us-airlines-let-passengers-book-tickets-with-gender-neutral-option-2022-07-01/.

Sherman, Carter. "Cops Sexually Assault Women Way More Often than Most People Think." *Vice*, June 10, 2021. www.vice.com/en/article/m7e77y/sarah-everard-cops-sexually-assault-people.

Shimabukuro, Jon O. "Fetal Viability and the Alabama Human Life Protection Act." Congressional Research Service, May 16, 2019. https://sgp.fas.org/crs/misc/LSB10299.pdf.

Shulman, Alix Kates, and Honor Moore, eds. *Women's Liberation! Feminist Writings That Inspired a Revolution & Still Can*. New York: Library of America, 2021.

Sid Miller v. Tom Vilsack. No. 4:21-cv-00595 (N.D. Tex.). www.courthousenews.com/wp-content/uploads/2021/04/177114170174.pdf.

Siegel, Neil S., and Riva B. Siegel. "Equality Arguments for Abortion Rights." *UCLA Law Review*, April 6, 2013. www.uclalawreview.org/the-equality-argument-for-abortion-rights/.

Singh, Gopal K. "Trends and Social Inequalities in Maternal Mortality in the United States, 1969–2018." *International Journal of Maternal and Child Health and AIDS* 10, no. 1 (December 30, 2020): 29–42. https://doi.org/10.21106/ijma.444.

Sins Invalid. "What Is Disability Justice?" June 16, 2020. www.sinsinvalid.org/news-1/2020/6/16/what-is-disability-justice.

Sisson, Gretchen, Lauren Ralph, Heather Gould, and Diana Greene Foster. "Adoption Decision Making Among Women Seeking Abortion." *Women's Health Issues* 27, no. 2 (March–April 2017): 136–144.

SisterSong. www.sistersong.net.

Smith, Barbara, ed. *Home Girls: A Black Feminist Anthology*. New Brunswick, NJ: Rutgers University Press, 1983.

Smith, Barbara. "Racism and Women's Studies." In *Women's Liberation! Feminist Writings That Inspired a Revolution & Still Can*, edited by Alix Kates Shulman and Honor Moore, 377–380. New York: Library of America, 2021.

smith, s. e. "The Beauty of Spaces Created by and for Disabled People." An Unquiet Mind. *Catapult*, October 22, 2018. https://catapult.co/stories/the-beauty-of-spaces-created -for-and-by-disabled-people.

smith, s. e. "Give Disability Feminism the Respect It Deserves." An Unquiet Mind. *Catapult*, September 20, 2021. https://catapult.co/stories/se-smith-column-disability -feminism-long-covid.

smith, s. e. "What If Accessibility Was Also Inclusive?" An Unquiet Mind. *Catapult*, July 28, 2020. https://catapult.co/stories/what-if-accessibility-was-also-inclusive-column -unquiet-mind-s-e-smith.

Smith, Zadie. *Feel Free: Essays*. New York: Penguin Books, 2018.

Smith, Zadie. *Intimations: Six Essays*. New York: Penguin Books, 2020.

Snitow, Ann. *The Feminism of Uncertainty: A Gender Diary*. Durham, NC: Duke University Press, 2015.

Sojourner Truth Project. "Compare the Two Speeches." www.thesojournertruthproject .com/compare-the-speeches/.

"Southern Manifesto." *Congressional Record* 102, part 4 (March 12, 1956). Washington, DC: Governmental Printing Office, 1956: 4459–4460. https://www.thirteen.org /wnet/supremecourt/rights/sources_document2.html.

Spade, Dean. *Mutual Aid: Building Solidarity During This Crisis (and the Next)*. New York: Verso, 2020.

Spade, Dean. *Normal Life: Administrative Violence, Critical Trans Politics, and the Limits of the Law*. Brooklyn: South End Press, 2011.

Spade, Dean. "Solidarity Not Charity: Mutual Aid for Mobilization and Survival." *Social Text* 38, no. 1 (March 2020): 131–151.

Spears, Britney (britneyspears). Instagram. www.instagram.com/britneyspears.

Spears, Britney (@britneyspears). Twitter. https://twitter.com/britneyspears.

Spindelman, Marc. "What 'Dobbs' Means for Women's Equality." *American Prospect*, June 20, 2022. https://prospect.org/justice/what-dobbs-means-for-womens-equality/.

Spinoza, Benedict de. *Ethics*. Edited and translated by Edwin Curley. New York: Penguin Books, 1996.

Stanton, Elizabeth Cady. "Declaration of Sentiments and Resolutions." 1848. In *The Essential Feminist Reader*, edited by Estelle B. Freedman, 57–62. New York: The Modern Library, 2007.

Steinem, Gloria. *My Life on the Road*. New York: Random House, 2015.

Stemen, Don. *The Prison Paradox: More Incarceration Will Not Make Us Safer*. Vera Institute of Justice, July 2017. www.vera.org/downloads/publications/for-the-record -prison-paradox_02.pdf.

Bibliography

Stinson, Philip Matthew, John Liederbach, Stephen L. Brewer, and Brooke E. Mathna. "Police Sexual Misconduct: A National Scale Study of Arrested Officers." *Criminal Justice Faculty Publications* 30 (2014). www.bwjp.org/assets/documents/pdfs/webinars/dhhs-police-sexual-misconduct-a-national-scale-study.pdf.

Stinson, Philip Matthew, John Liederbach, Steven P. Lab, and Stephen L. Brewer. *Police Integrity Lost: A Study of Law Enforcement Officers Arrested*. US Department of Justice, April 2016. https://www.ojp.gov/pdffiles1/nij/grants/249850.pdf.

Stinson, Philip Matthew, Robert W. Taylor, and John Liederbach. "The Situational Context of Police Sexual Violence: Data and Policy Implications." *Family & Intimate Partner Violence Quarterly* 12, no. 4 (Spring 2020): 59–68. www.ncbi.nlm.nih.gov/pmc/articles/PMC9365085/.

Stop Street Harassment and UCSD Center on Gender Equity and Health. *2019 Study on Sexual Harassment and Assault*. https://stopstreetharassment.org/our-work/national study/2019study/.

Stovall, Tyler. *White Freedom: The Racial History of an Idea*. Princeton, NJ: Princeton University Press, 2021.

Strauss, Valerie. "65 Years After Supreme Court's Historic Brown v. Board of Education Ruling: 'We Are Right Back Where We Started.'" *Washington Post*, April 30, 2019. www.washingtonpost.com/education/2019/04/30/years-after-supreme-courts-historic-brown-v-board-education-ruling-we-are-right-back-where-we-started/.

Students for Fair Admissions. https://studentsforfairadmissions.org/.

Students for Fair Admissions, Inc. v. President and Fellows of Harvard College, __US__ (2022).

Students for Fair Admissions, Inc. v. University of North Carolina, __US__ (2022).

Stump, Scott. "Athlete Calls Out Men's and Women's Weight Room Disparities at March Madness, Sparking Outrage." *Today*, March 19, 2021. www.today.com/news/viral-video-shows-men-s-women-s-weight-room-disparities-t212338.

Sullivan, Melissa A. "I Can't Outrun the Risks of Being a Woman Runner. And I'm Sick of It." *Washington Post*, September 10, 2022. www.washingtonpost.com/opinions/2022/09/10/eliza-fletcher-women-runner-harassment-threats-risk/.

Syrda, Joanna. "Gendered Housework: Spousal Relative Income, Parenthood and Traditional Gender Identity Norms." *Work, Employment and Society* (March 9, 2022). https://journals.sagepub.com/doi/10.1177/09500170211069780.

Táíwò, Olúfémi O. "Liberty for Whom?" *The Nation*, May 3, 2021.

Talbot, Margaret. "How the Real Jane Roe Shaped the Abortion Wars." *New Yorker*, September 13, 2021. www.newyorker.com/magazine/2021/09/20/how-the-real-jane-roe-shaped-the-abortion-wars.

Taylor, Astra. *Democracy May Not Exist, but We'll Miss It When It's Gone*. New York: Metropolitan Books, 2019.

Taylor, Keeanga-Yamahtta. "The Black Plague." *New Yorker*, April 16, 2020. www.newyorker.com/news/our-columnists/the-black-plague.

Bibliography

Taylor, Keeanga-Yamahtta, ed. *How We Get Free: Black Feminism and the Combahee River Collective*. Chicago: Haymarket Books, 2017.

Testa, Jessica. "How Police Caught the Cop Who Allegedly Sexually Abused Black Women." *BuzzFeed News*, September 5, 2014. www.buzzfeednews.com/article/jtes/daniel-holtzclaw-alleged-sexual-assault-oklahoma-city#.hm7amV1JW.

Thalos, Miriam. "Resist and Be Free." *Aeon*, April 4, 2019. https://aeon.co/essays/more-than-having-options-freedom-is-being-true-to-yourself.

Thalos, Miriam. *A Social Theory of Freedom*. New York: Routledge, 2016.

Thames, Alanis. "Despite 50 Years of Title IX, Racial Gaps in Equity Persist." *New York Times*, July 2, 2022.

Thompson, Dennis. "How 1.3 Million Americans Became Controlled by Conservatorships." *U.S. News & World Report*, October 18, 2021. www.usnews.com/news/health-news/articles/2021-10-18/how-13-million-americans-became-controlled-by-conservatorships.

Thompson, Derek. "Colleges Have a Guy Problem." *Atlantic*, September 14, 2021. www.theatlantic.com/ideas/archive/2021/09/young-men-college-decline-gender-gap-higher-education/620066/.

Thomson, Ainsley. "New Zealand's Public Sector Gender Pay Gap Narrows to Record Low." *Bloomberg*, November 14, 2021. www.bloomberg.com/news/articles/2021-11-15/new-zealand-s-public-sector-gender-pay-gap-narrows-to-record-low.

Tierce, Merrit. "The Abortion I Didn't Have." *New York Times Magazine*, December 2, 2021. www.nytimes.com/2021/12/02/magazine/abortion-parent-mother-child.html.

"Title IX: Falling Short at 50." *USA Today*, June 16, 2022. www.usatoday.com/in-depth/news/investigations/2022/05/26/title-ix-falling-short-50-exposes-how-colleges-still-fail-women/9722521002/.

Tolentino, Jia. "Another Risk in Overturning Roe." *New Yorker*, February 20, 2022. www.newyorker.com/magazine/2022/02/28/another-risk-in-overturning-roe-v-wade-abortion.

Tolentino, Jia. "We're Not Going Back to the Time Before Roe. We're Going Somewhere Worse." *New Yorker*, June 24, 2022. www.newyorker.com/magazine/2022/07/04/we-are-not-going-back-to-the-time-before-roe-we-are-going-somewhere-worse.

Transrespect versus Transphobia Worldwide. "Trans Murder Monitoring." November 8, 2022. https://transrespect.org/en/tmm-update-tdor-2022/.

Treatment Advocacy Center. *Overlooked and Undercounted: The Role of Mental Illness in Fatal Law Enforcement Encounters*. 2015. www.treatmentadvocacycenter.org/storage/documents/overlooked-in-the-undercounted.pdf.

Treisman, Rachel. "The Missouri House Tightens Its Dress Code for Women, to the Dismay of Democrats." NPR, January 13, 2023. www.npr.org/2023/01/13/1149057491/missouri-house-dress-code-women-cardigan.

Unger, Roberto Mangabeira. "Deep Freedom: Why the Left Should Abandon Equality." IPPR, October 24, 2013. www.ippr.org/juncture/deep-freedom-why-the-left-should-abandon-equality.

Bibliography

University of Bath. "Married Mothers Who Earn More Than Their Husbands Take on an Even Greater Share of the Housework—New Research." News release. March 31, 2022. www.bath.ac.uk/announcements/married-mothers-who-earn-more-than-their -husbands-take-on-an-even-greater-share-of-housework/.

Urban Indian Health Institute. *Missing and Murdered Indigenous Women & Girls: A Snapshot of Data from 71 Urban Cities in the United States.* 2018. www.uihi.org/wp-content /uploads/2018/11/Missing-and-Murdered-Indigenous-Women-and-Girls-Report.pdf.

US Department of Justice. *FY 2023 Budget Summary.* www.justice.gov/jmd/page/file /1489621/download.

US Equal Employment Opportunity Commission. "Equal Pay Act of 1963." www.eeoc .gov/statutes/equal-pay-act-1963.

US Senate Committee on Armed Services. *Summary of the Fiscal Year 2023 National Defense Authorization Act.* https://www.armed-services.senate.gov/imo/media/doc /fy23_ndaa_agreement_summary.pdf.

US Senate Permanent Subcommittee on Investigations. *Sexual Abuse of Female Inmates in Federal Prisons.* December 13, 2022. www.hsgac.senate.gov/wp-content/uploads /imo/media/doc/2022-12-13%20PSI%20Staff%20Report%20-%20Sexual%20Abuse %20of%20Female%20Inmates%20in%20Federal%20Prisons.pdf.

US Soccer Federation. "U.S. Soccer Federation, Women's and Men's National Team Unions Agree to Historic Collective Bargaining Agreements." May 18, 2022. www .ussoccer.com/stories/2022/05/ussf-womens-and-mens-national-team-unions -agree-to-historic-collective-bargaining-agreements.

Utaraité, Neringa. "18 Saddening Replies to the Question 'What Would You Do If There Were No Men on Earth for 24 Hours?' Shared on TikTok." Bored Panda. www .boredpanda.com/no-men-on-earth-for-24-hours-tik-tok.

Vakil, Caroline. "Cherelle Griner Says Brittney Griner Is 'Struggling': 'I Will Not Be Quiet Anymore.'" *The Hill,* July 5, 2022. https://thehill.com/blogs/in-the-know/3546080 -cherelle-griner-says-brittney-griner-is-struggling-i-will-not-be-quiet-anymore/.

Valenti, Jessica. *Abortion, Every Day* (Substack). https://jessica.substack.com/.

Vera-Gray, Fiona. *The Right Amount of Panic: How Women Trade Freedom for Safety.* Bristol: Policy Press, 2018.

Vera-Gray, Fiona, and Liz Kelly. "Contested Gendered Space: Public Sexual Harassment and Women's Safety Work." *International Journal of Comparative and Applied Criminal Justice* 44, no. 4 (2020): 265–275.

Villarosa, Linda. *Under the Skin: The Hidden Toll of Racism on American Lives and on the Health of Our Nation.* New York: Doubleday, 2022.

Villarosa, Linda. "Why America's Black Mothers and Babies Are in a Life-or-Death Crisis." *New York Times Magazine,* April 11, 2018. www.nytimes.com/2018/04/11/magazine /black-mothers-babies-death-maternal-mortality.html.

Vossel, Holly. "Pandemic Pushes Death Doula Awareness, Hospices Seek Strengthened Ties." *Hospice News,* April 11, 2022. https://hospicenews.com/2022/04/11/pandemic -pushes-death-doula-awareness-hospices-seek-strengthened-ties/.

Wall, Steven. "Self-Mastery and the Quality of Life." In *Positive Freedom: Past, Present, and Future,* edited by John Christman. New York: Cambridge University Press, 2021. https://doi.org/10.1017/9781108768276.007.

Ward, Jane. *The Tragedy of Heterosexuality.* New York: New York University Press, 2020.

Ware, Susan. *Why They Marched: Untold Stories of the Women Who Fought for the Right to Vote.* Cambridge, MA: Belknap Press of Harvard University Press, 2019.

Washington Post. "Fatal Force." www.washingtonpost.com/graphics/investigations/police -shootings-database/.

We Are BG. https://wearebg.org/.

Wegman, Jesse. "Why Can't We Make Women's Equality the Law of the Land?" *New York Times,* January 28, 2022. www.nytimes.com/2022/01/28/opinion/equal -rights-amendment-ratification.html.

White House. "Fact Sheet: President Biden's Budget Invests in Reducing Gun Crime to Make Our Communities Safer." Press release. March 28, 2022. www.whitehouse.gov /omb/briefing-room/2022/03/28/fact-sheet-president-bidens-budget-invests-in -reducing-gun-crime-to-make-our-communities-safer/.

Widdicombe, Lizzie. "What Does an At-Home Abortion Look Like?" *New Yorker,* November 11, 2021. www.newyorker.com/news/news-desk/what-does-an-at-home -abortion-look-like.

Wilkerson, Isabel. *Caste: The Origins of Our Discontents.* New York: Random House, 2020.

Williams Institute. "Transgender People Over Four Times More Likely Than Cisgender People to Be Victims of Violent Crime." Press release. March 23, 2021. https:// williamsinstitute.law.ucla.edu/press/ncvs-trans-press-release/.

Williams, Serena. "How Serena Williams Saved Her Own Life." *Elle,* April 5, 2022. www .elle.com/life-love/a39586444/how-serena-williams-saved-her-own-life/.

Willingham, Emily. "People Think Minority Groups Are Bigger Than They Really Are." *Scientific American,* April 27, 2022. www.scientificamerican.com/article/people -think-minority-groups-are-bigger-than-they-really-are/.

Willis, Ellen. "Toward a Feminist Sexual Revolution." In *Women's Liberation! Feminist Writings That Inspired a Revolution & Still Can,* edited by Alix Kates Shulman and Honor Moore, 433–443. New York: Library of America, 2021.

Willke, Jack C., and Barbara Willke. *Handbook on Abortion.* Cincinnati, OH: Hiltz, 1972.

Wilmot-Smith, Frederick. *Equal Justice: Fair Legal Systems in an Unfair World.* Cambridge, MA: Harvard University Press, 2019.

Wilson, Jeremy. "Lia Thomas Banned from Competing Against Women as Swimming Cracks Down on Transgender Athletes." *Telegraph,* June 19, 2022. www.telegraph.co .uk/swimming/2022/06/19/lia-thomas-banned-competing-against-women-swim ming-cracks-transgender/.

Winnubst, Shannon. *Queering Freedom.* Bloomington: Indiana University Press, 2006.

Winterson, Jeanette. *12 Bytes: How We Got Here. Where We Might Go Next.* New York: Grove Press, 2022.

Bibliography

Witchel, Alex. "Life After 'Sex.'" *New York Times*, January 19, 2012. www.nytimes.com /2012/01/22/magazine/cynthia-nixon-wit.html.

Wittig, Monique. "The Straight Mind." In *The Straight Mind and Other Essays*. Boston: Beacon Press, 1992.

WNBA. "WNBA and WNBPA Reach Tentative Agreement on Groundbreaking Eight-Year Collective Bargaining Agreement." Press release. January 14, 2020. www.wnba .com/news/wnba-and-wnbpa-reach-tentative-agreement-on-groundbreaking -eight-year-collective-bargaining-agreement/.

Wollstonecraft, Mary. *A Vindication of the Rights of Woman*. Mineola, NY: Dover Publications, 1996.

Women Count USA: Femicide Accountability Project. https://womencountusa.org/.

Woodhull, Victoria. *Selected Writings of Victoria Woodhull: Suffrage, Free Love, and Eugenics*. Edited by Cari M. Carpenter. Lincoln: University of Nebraska Press, 2010.

Woodhull, Victoria, and Tennessee Claflin. "Virtue: What It Is, and What It Is Not." In *Feminism: The Essential Historical Writings*, edited by Miriam Schneir, 143–146. New York: Vintage Books, 1994.

Woolf, Virginia. *A Room of One's Own*. 1929. Reprint, New York: Harcourt, 1981.

World Population Review. "Marital Rape States 2023." https://worldpopulationreview.com /state-rankings/marital-rape-states.

Yang, Maya. "Airbnb Apologizes for Slave Cabin for Rent in Mississippi." *Guardian*, August 3, 2022. www.theguardian.com/technology/2022/aug/03/airbnb-slave-cabin -mississippi.

Yousif, Nadine. "Ron DeSantis Government Bans New Advanced African American History Course." BBC News, January 20, 2023. www.bbc.com/news/world-us-canada -64348902.

Yurcaba, Jo. "Louisiana Becomes 18th State to Enact a Transgender Athlete Ban." NBC Out, June 7, 2022. www.nbcnews.com/nbc-out/out-politics-and-policy/louisiana -becomes-18th-state-enact-transgender-athlete-ban-rcna32328.

Zakaria, Rafia. *Against White Feminism: Notes on Disruption*. New York: W. W. Norton, 2021.

Zeisler, Andi. *We Were Feminists Once: From Riot Grrrl to CoverGirl®, the Buying and Selling of a Political Movement*. New York: PublicAffairs, 2016.

Zerilli, Linda M. G. *Feminism and the Abyss of Freedom*. Chicago: University of Chicago Press, 2005.

Ziegler, Mary. "The Abortion Fight Has Never Been About Just *Roe v. Wade*." *Atlantic*, May 20, 2021. www.theatlantic.com/ideas/archive/2021/05/abortion-fight-roe-v -wade/618930/.

Zill, Nicholas. "The Changing Face of Adoption in the United States." Institute for Family Studies, August 8, 2017. https://ifstudies.org/blog/the-changing-face-of-adoption -in-the-united-states.

INDEX

ABOUT THE AUTHOR

Kristin Cofer

Marcie Bianco is a writer, editor, and cultural critic. She has written, taught, and lectured about feminism, ethics, literature, and culture for more than fifteen years. A 2013 Lambda Literary Fellow, her writing has appeared at CNN and NBC Think and in *Vanity Fair,* among other outlets and academic publications. Bianco is a columnist at the Women's Media Center and a SheSource expert. She currently is an editor at *Stanford Social Innovation Review,* an award-winning quarterly print magazine. Bianco resides in California with her cats, Simone de Beauvoir, Freddie Nietzsche, (Amanda) Gorman, and Audre THEE Lorde.

PublicAffairs is a publishing house founded in 1997. It is a tribute to the standards, values, and flair of three persons who have served as mentors to countless reporters, writers, editors, and book people of all kinds, including me.

I. F. STONE, proprietor of *I. F. Stone's Weekly*, combined a commitment to the First Amendment with entrepreneurial zeal and reporting skill and became one of the great independent journalists in American history. At the age of eighty, Izzy published *The Trial of Socrates*, which was a national bestseller. He wrote the book after he taught himself ancient Greek.

BENJAMIN C. BRADLEE was for nearly thirty years the charismatic editorial leader of *The Washington Post*. It was Ben who gave the *Post* the range and courage to pursue such historic issues as Watergate. He supported his reporters with a tenacity that made them fearless and it is no accident that so many became authors of influential, best-selling books.

ROBERT L. BERNSTEIN, the chief executive of Random House for more than a quarter century, guided one of the nation's premier publishing houses. Bob was personally responsible for many books of political dissent and argument that challenged tyranny around the globe. He is also the founder and longtime chair of Human Rights Watch, one of the most respected human rights organizations in the world.

.   .   .

For fifty years, the banner of Public Affairs Press was carried by its owner Morris B. Schnapper, who published Gandhi, Nasser, Toynbee, Truman, and about 1,500 other authors. In 1983, Schnapper was described by *The Washington Post* as "a redoubtable gadfly." His legacy will endure in the books to come.

Peter Osnos, *Founder*